SKY PIRATES
OF NEO TERRA

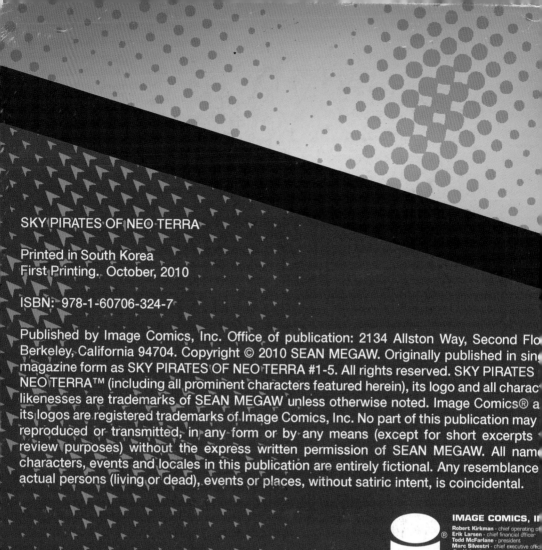

SKY PIRATES OF NEO TERRA

Printed in South Korea
First Printing. October, 2010

ISBN: 978-1-60706-324-7

Published by Image Comics, Inc. Office of publication: 2134 Allston Way, Second Flo Berkeley, California 94704.

IMAGE COMICS, I

Robert Kirkman - chief operating o
Erik Larsen - chief financial officer
Todd McFarlane - president
Marc Silvestri - chief executive offic
Jim Valentino - vice-president

Eric Stephenson - publisher
Todd Martinez - sales & licensing co
Betsy Gomez - pr & marketing coord
Branwyn Bigglestone - accounts ma
Sarah deLaine - administrative assis
Tyler Shainline - production manage
Drew Gill - art director
Jonathan Chan - production artist
Monica Howard - production artist
Vincent Kukua - production artist
Kevin Yuen - production artist

www.imagecomics.c

International Rights Representative: Christine Meyer (christine@gfloystu

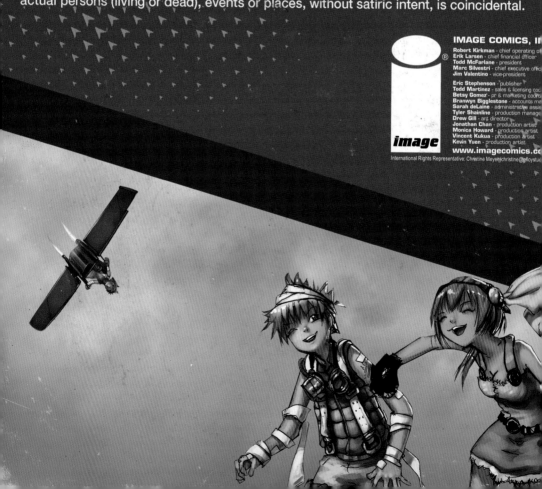

WORDS JOSH WAGNER

ART CAMILLA D'ERRICO

COLORS

SIMON BORK   PATIPAT ASAVASENA

DESIGN
TIM DANIEL

LETTERS
ED BRISSON

ASSISTANT EDITOR
SARAH CARBIENER

EDITOR
SEAN MEGAW

CREATED BY SEAN MEGAW & CAMILLA D'ERRICO
WORLD CREATED BY TYLER SIGMAN & JEFF SIMPSON

GREG MORK - CEO
TORVAL MORK - President
SEAN MEGAW - Director, Business Development
DAY 21 STUDIOS INC.

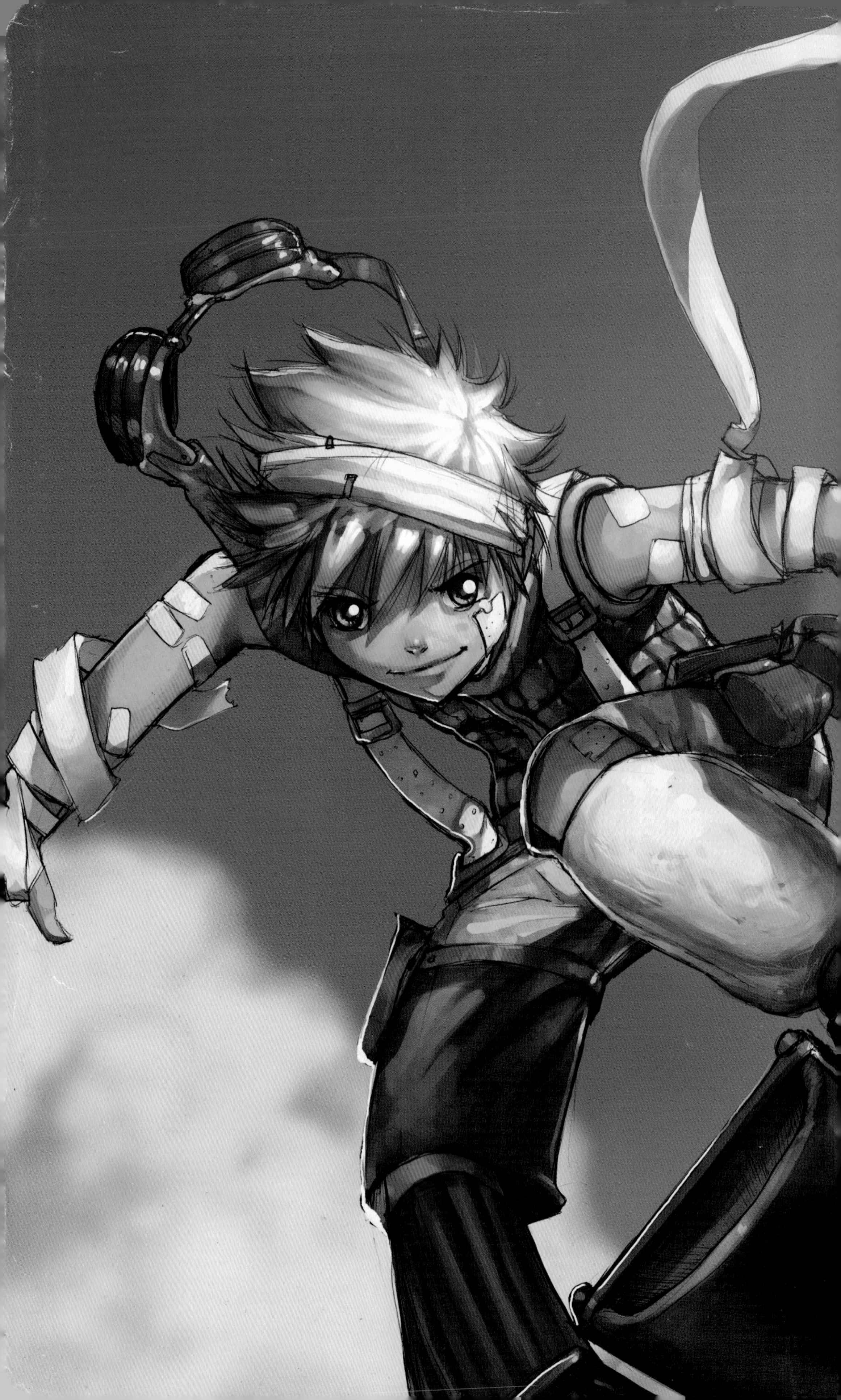

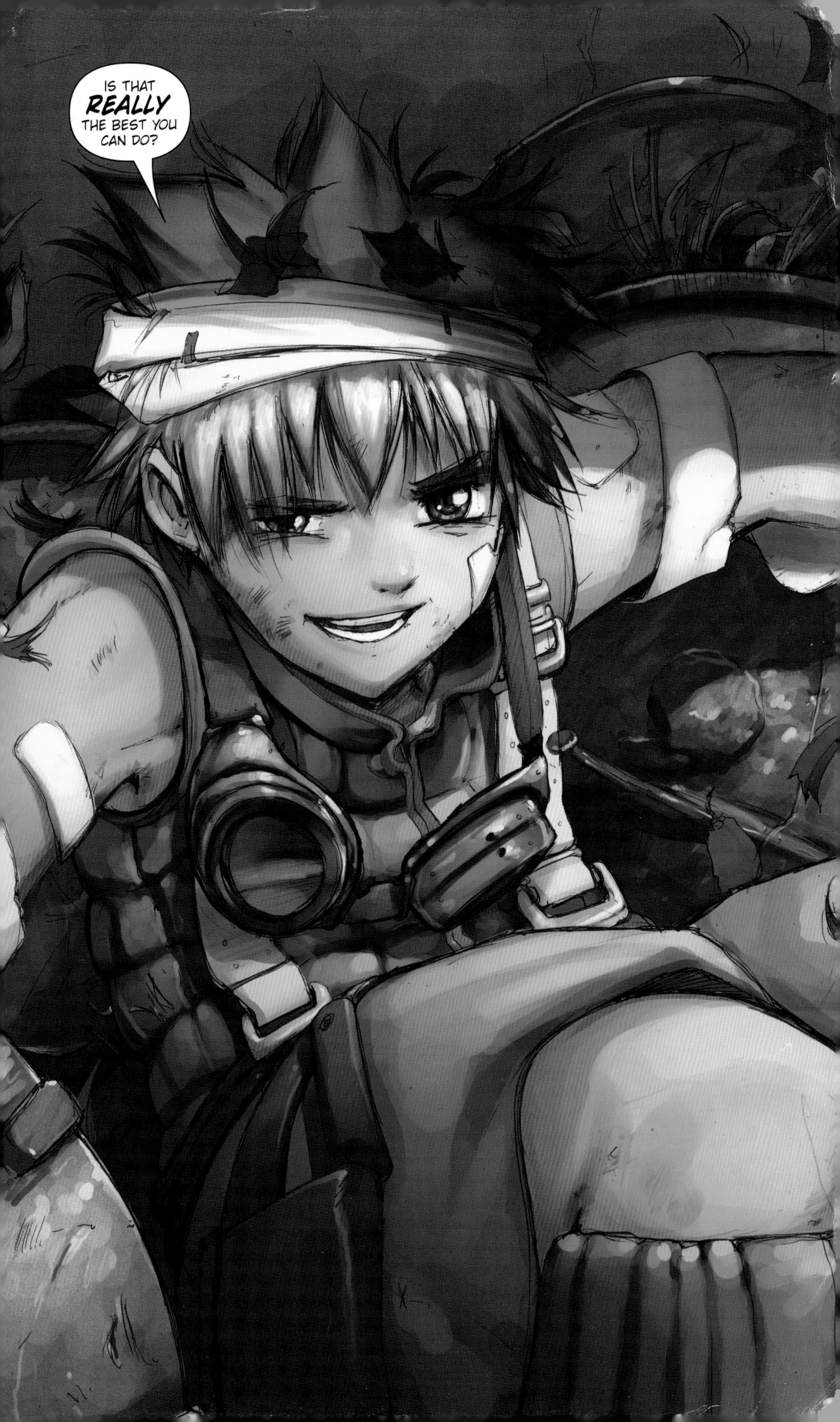
IS THAT REALLY THE BEST YOU CAN DO?

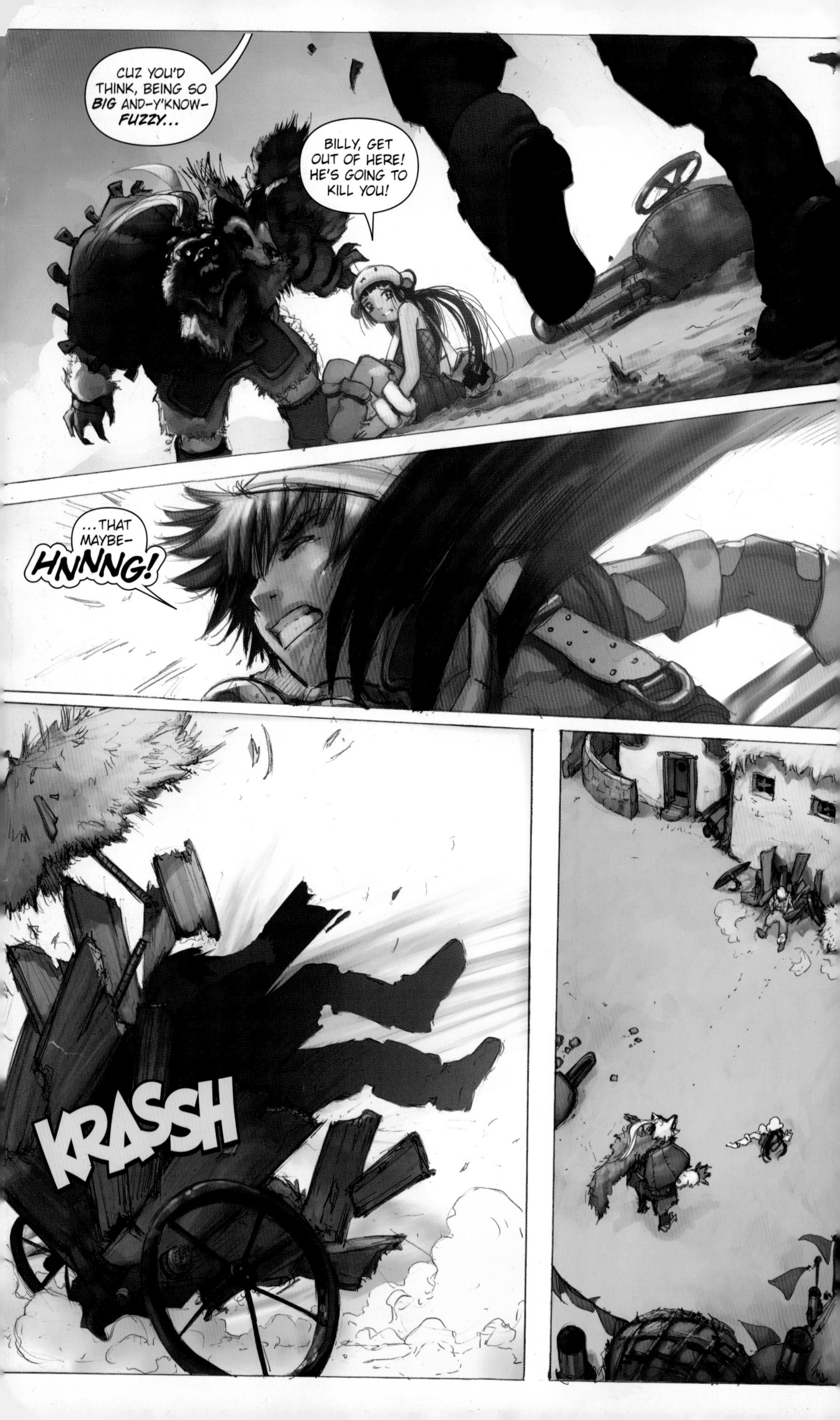
CUZ YOU'D THINK, BEING SO BIG AND-Y'KNOW-FUZZY...
BILLY, GET OUT OF HERE! HE'S GOING TO KILL YOU!
...THAT MAYBE-
HNNNG!
KRASSH

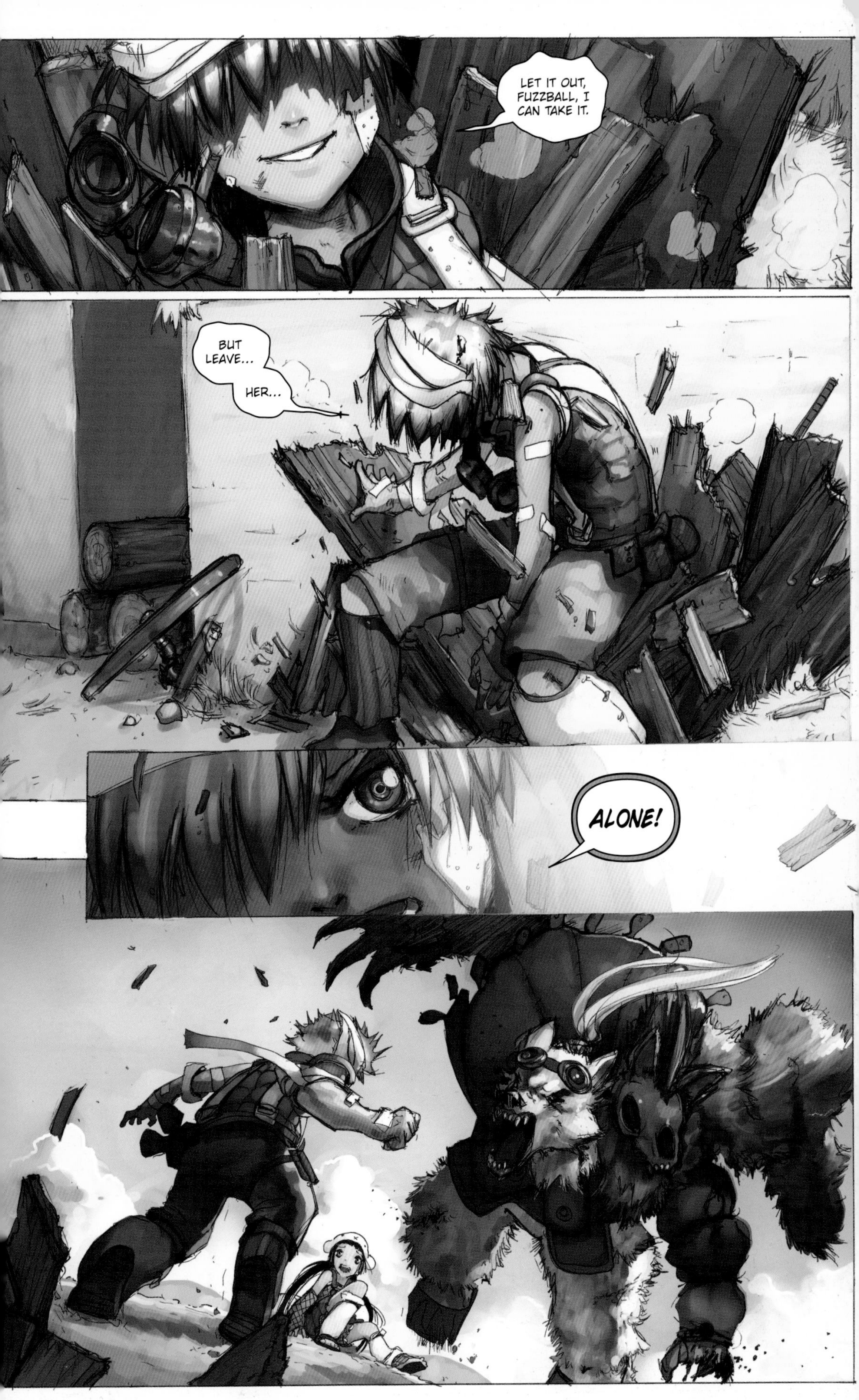
LET IT OUT, FUZZBALL, I CAN TAKE IT.
BUT LEAVE...
HER...
ALONE!

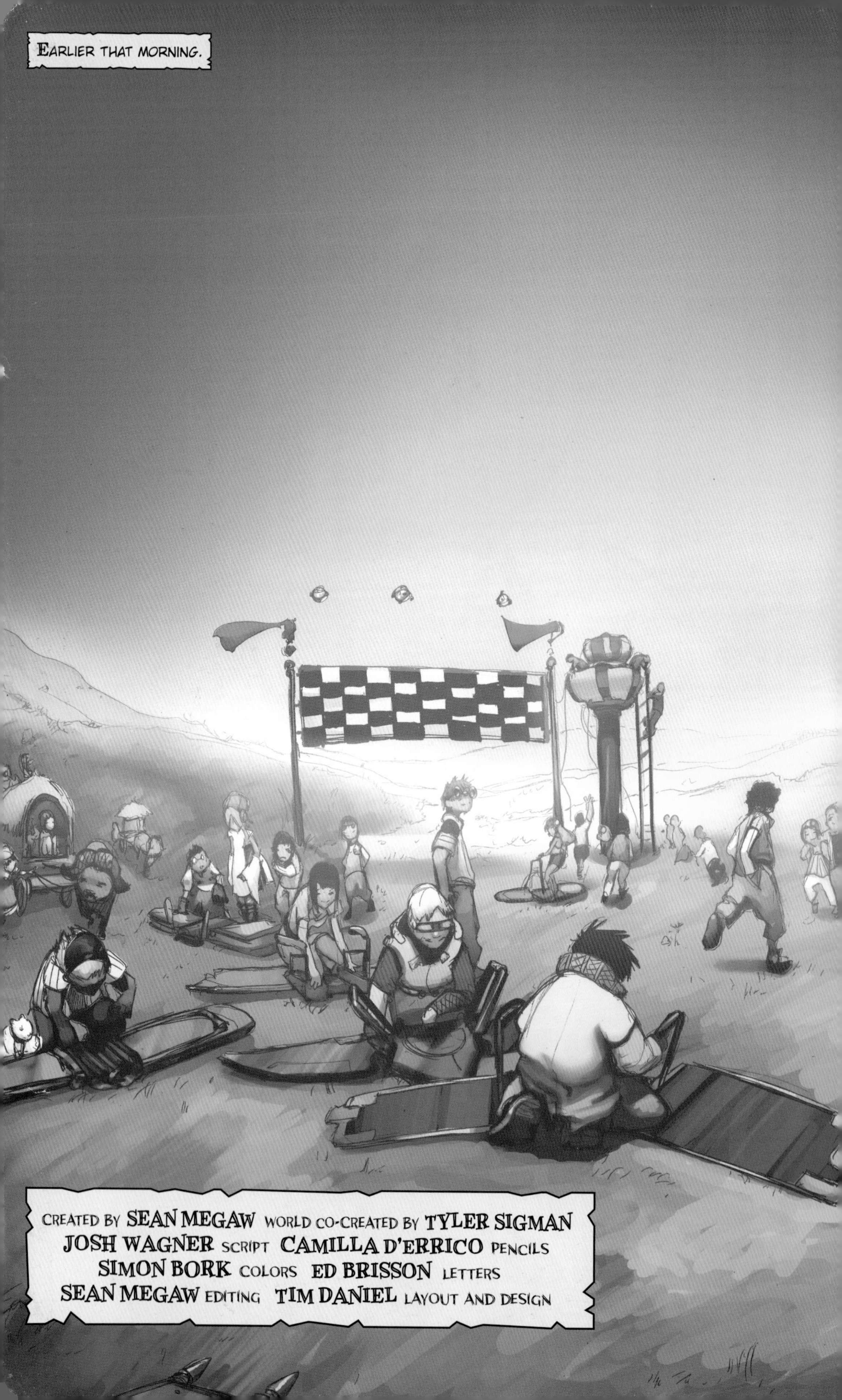
EARLIER THAT MORNING.
CREATED BY SEAN MEGAW WORLD CO-CREATED BY TYLER SIGMAN
JOSH WAGNER SCRIPT CAMILLA D'ERRICO PENCILS
SIMON BORK COLORS ED BRISSON LETTERS
SEAN MEGAW EDITING TIM DANIEL LAYOUT AND DESIGN

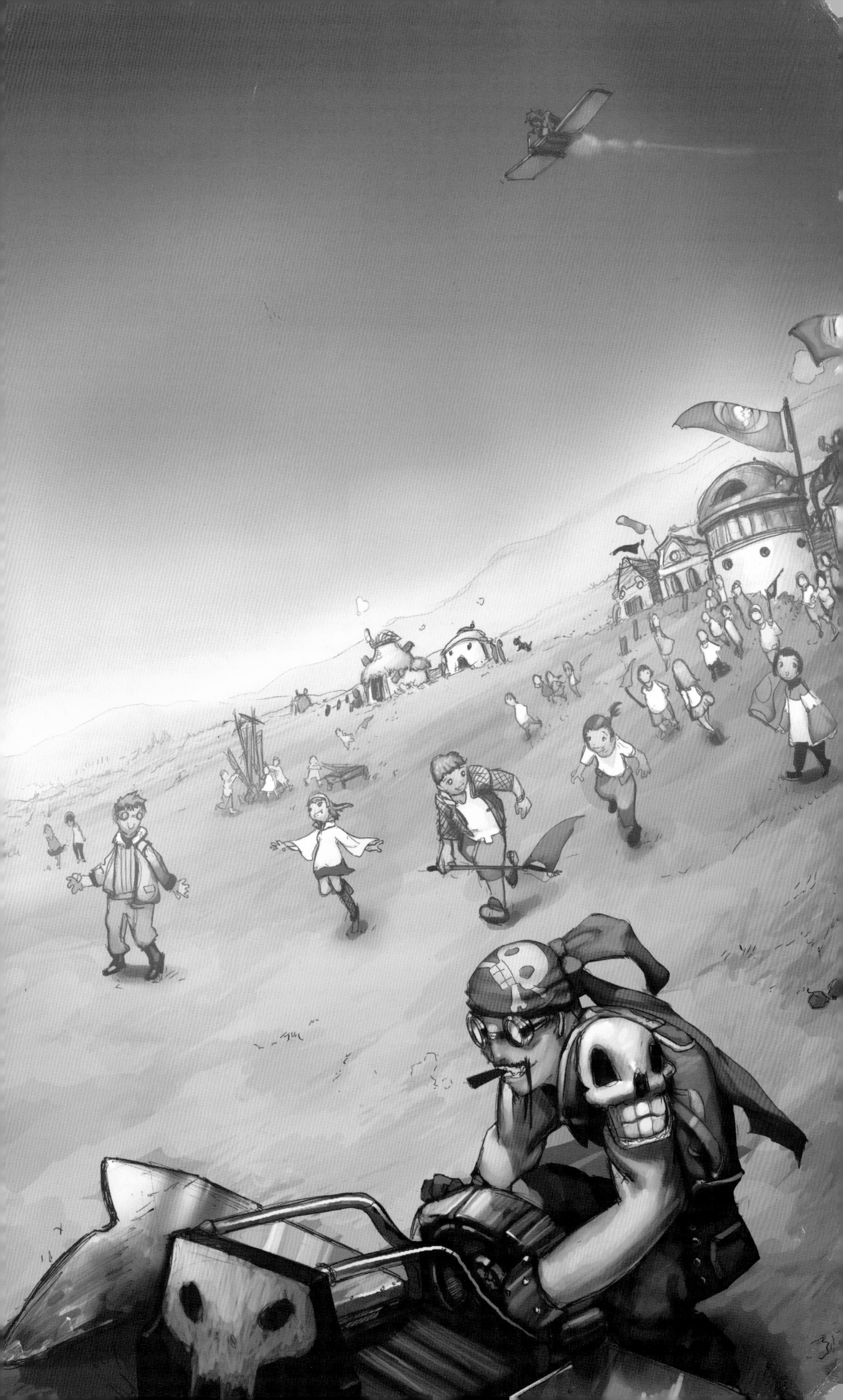

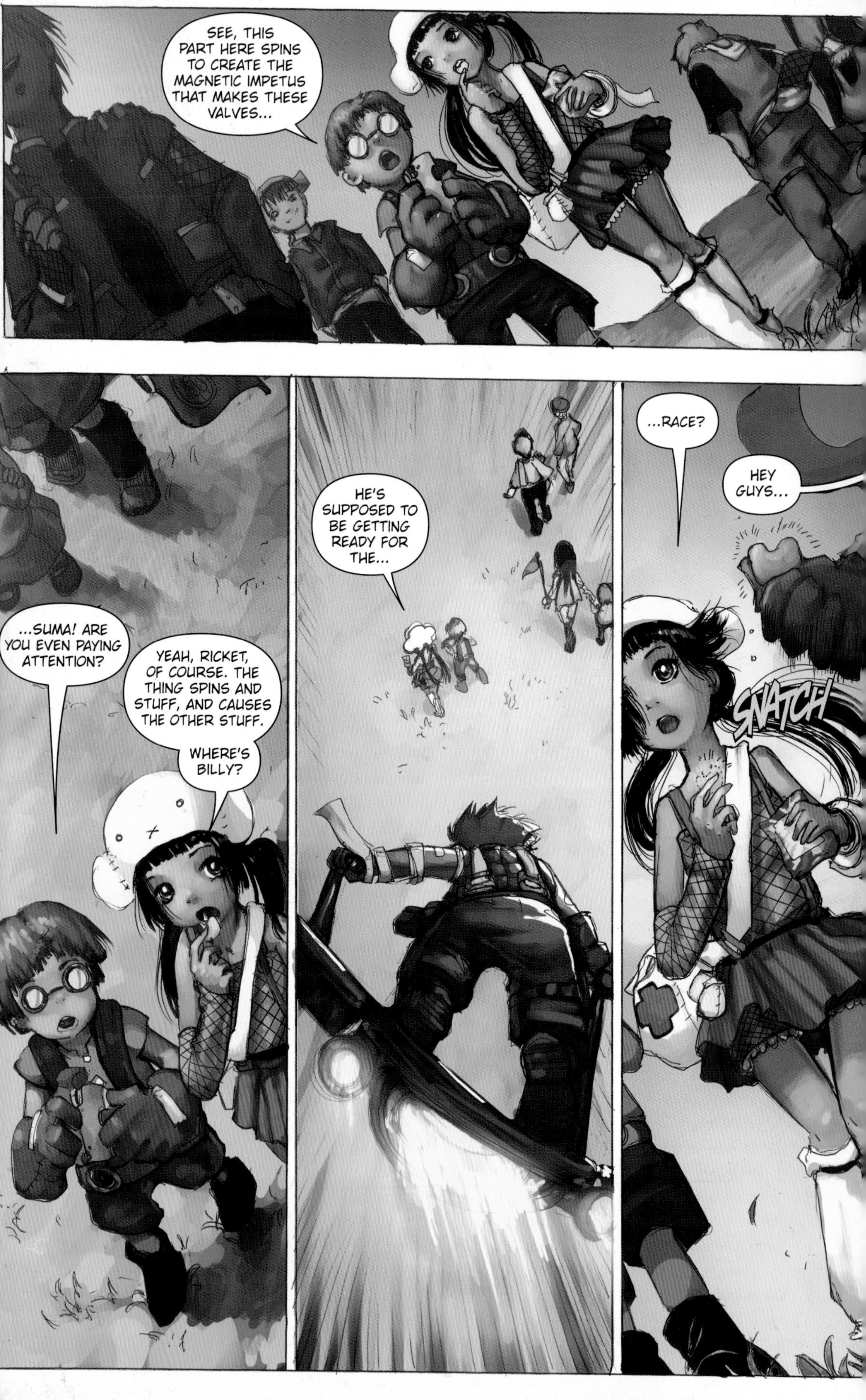
SEE, THIS PART HERE SPINS TO CREATE THE MAGNETIC IMPETUS THAT MAKES THESE VALVES...
...SUMA! ARE YOU EVEN PAYING ATTENTION?
YEAH, RICKET, OF COURSE. THE THING SPINS AND STUFF, AND CAUSES THE OTHER STUFF.
WHERE'S BILLY?
HE'S SUPPOSED TO BE GETTING READY FOR THE...
...RACE?
HEY GUYS...
SNATCH

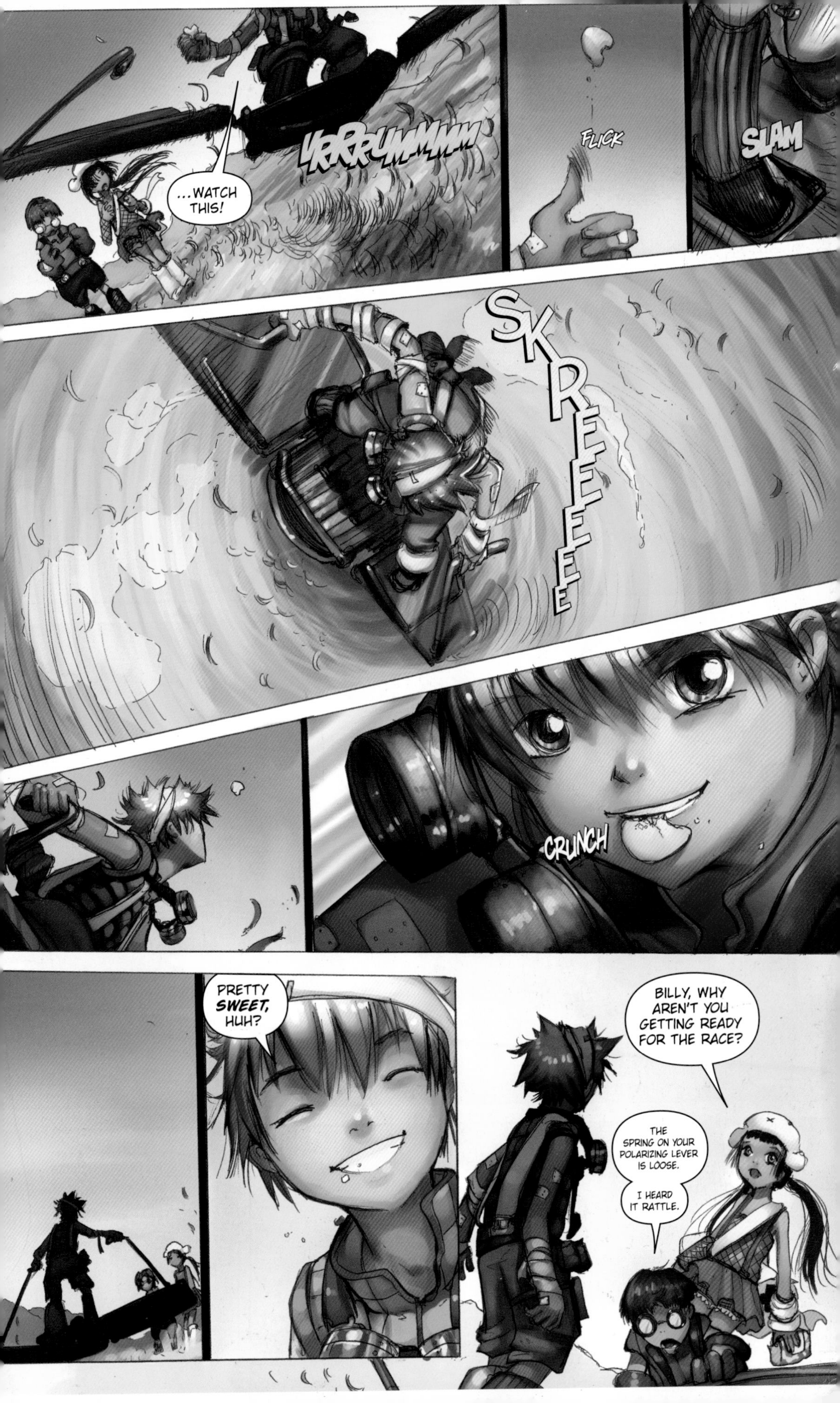
...WATCH THIS!
VRRRUMMMMM
FLICK
SLAM
SKREEEEEE
CRUNCH
PRETTY SWEET, HUH?
BILLY, WHY AREN'T YOU GETTING READY FOR THE RACE?
THE SPRING ON YOUR POLARIZING LEVER IS LOOSE.
I HEARD IT RATTLE.

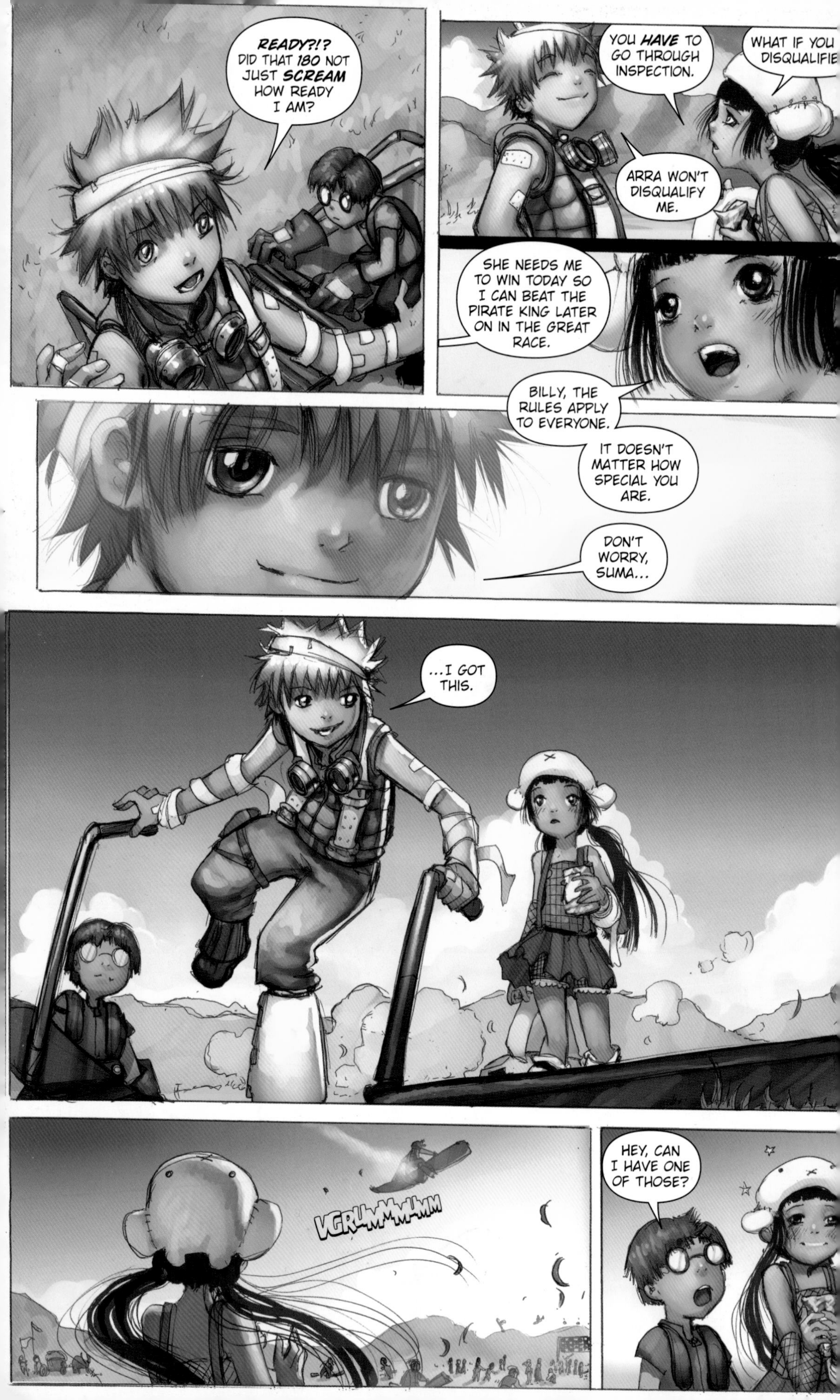
READY?!? DID THAT 180 NOT JUST SCREAM HOW READY I AM?
YOU HAVE TO GO THROUGH INSPECTION.
WHAT IF YOU DISQUALIFIE
ARRA WON'T DISQUALIFY ME.
SHE NEEDS ME TO WIN TODAY SO I CAN BEAT THE PIRATE KING LATER ON IN THE GREAT RACE.
BILLY, THE RULES APPLY TO EVERYONE.
IT DOESN'T MATTER HOW SPECIAL YOU ARE.
DON'T WORRY, SUMA...
...I GOT THIS.
VGRUMMMUMM
HEY, CAN I HAVE ONE OF THOSE?

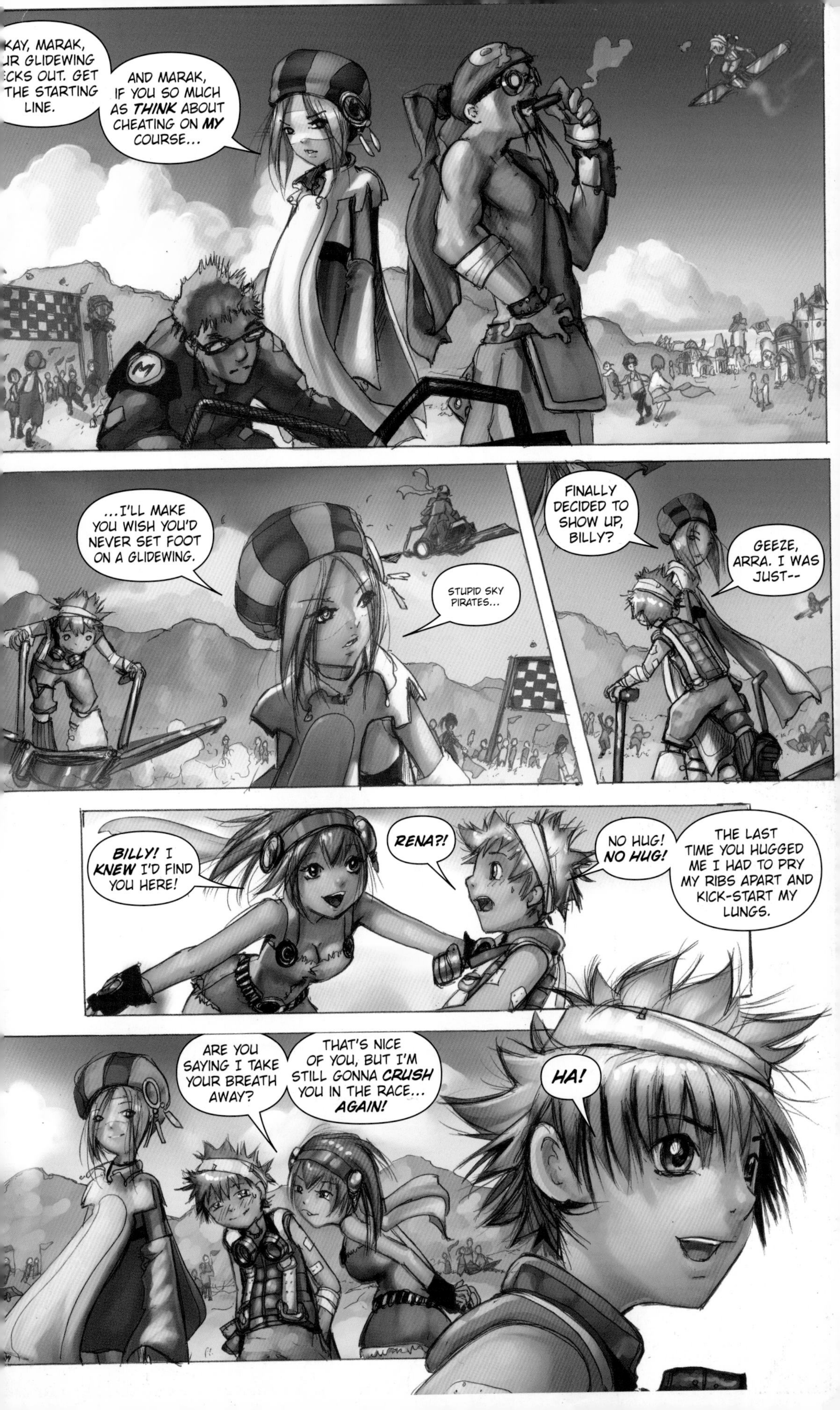
KAY, MARAK, UR GLIDEWING ECKS OUT. GET THE STARTING LINE.
AND MARAK, IF YOU SO MUCH AS THINK ABOUT CHEATING ON MY COURSE...
...I'LL MAKE YOU WISH YOU'D NEVER SET FOOT ON A GLIDEWING.
STUPID SKY PIRATES...
FINALLY DECIDED TO SHOW UP, BILLY?
GEEZE, ARRA. I WAS JUST--
BILLY! I KNEW I'D FIND YOU HERE!
RENA?!
NO HUG! NO HUG!
THE LAST TIME YOU HUGGED ME I HAD TO PRY MY RIBS APART AND KICK-START MY LUNGS.
ARE YOU SAYING I TAKE YOUR BREATH AWAY?
THAT'S NICE OF YOU, BUT I'M STILL GONNA CRUSH YOU IN THE RACE... AGAIN!
HA!

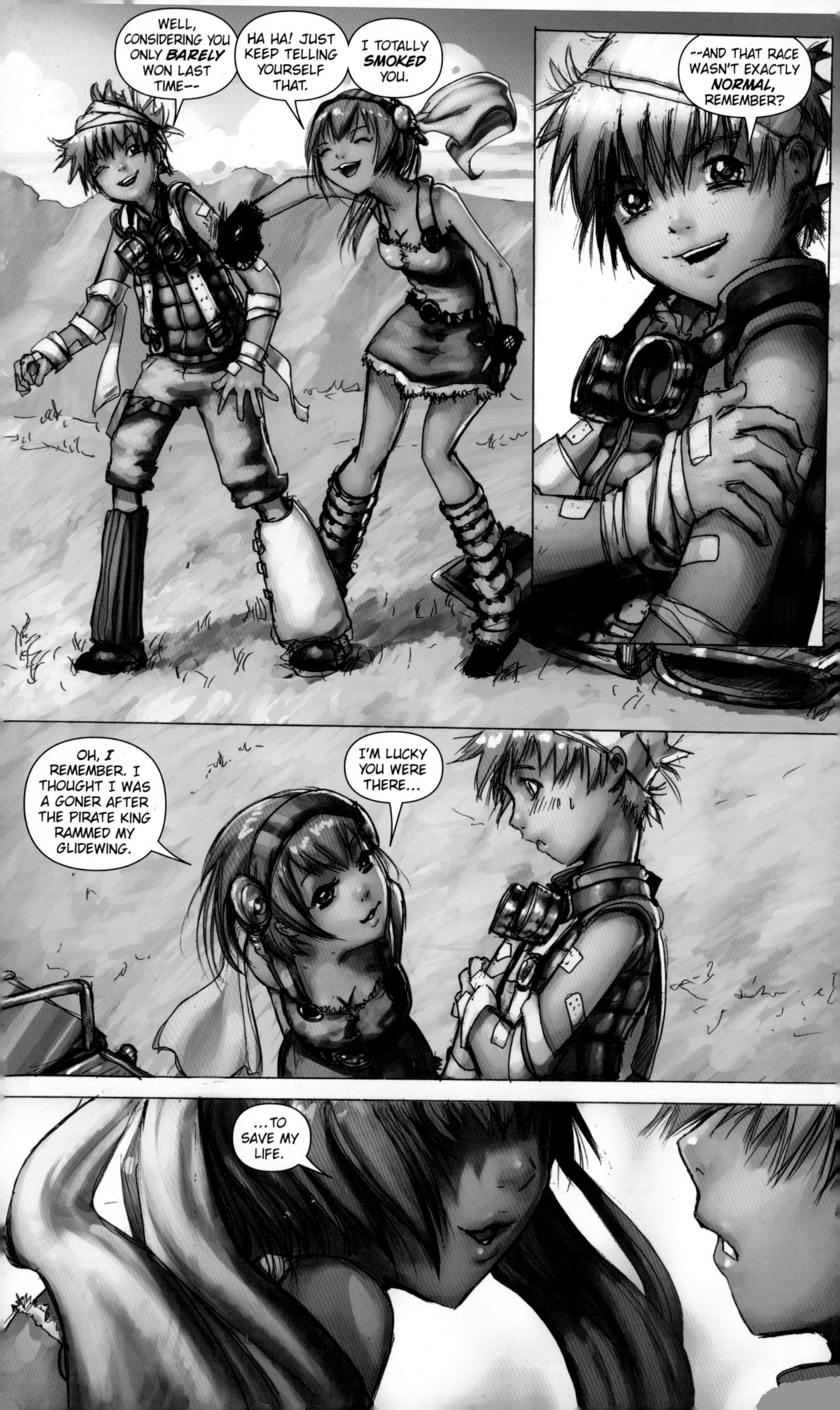
WELL, CONSIDERING YOU ONLY BARELY WON LAST TIME--
HA HA! JUST KEEP TELLING YOURSELF THAT.
I TOTALLY SMOKED YOU.
--AND THAT RACE WASN'T EXACTLY NORMAL, REMEMBER?
OH, I REMEMBER. I THOUGHT I WAS A GONER AFTER THE PIRATE KING RAMMED MY GLIDEWING.
I'M LUCKY YOU WERE THERE...
...TO SAVE MY LIFE.

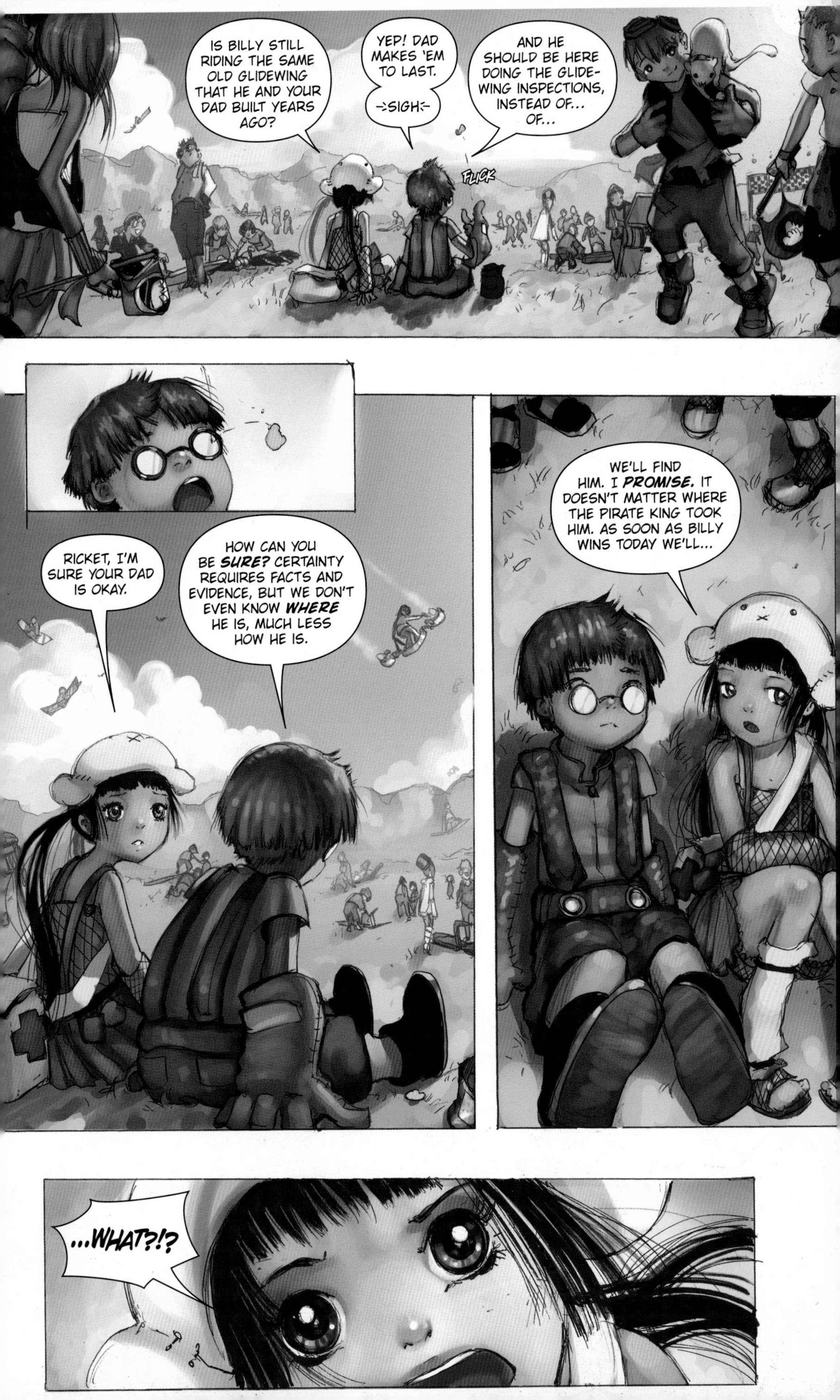
IS BILLY STILL RIDING THE SAME OLD GLIDEWING THAT HE AND YOUR DAD BUILT YEARS AGO?
YEP! DAD MAKES 'EM TO LAST.
-SIGH-
AND HE SHOULD BE HERE DOING THE GLIDE-WING INSPECTIONS, INSTEAD OF... OF...
FLICK
RICKET, I'M SURE YOUR DAD IS OKAY.
HOW CAN YOU BE SURE? CERTAINTY REQUIRES FACTS AND EVIDENCE, BUT WE DON'T EVEN KNOW WHERE HE IS, MUCH LESS HOW HE IS.
WE'LL FIND HIM. I PROMISE. IT DOESN'T MATTER WHERE THE PIRATE KING TOOK HIM. AS SOON AS BILLY WINS TODAY WE'LL...
...WHAT?!?

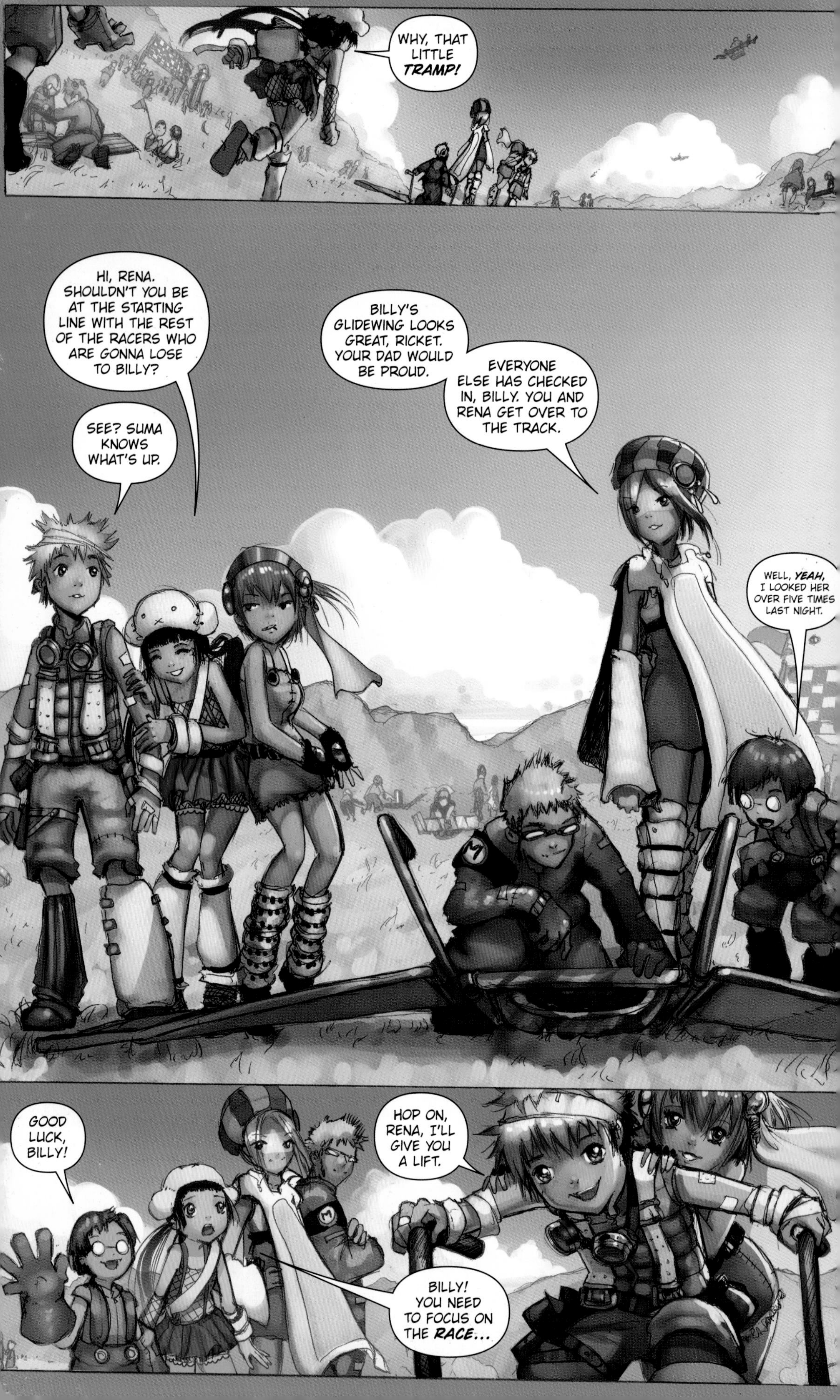
WHY, THAT LITTLE *TRAMP!*
HI, RENA. SHOULDN'T YOU BE AT THE STARTING LINE WITH THE REST OF THE RACERS WHO ARE GONNA LOSE TO BILLY?
SEE? SUMA KNOWS WHAT'S UP.
BILLY'S GLIDEWING LOOKS GREAT, RICKET. YOUR DAD WOULD BE PROUD.
EVERYONE ELSE HAS CHECKED IN, BILLY. YOU AND RENA GET OVER TO THE TRACK.
WELL, *YEAH,* I LOOKED HER OVER FIVE TIMES LAST NIGHT.
GOOD LUCK, BILLY!
HOP ON, RENA, I'LL GIVE YOU A LIFT.
BILLY! YOU NEED TO FOCUS ON THE *RACE...*

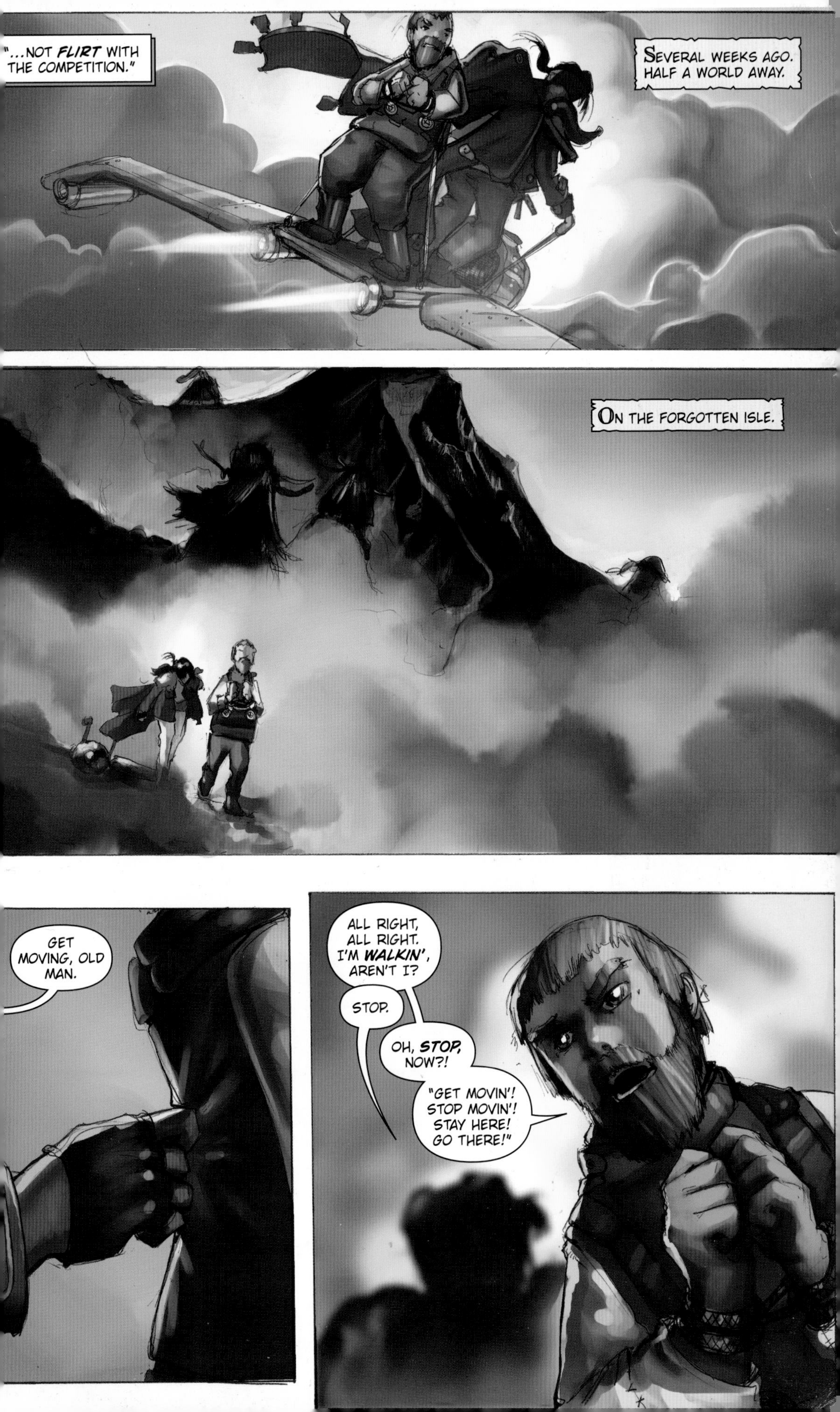
"...NOT FLIRT WITH THE COMPETITION."
SEVERAL WEEKS AGO. HALF A WORLD AWAY.
ON THE FORGOTTEN ISLE.
GET MOVING, OLD MAN.
ALL RIGHT, ALL RIGHT. I'M WALKIN', AREN'T I?
STOP.
OH, STOP, NOW?!
"GET MOVIN'! STOP MOVIN'! STAY HERE! GO THERE!"

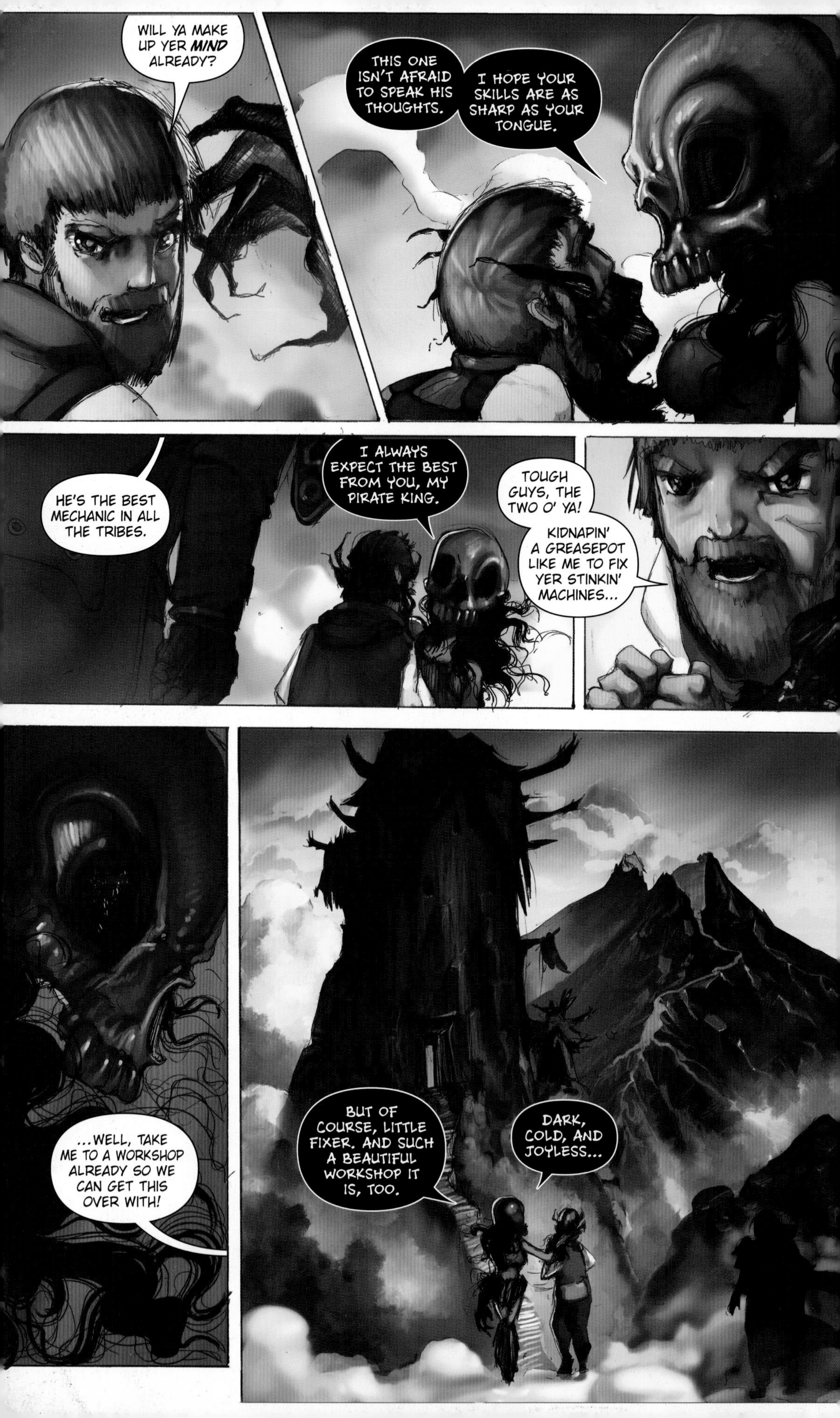
WILL YA MAKE UP YER MIND ALREADY?
THIS ONE ISN'T AFRAID TO SPEAK HIS THOUGHTS.
I HOPE YOUR SKILLS ARE AS SHARP AS YOUR TONGUE.
HE'S THE BEST MECHANIC IN ALL THE TRIBES.
I ALWAYS EXPECT THE BEST FROM YOU, MY PIRATE KING.
TOUGH GUYS, THE TWO O' YA!
KIDNAPIN' A GREASEPOT LIKE ME TO FIX YER STINKIN' MACHINES...
...WELL, TAKE ME TO A WORKSHOP ALREADY SO WE CAN GET THIS OVER WITH!
DARK, COLD, AND JOYLESS...
BUT OF COURSE, LITTLE FIXER. AND SUCH A BEAUTIFUL WORKSHOP IT IS, TOO.

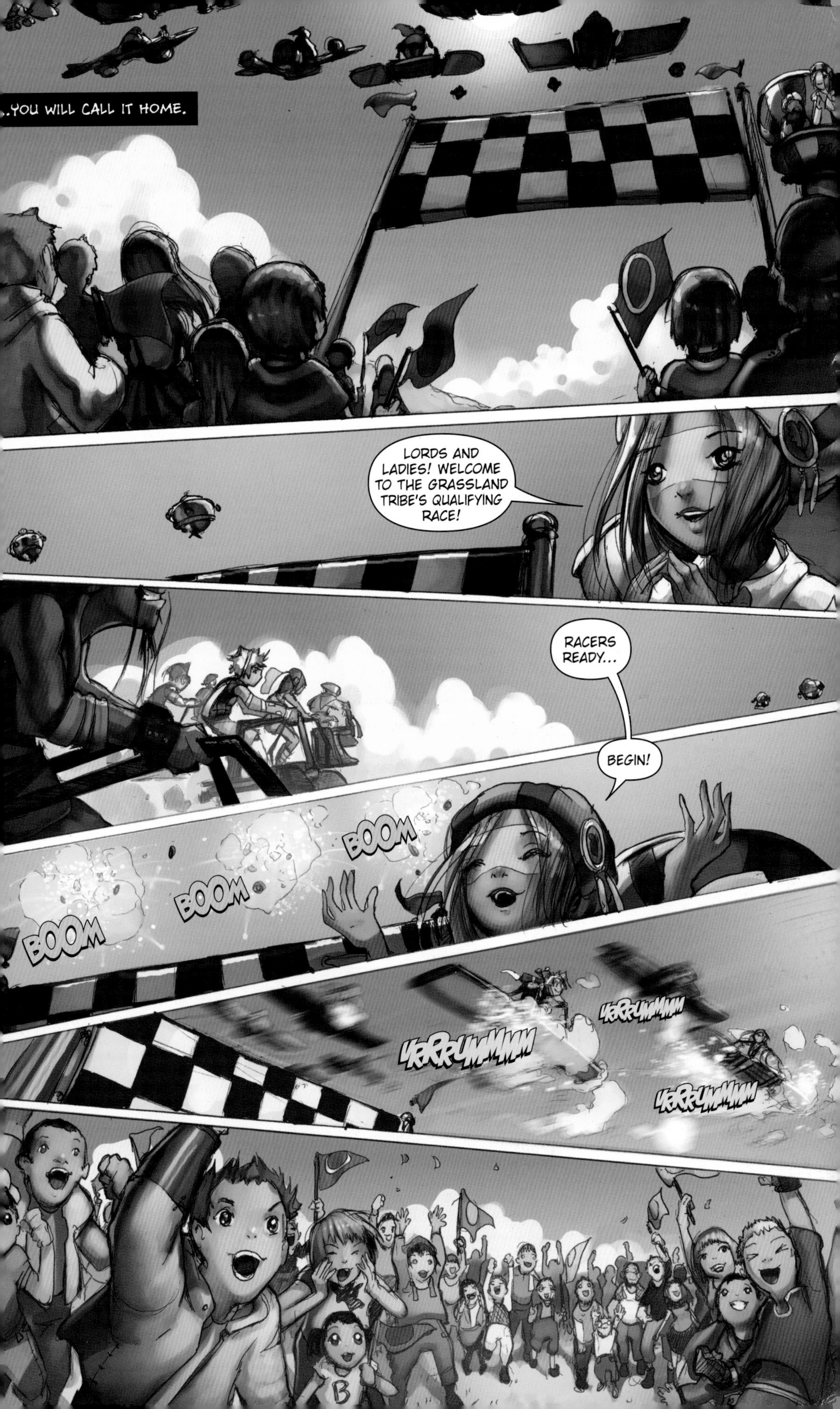
...YOU WILL CALL IT HOME.
LORDS AND LADIES! WELCOME TO THE GRASSLAND TRIBE'S QUALIFYING RACE!
RACERS READY...
BEGIN!
BOOM
BOOM
BOOM
VRRRUMMMM
VRRRUMMMM
VRRRUMMMM

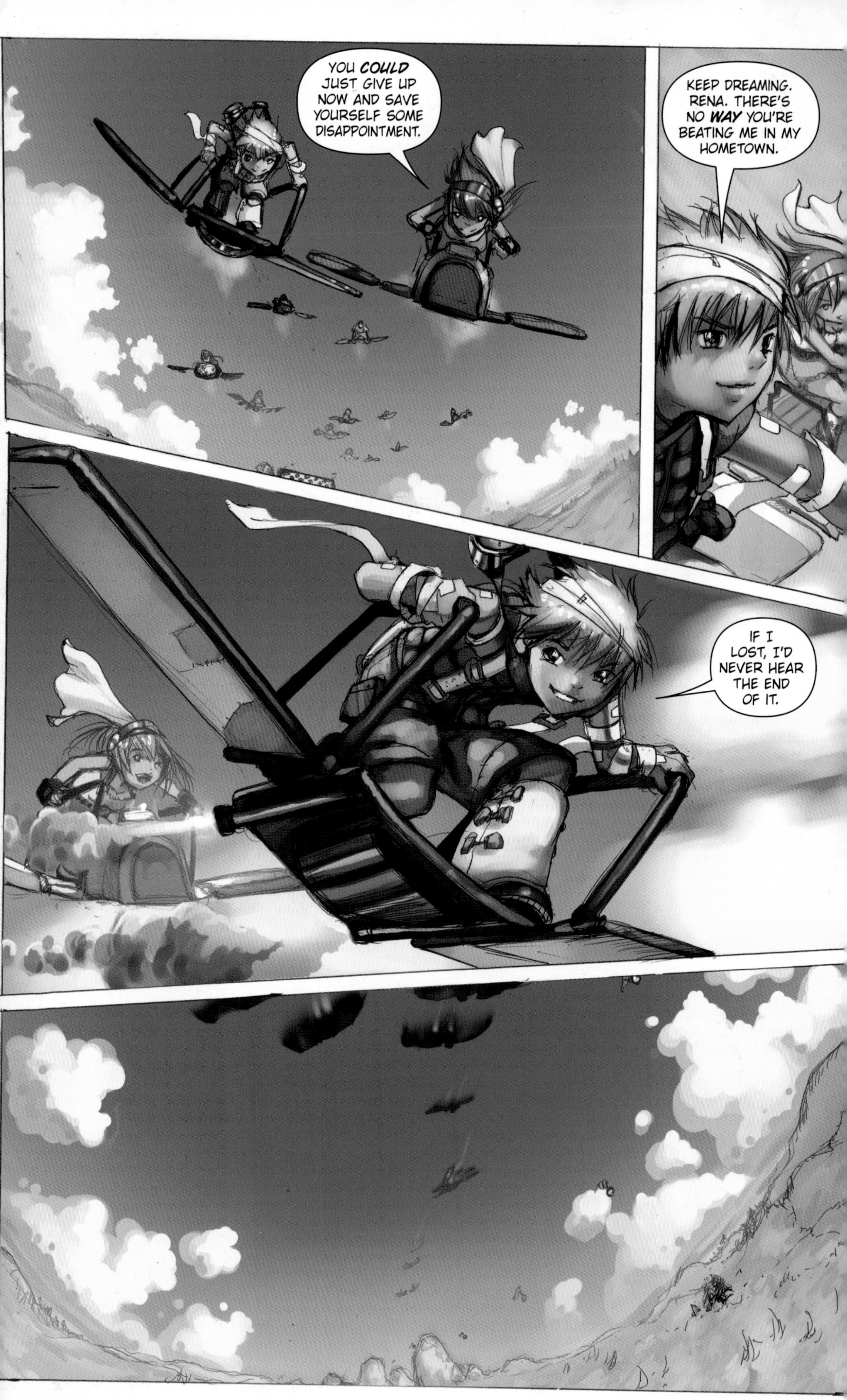
YOU **COULD** JUST GIVE UP NOW AND SAVE YOURSELF SOME DISAPPOINTMENT.
KEEP DREAMING. RENA. THERE'S NO **WAY** YOU'RE BEATING ME IN MY HOMETOWN.
IF I LOST, I'D NEVER HEAR THE END OF IT.

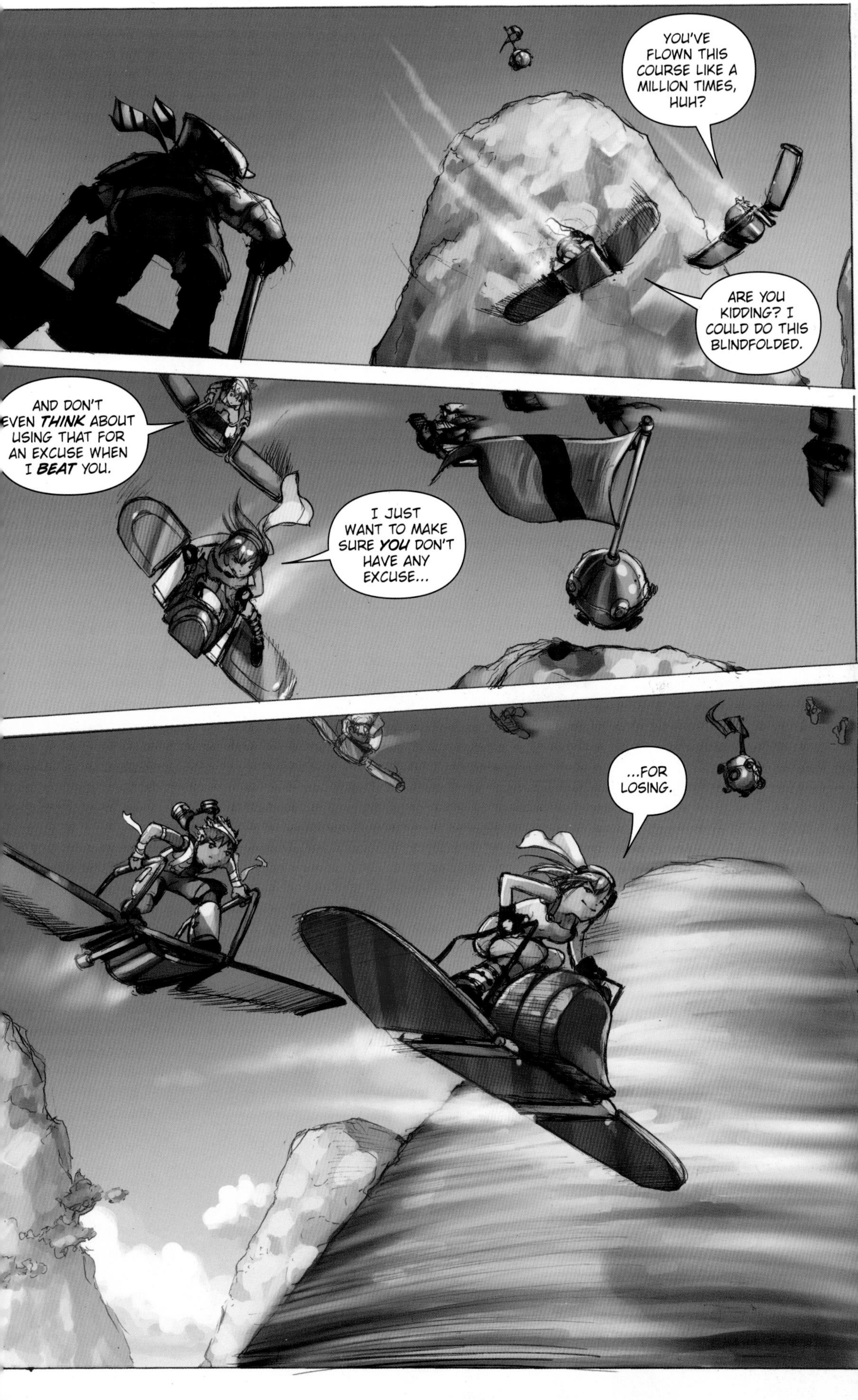
YOU'VE FLOWN THIS COURSE LIKE A MILLION TIMES, HUH?
ARE YOU KIDDING? I COULD DO THIS BLINDFOLDED.
AND DON'T EVEN *THINK* ABOUT USING THAT FOR AN EXCUSE WHEN I *BEAT* YOU.
I JUST WANT TO MAKE SURE *YOU* DON'T HAVE ANY EXCUSE...
...FOR LOSING.

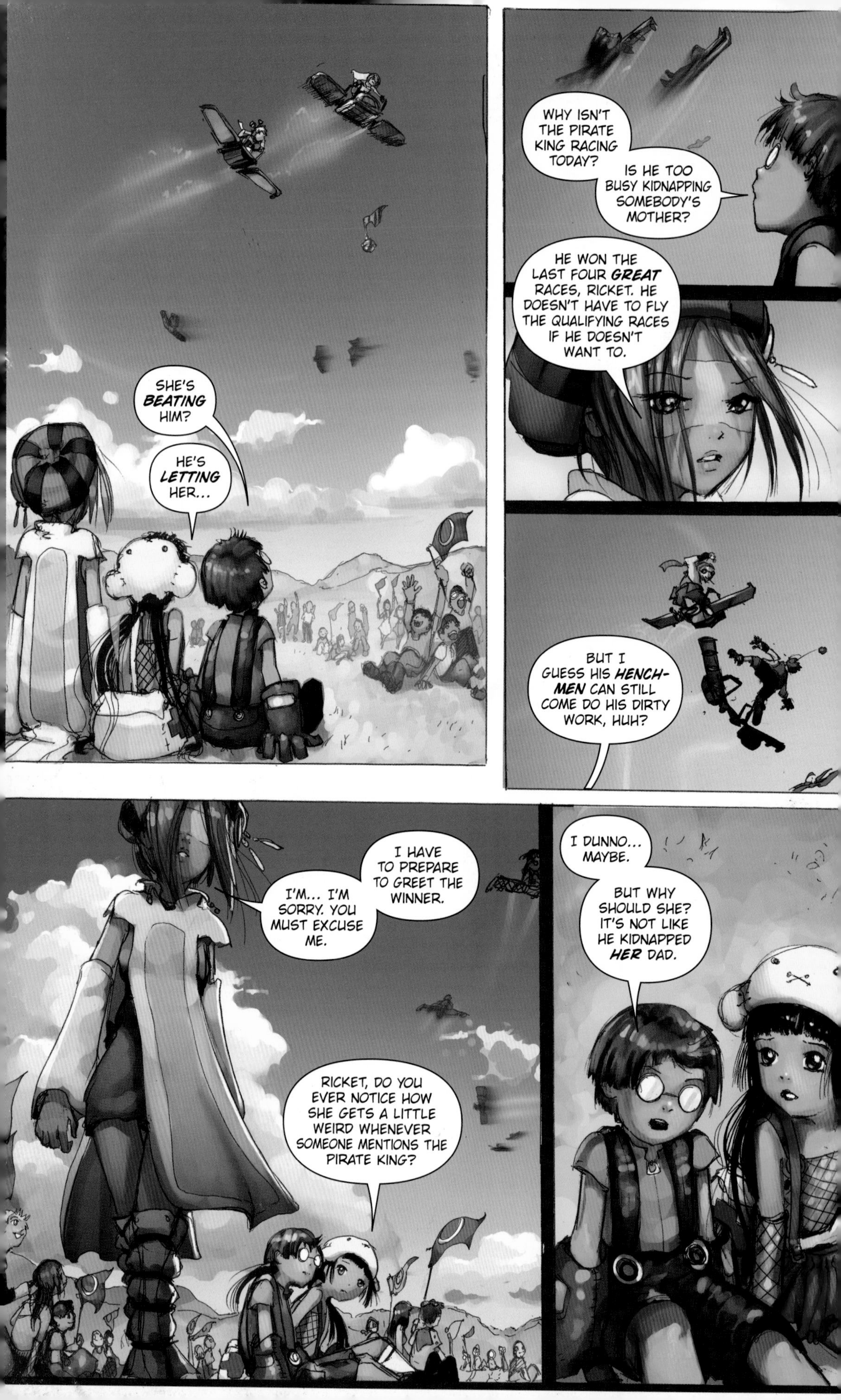
SHE'S **BEATING** HIM?
HE'S **LETTING** HER...
WHY ISN'T THE PIRATE KING RACING TODAY?
IS HE TOO BUSY KIDNAPPING SOMEBODY'S MOTHER?
HE WON THE LAST FOUR **GREAT** RACES, RICKET. HE DOESN'T HAVE TO FLY THE QUALIFYING RACES IF HE DOESN'T WANT TO.
BUT I GUESS HIS **HENCH-MEN** CAN STILL COME DO HIS DIRTY WORK, HUH?
I'M... I'M SORRY. YOU MUST EXCUSE ME.
I HAVE TO PREPARE TO GREET THE WINNER.
RICKET, DO YOU EVER NOTICE HOW SHE GETS A LITTLE WEIRD WHENEVER SOMEONE MENTIONS THE PIRATE KING?
I DUNNO... MAYBE.
BUT WHY SHOULD SHE? IT'S NOT LIKE HE KIDNAPPED **HER** DAD.

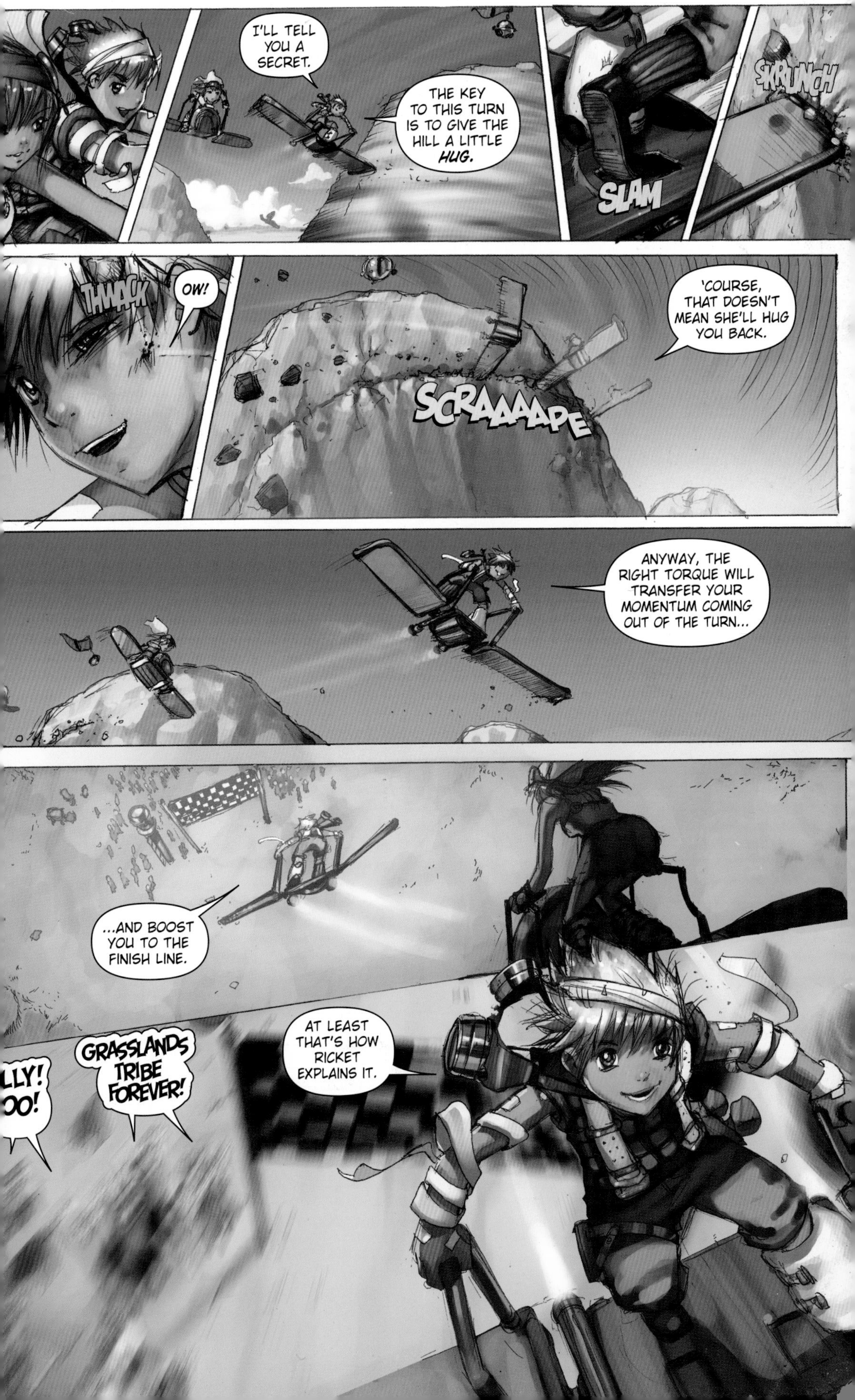

I'LL TELL YOU A SECRET.
THE KEY TO THIS TURN IS TO GIVE THE HILL A LITTLE HUG.
SLAM
SKRUNCH
THWACK
OW!
'COURSE, THAT DOESN'T MEAN SHE'LL HUG YOU BACK.
SCRAAAAPE
ANYWAY, THE RIGHT TORQUE WILL TRANSFER YOUR MOMENTUM COMING OUT OF THE TURN...
...AND BOOST YOU TO THE FINISH LINE.
GRASSLANDS TRIBE FOREVER!
AT LEAST THAT'S HOW RICKET EXPLAINS IT.

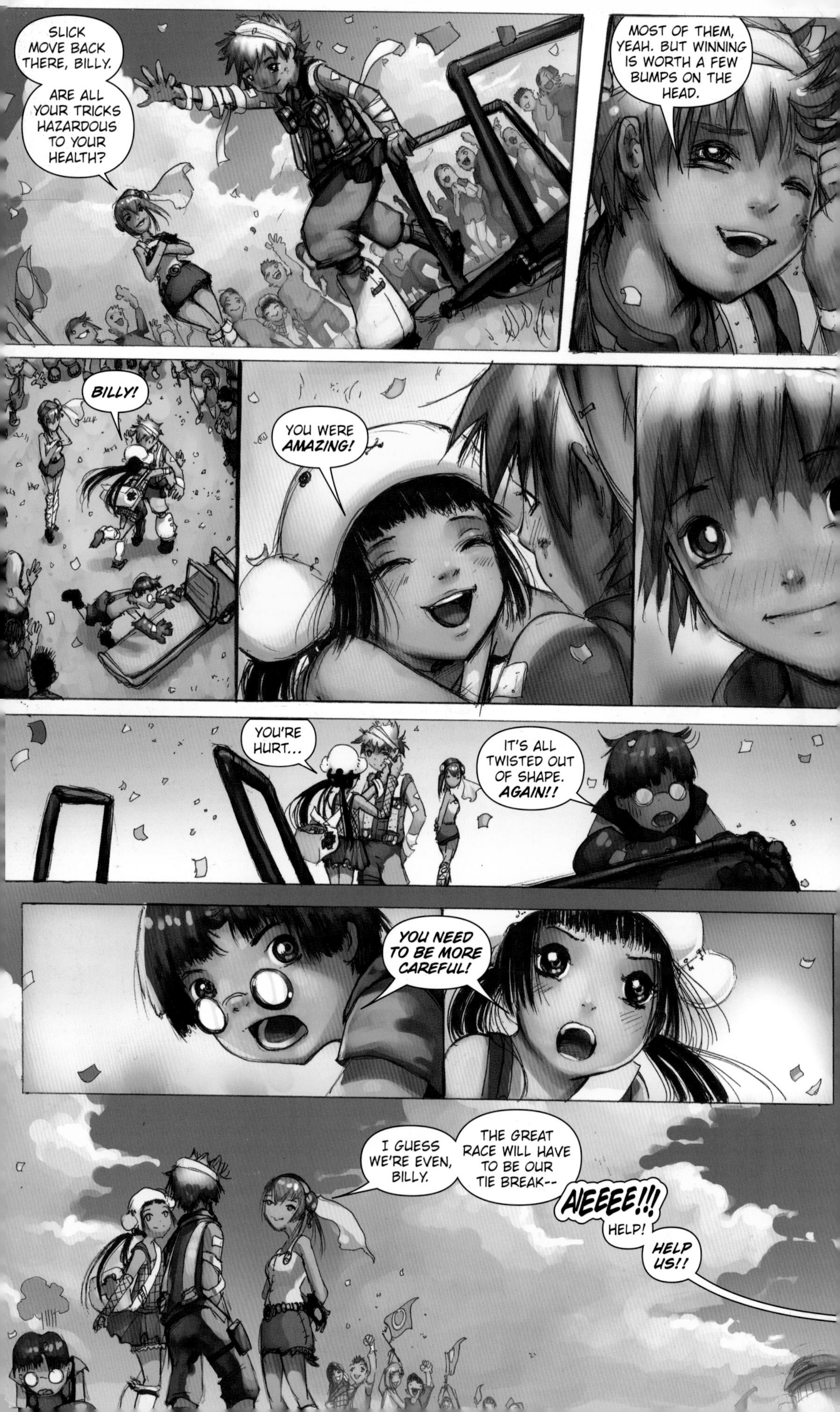
SLICK MOVE BACK THERE, BILLY.
ARE ALL YOUR TRICKS HAZARDOUS TO YOUR HEALTH?
MOST OF THEM, YEAH. BUT WINNING IS WORTH A FEW BUMPS ON THE HEAD.
BILLY!
YOU WERE AMAZING!
YOU'RE HURT...
IT'S ALL TWISTED OUT OF SHAPE. AGAIN!!
YOU NEED TO BE MORE CAREFUL!
I GUESS WE'RE EVEN, BILLY.
THE GREAT RACE WILL HAVE TO BE OUR TIE BREAK--
AIEEEE!!!
HELP!
HELP US!!

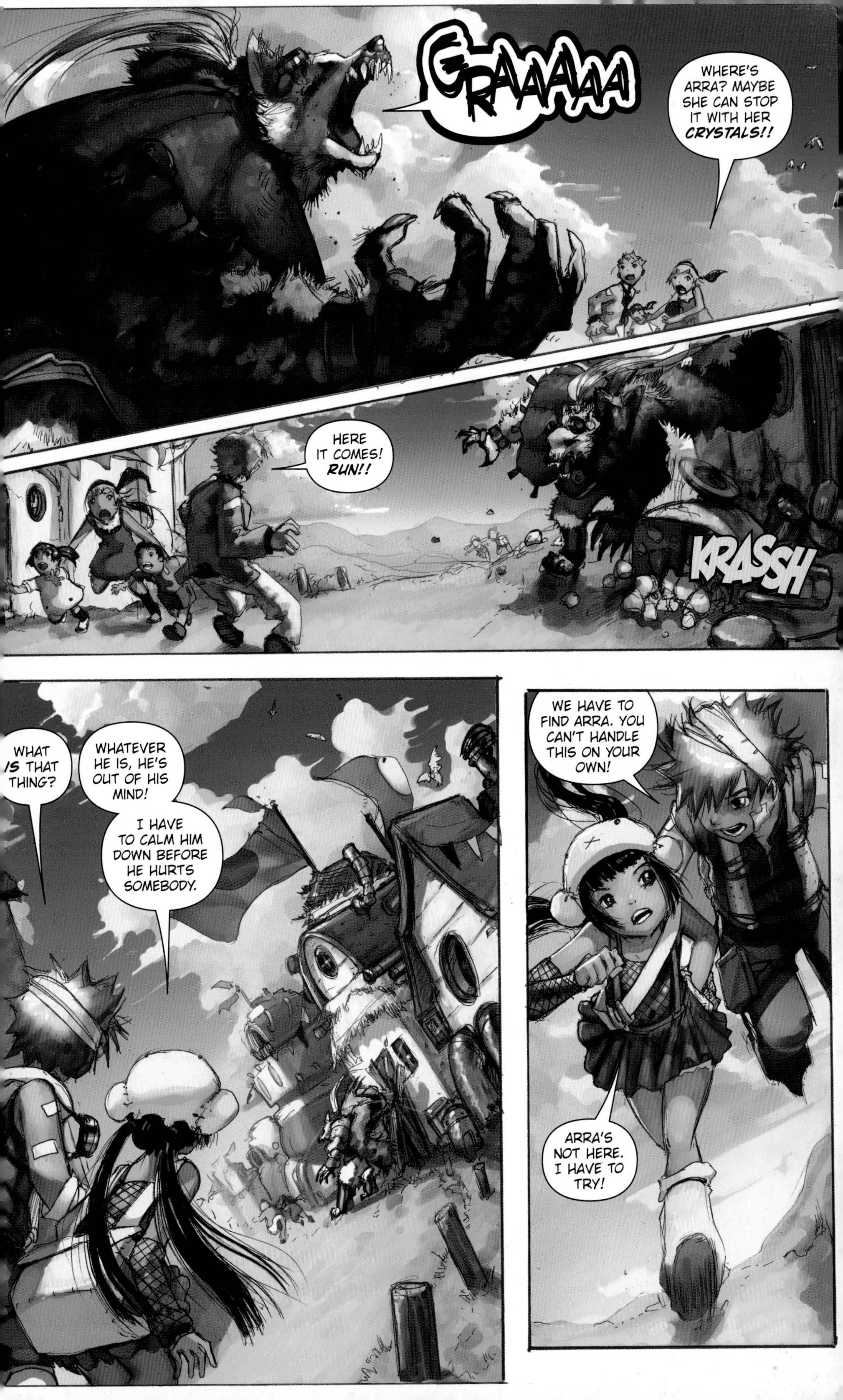
GRAAAAAA
WHERE'S ARRA? MAYBE SHE CAN STOP IT WITH HER CRYSTALS!!
HERE IT COMES! RUN!!
KRASSH
WHAT IS THAT THING?
WHATEVER HE IS, HE'S OUT OF HIS MIND!
I HAVE TO CALM HIM DOWN BEFORE HE HURTS SOMEBODY.
WE HAVE TO FIND ARRA. YOU CAN'T HANDLE THIS ON YOUR OWN!
ARRA'S NOT HERE. I HAVE TO TRY!

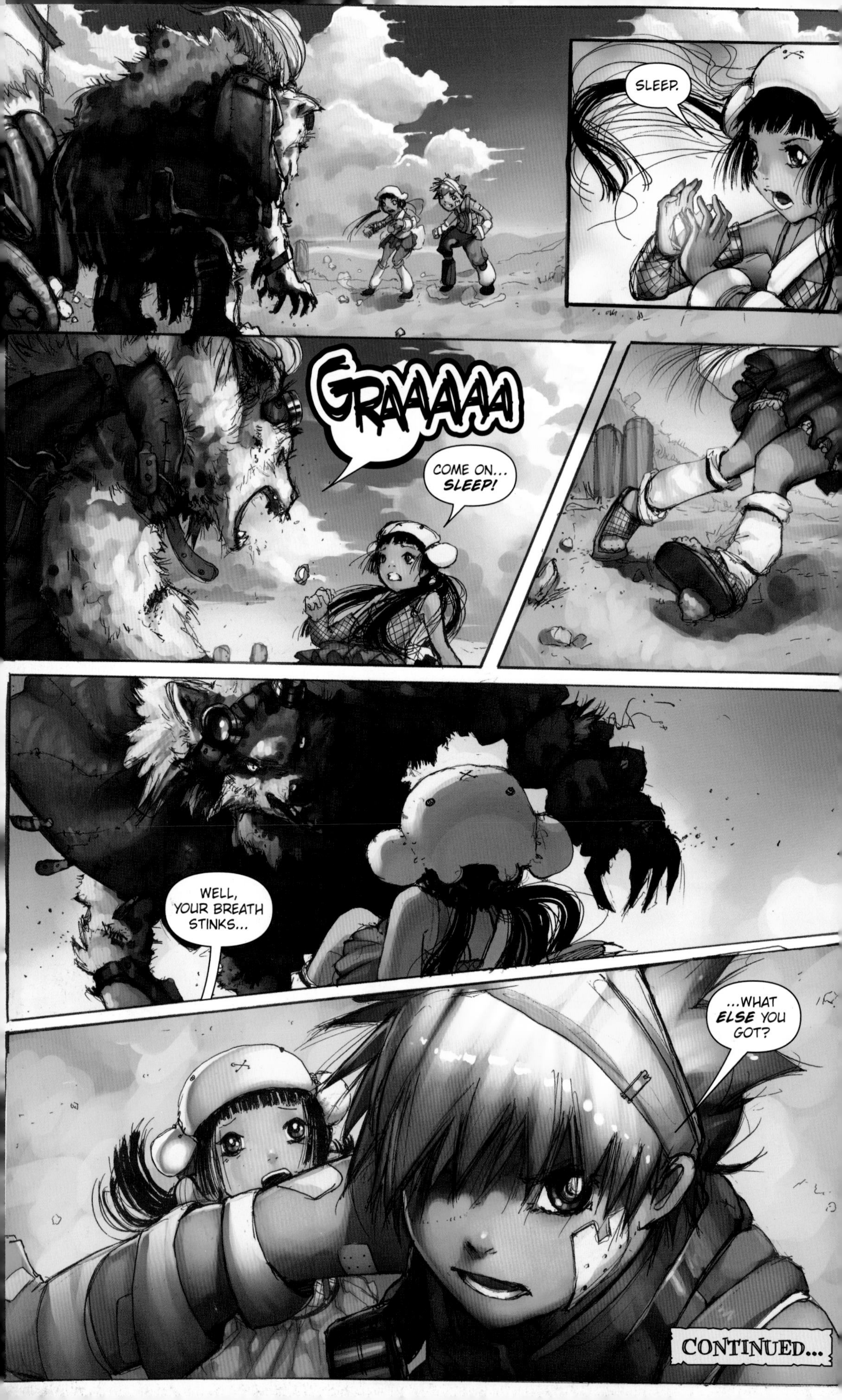
SLEEP.
GRAAAAAA
COME ON... SLEEP!
WELL, YOUR BREATH STINKS...
...WHAT ELSE YOU GOT?
CONTINUED...

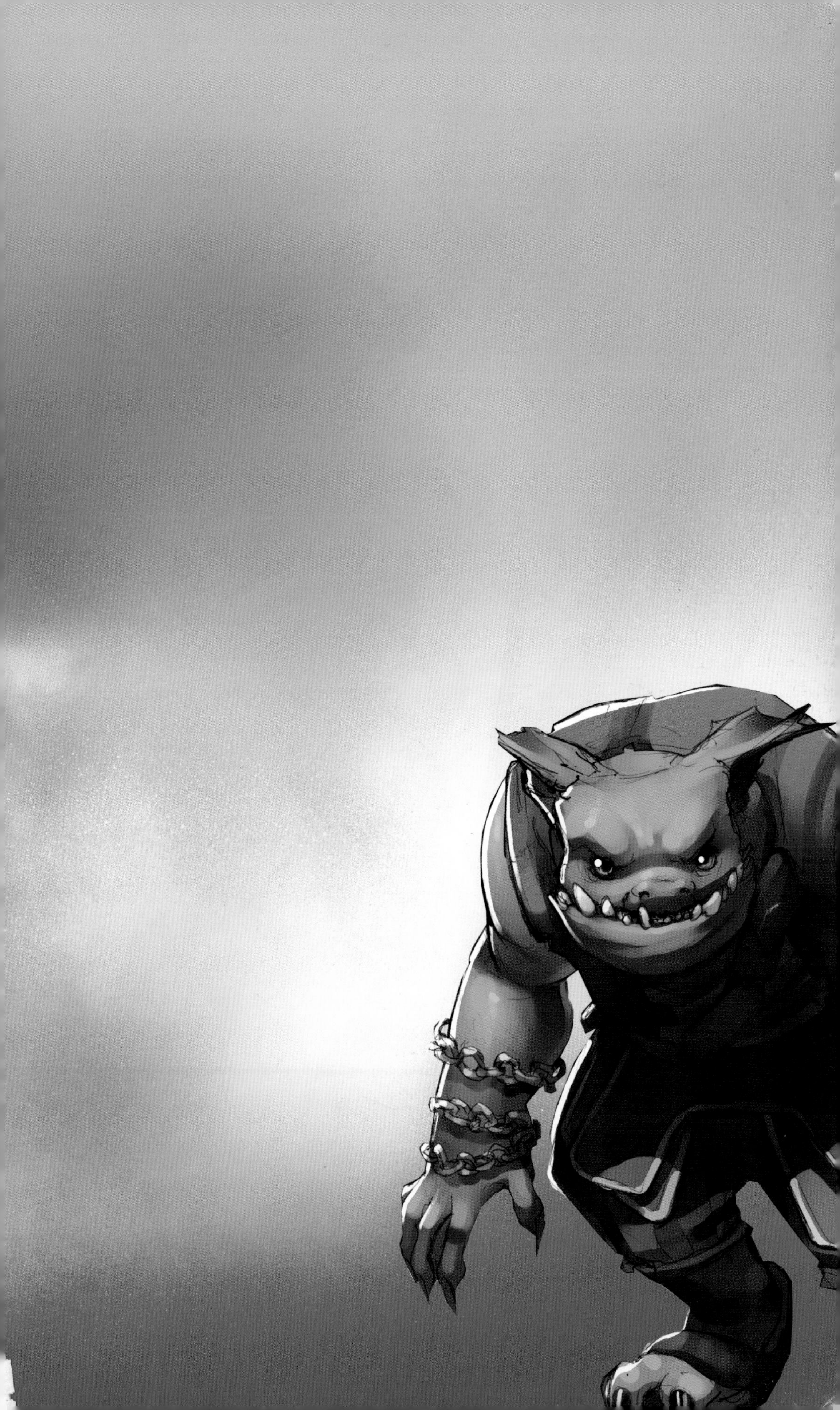

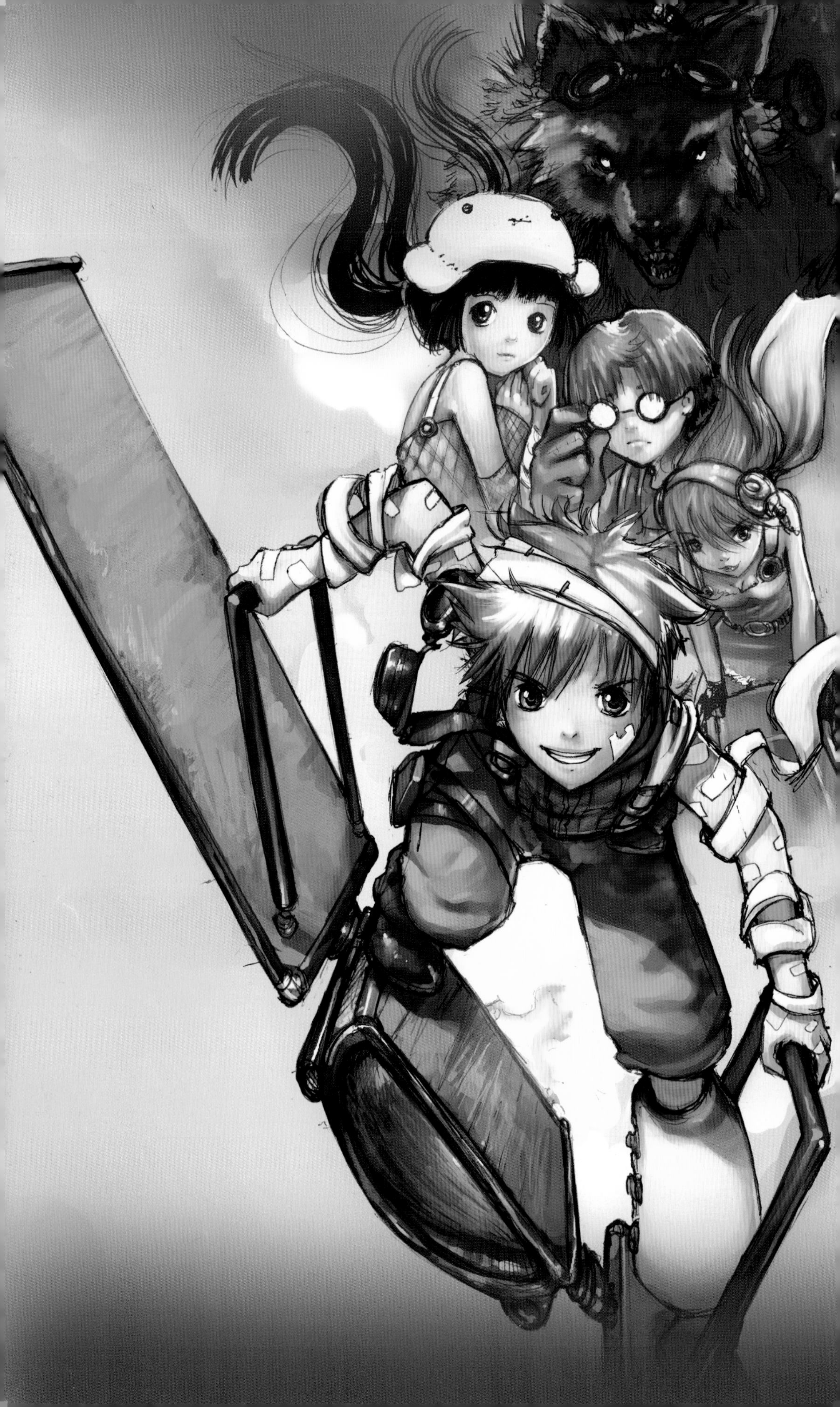

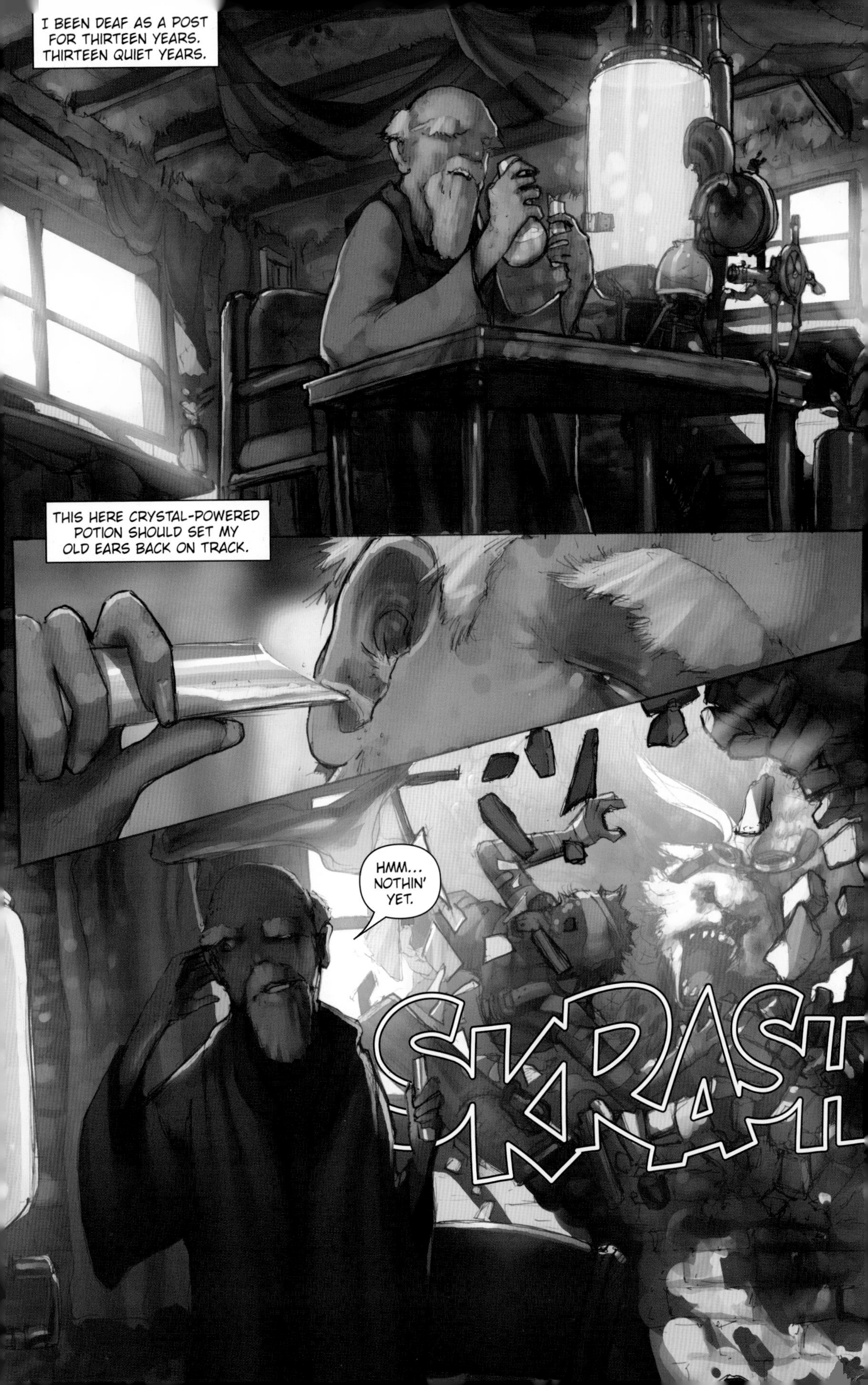
I BEEN DEAF AS A POST FOR THIRTEEN YEARS. THIRTEEN QUIET YEARS.
THIS HERE CRYSTAL-POWERED POTION SHOULD SET MY OLD EARS BACK ON TRACK.
HMM... NOTHIN' YET.
SKRASH

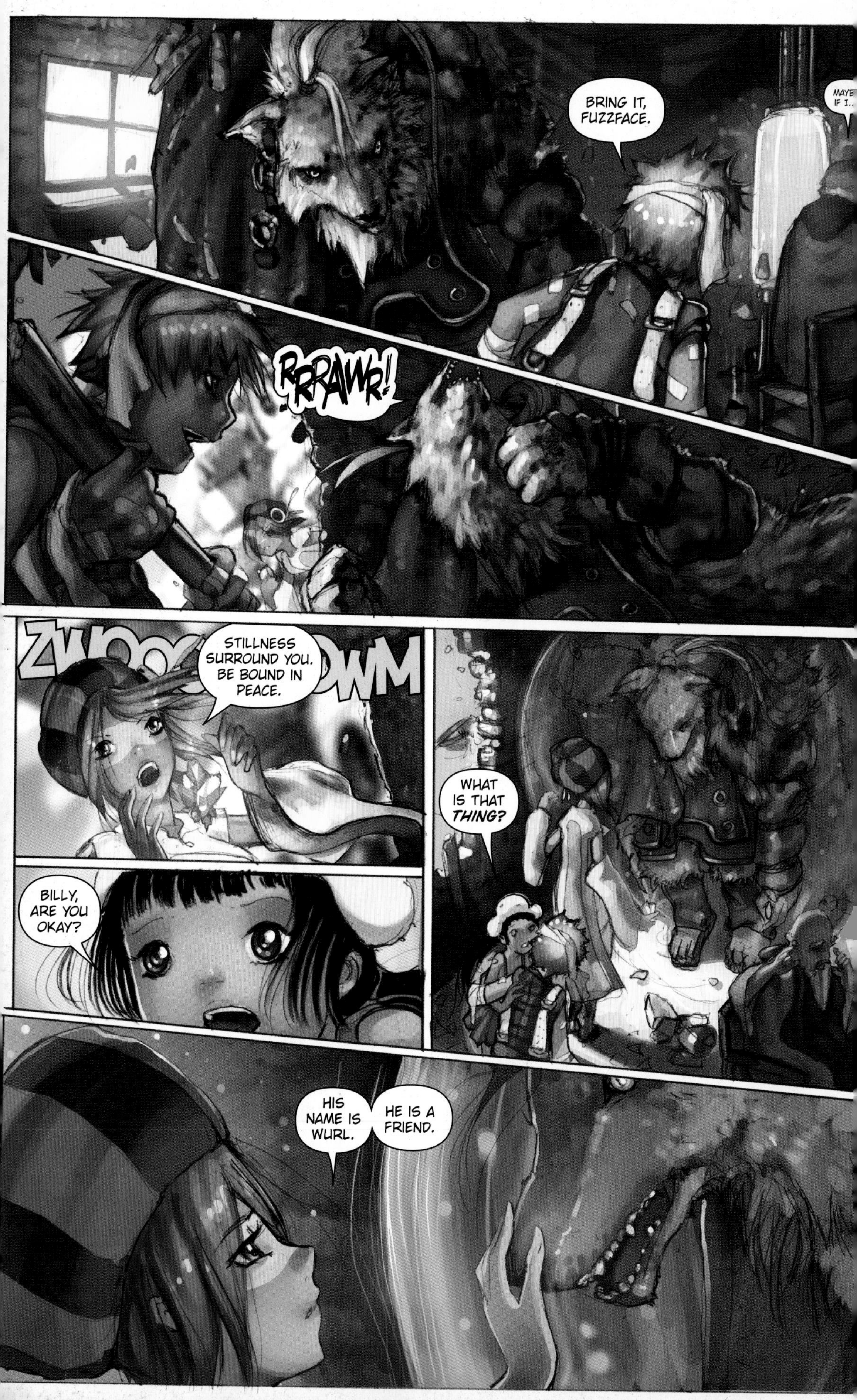
BRING IT, FUZZFACE.
RRRAWR!
STILLNESS SURROUND YOU. BE BOUND IN PEACE.
WHAT IS THAT *THING?*
BILLY, ARE YOU OKAY?
HIS NAME IS WURL.
HE IS A FRIEND.

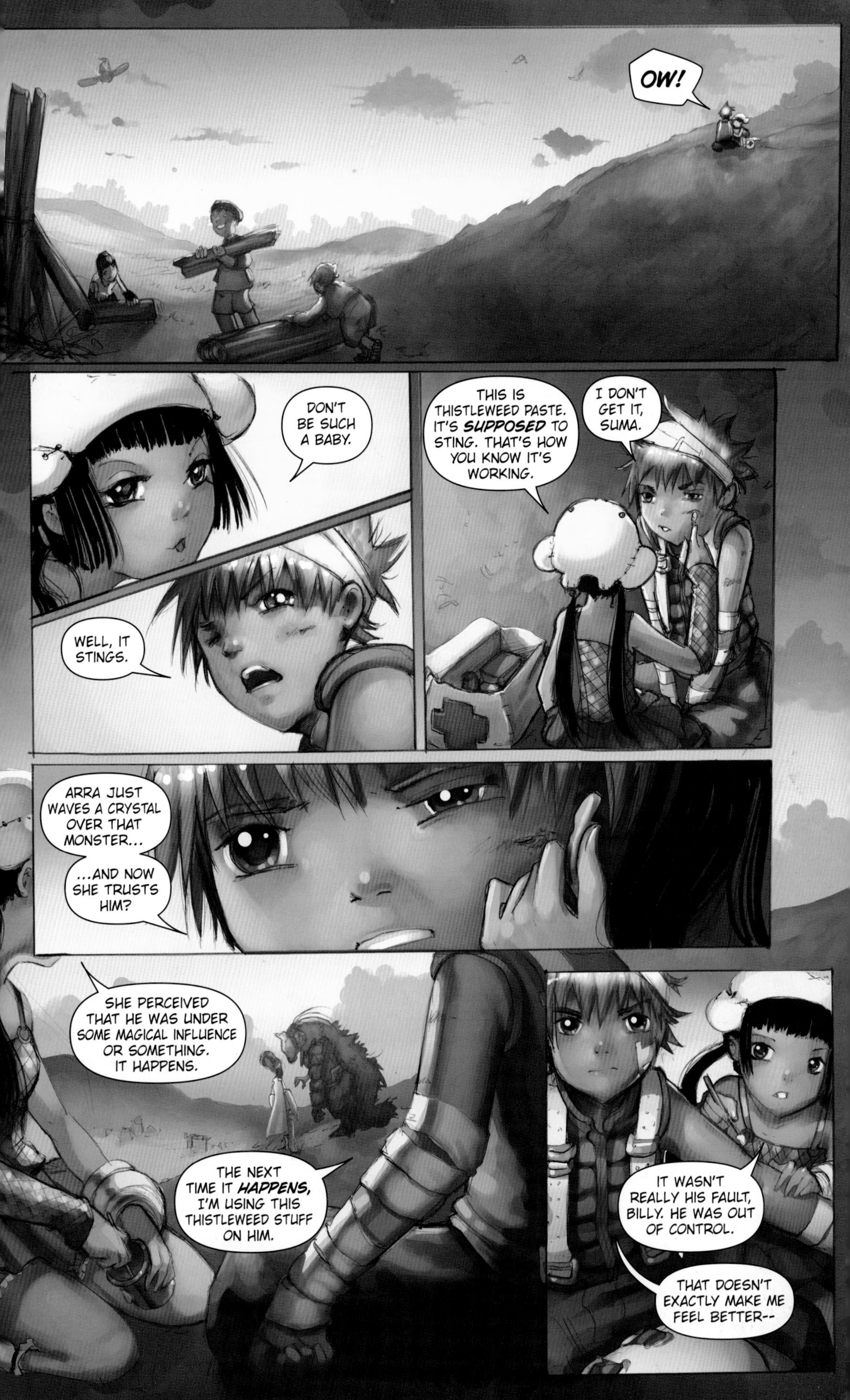
OW!
DON'T BE SUCH A BABY.
WELL, IT STINGS.
THIS IS THISTLEWEED PASTE. IT'S *SUPPOSED* TO STING. THAT'S HOW YOU KNOW IT'S WORKING.
I DON'T GET IT, SUMA.
ARRA JUST WAVES A CRYSTAL OVER THAT MONSTER...
...AND NOW SHE TRUSTS HIM?
SHE PERCEIVED THAT HE WAS UNDER SOME MAGICAL INFLUENCE OR SOMETHING. IT HAPPENS.
THE NEXT TIME IT *HAPPENS,* I'M USING THIS THISTLEWEED STUFF ON HIM.
IT WASN'T REALLY HIS FAULT, BILLY. HE WAS OUT OF CONTROL.
THAT DOESN'T EXACTLY MAKE ME FEEL BETTER--

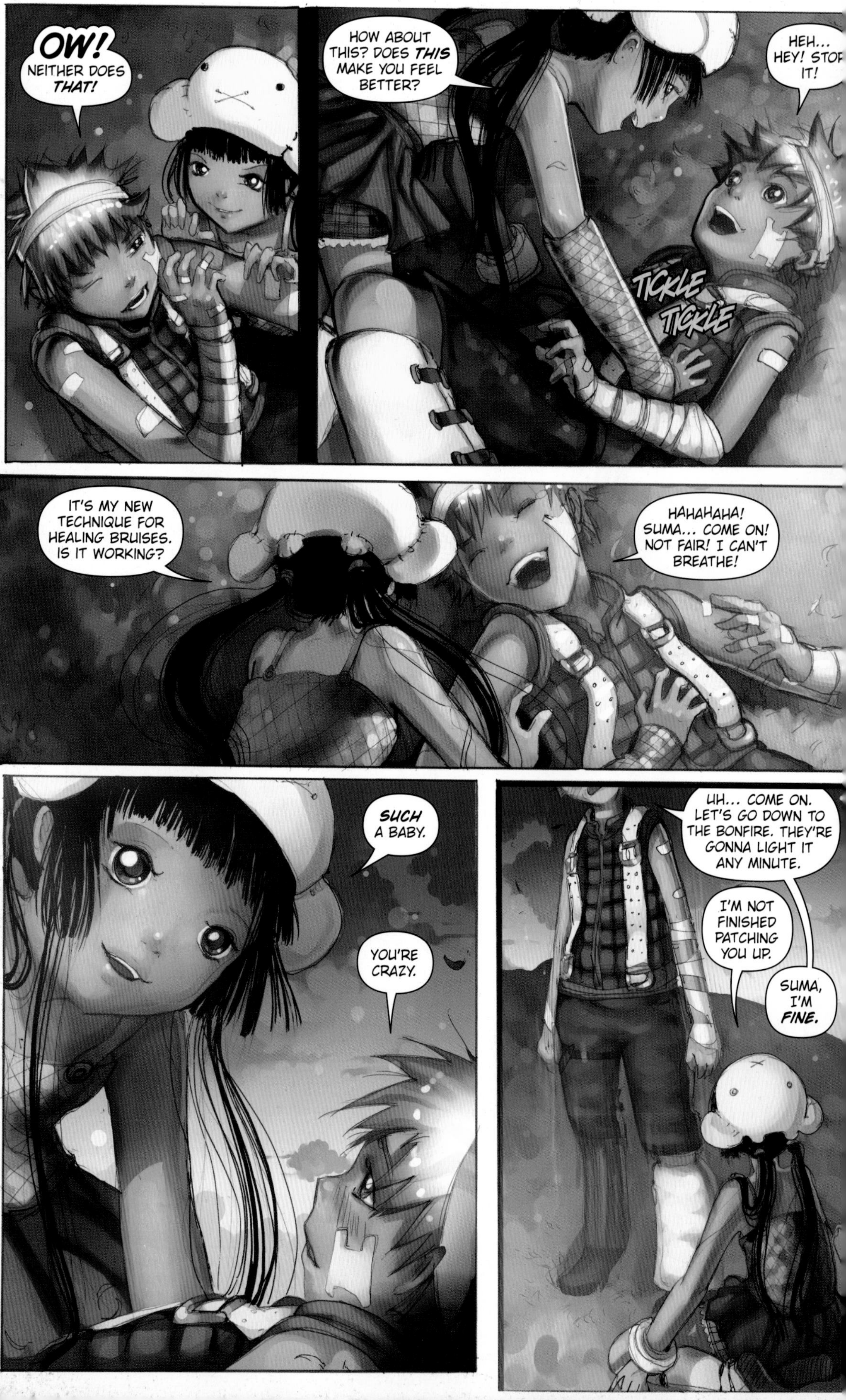
OW! NEITHER DOES THAT!
HOW ABOUT THIS? DOES THIS MAKE YOU FEEL BETTER?
HEH... HEY! STOP IT!
TICKLE TICKLE
IT'S MY NEW TECHNIQUE FOR HEALING BRUISES. IS IT WORKING?
HAHAHAHA! SUMA... COME ON! NOT FAIR! I CAN'T BREATHE!
SUCH A BABY.
YOU'RE CRAZY.
UH... COME ON. LET'S GO DOWN TO THE BONFIRE. THEY'RE GONNA LIGHT IT ANY MINUTE.
I'M NOT FINISHED PATCHING YOU UP.
SUMA, I'M FINE.

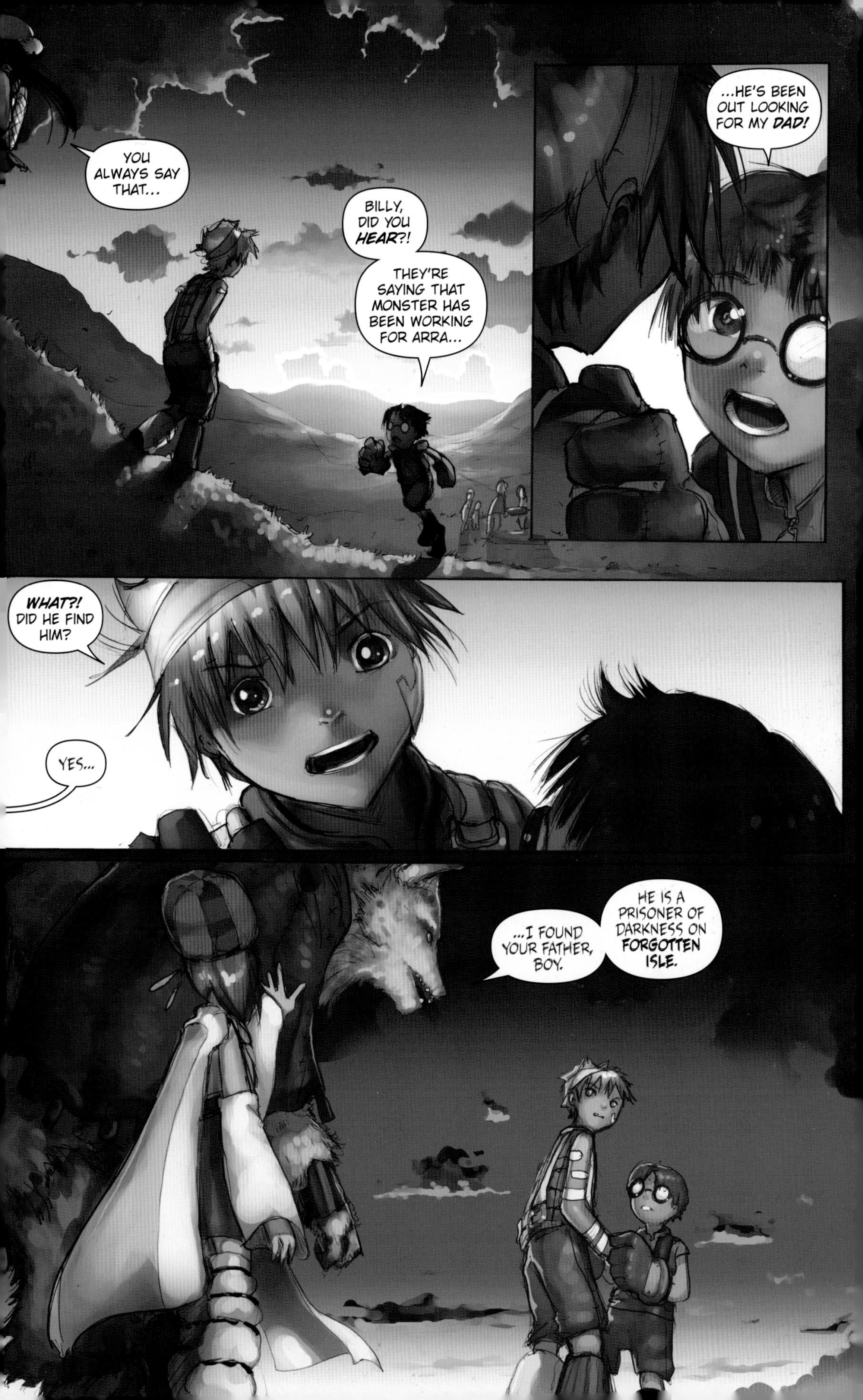
YOU ALWAYS SAY THAT...
BILLY, DID YOU HEAR?!
THEY'RE SAYING THAT MONSTER HAS BEEN WORKING FOR ARRA...
...HE'S BEEN OUT LOOKING FOR MY DAD!
WHAT?! DID HE FIND HIM?
YES...
...I FOUND YOUR FATHER, BOY.
HE IS A PRISONER OF DARKNESS ON FORGOTTEN ISLE.

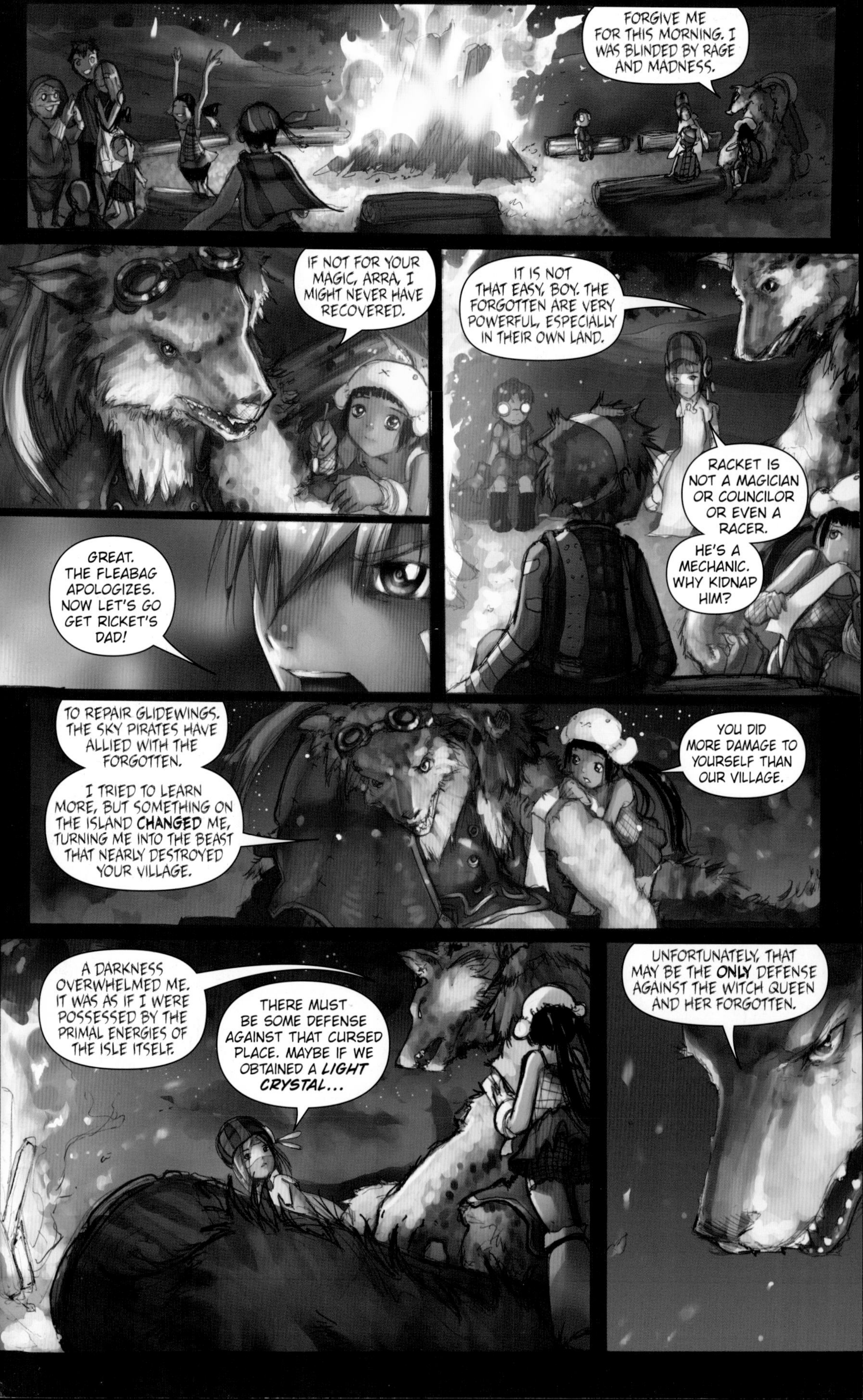
FORGIVE ME FOR THIS MORNING. I WAS BLINDED BY RAGE AND MADNESS.
IF NOT FOR YOUR MAGIC, ARRA, I MIGHT NEVER HAVE RECOVERED.
GREAT. THE FLEABAG APOLOGIZES. NOW LET'S GO GET RICKET'S DAD!
IT IS NOT THAT EASY, BOY. THE FORGOTTEN ARE VERY POWERFUL, ESPECIALLY IN THEIR OWN LAND.
RACKET IS NOT A MAGICIAN OR COUNCILOR OR EVEN A RACER.
HE'S A MECHANIC. WHY KIDNAP HIM?
TO REPAIR GLIDEWINGS. THE SKY PIRATES HAVE ALLIED WITH THE FORGOTTEN.
I TRIED TO LEARN MORE, BUT SOMETHING ON THE ISLAND **CHANGED** ME, TURNING ME INTO THE BEAST THAT NEARLY DESTROYED YOUR VILLAGE.
YOU DID MORE DAMAGE TO YOURSELF THAN OUR VILLAGE.
A DARKNESS OVERWHELMED ME. IT WAS AS IF I WERE POSSESSED BY THE PRIMAL ENERGIES OF THE ISLE ITSELF.
THERE MUST BE SOME DEFENSE AGAINST THAT CURSED PLACE. MAYBE IF WE OBTAINED A ***LIGHT CRYSTAL...***
UNFORTUNATELY, THAT MAY BE THE **ONLY** DEFENSE AGAINST THE WITCH QUEEN AND HER FORGOTTEN.

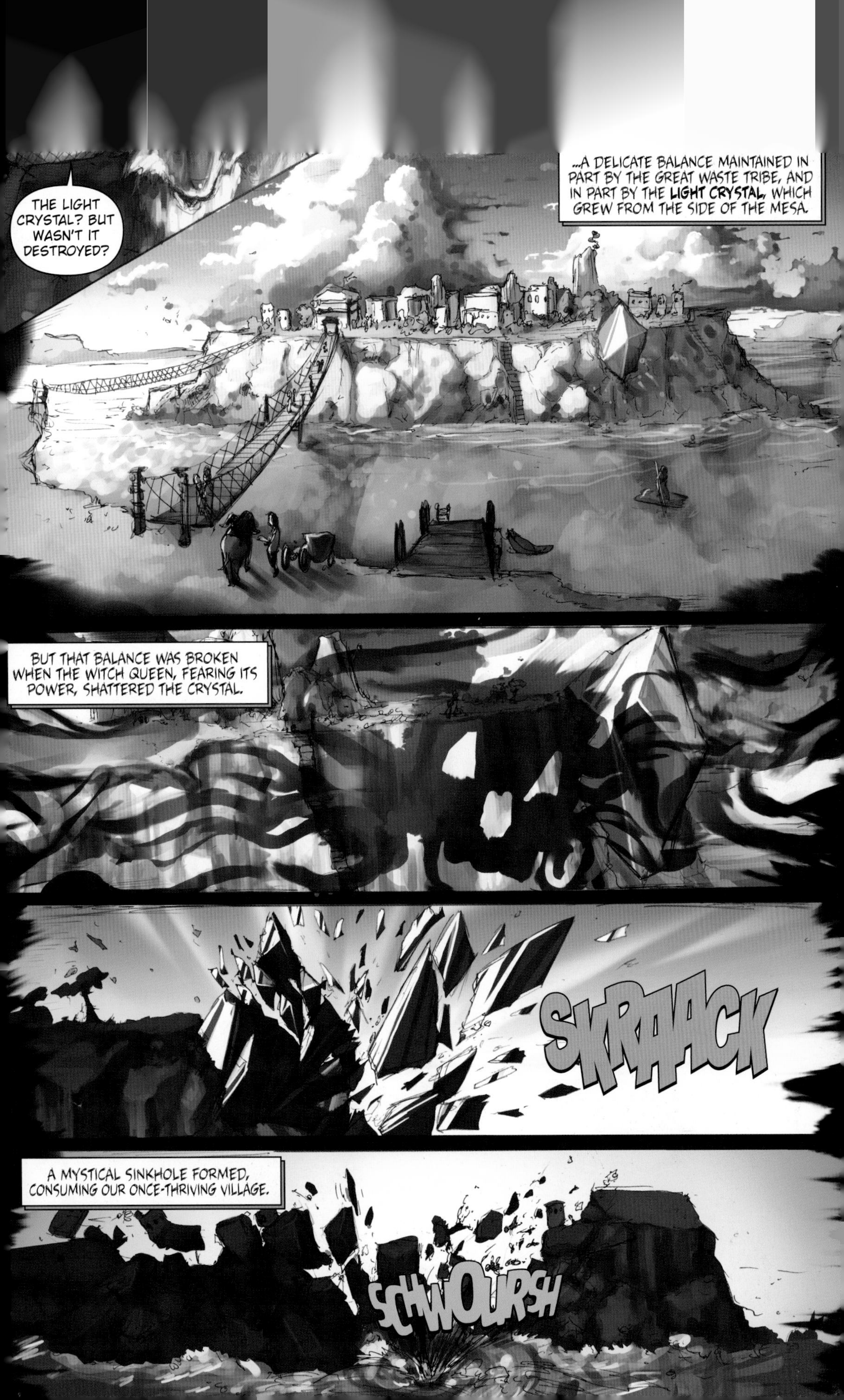

THE LIGHT CRYSTAL? BUT WASN'T IT DESTROYED?
...A DELICATE BALANCE MAINTAINED IN PART BY THE GREAT WASTE TRIBE, AND IN PART BY THE LIGHT CRYSTAL, WHICH GREW FROM THE SIDE OF THE MESA.
BUT THAT BALANCE WAS BROKEN WHEN THE WITCH QUEEN, FEARING ITS POWER, SHATTERED THE CRYSTAL.
SKRAACK
A MYSTICAL SINKHOLE FORMED, CONSUMING OUR ONCE-THRIVING VILLAGE.
SCHWOURSH

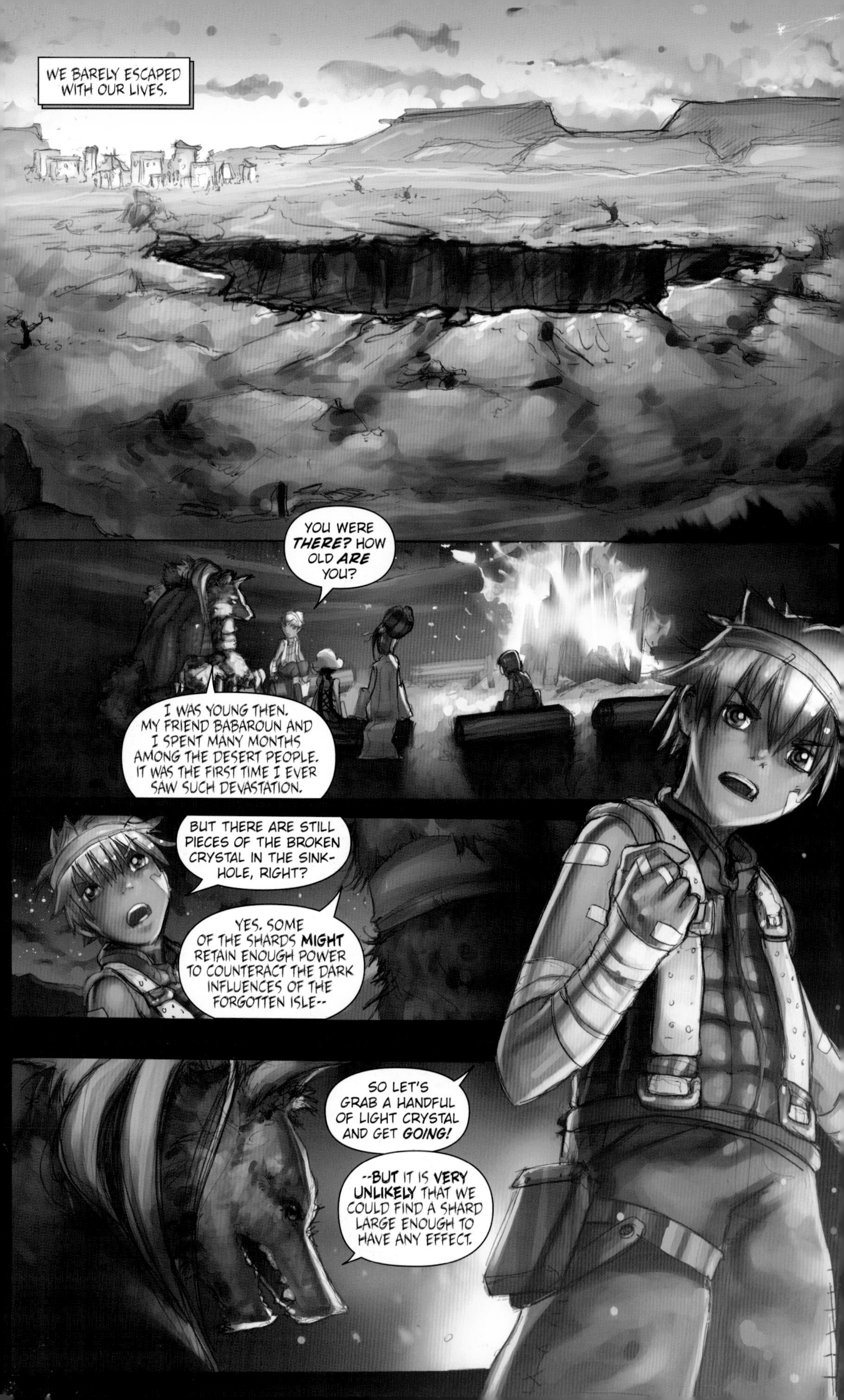
WE BARELY ESCAPED WITH OUR LIVES.
YOU WERE THERE? HOW OLD ARE YOU?
I WAS YOUNG THEN. MY FRIEND BABAROUN AND I SPENT MANY MONTHS AMONG THE DESERT PEOPLE. IT WAS THE FIRST TIME I EVER SAW SUCH DEVASTATION.
BUT THERE ARE STILL PIECES OF THE BROKEN CRYSTAL IN THE SINK-HOLE, RIGHT?
YES. SOME OF THE SHARDS MIGHT RETAIN ENOUGH POWER TO COUNTERACT THE DARK INFLUENCES OF THE FORGOTTEN ISLE--
SO LET'S GRAB A HANDFUL OF LIGHT CRYSTAL AND GET GOING!
--BUT IT IS VERY UNLIKELY THAT WE COULD FIND A SHARD LARGE ENOUGH TO HAVE ANY EFFECT.

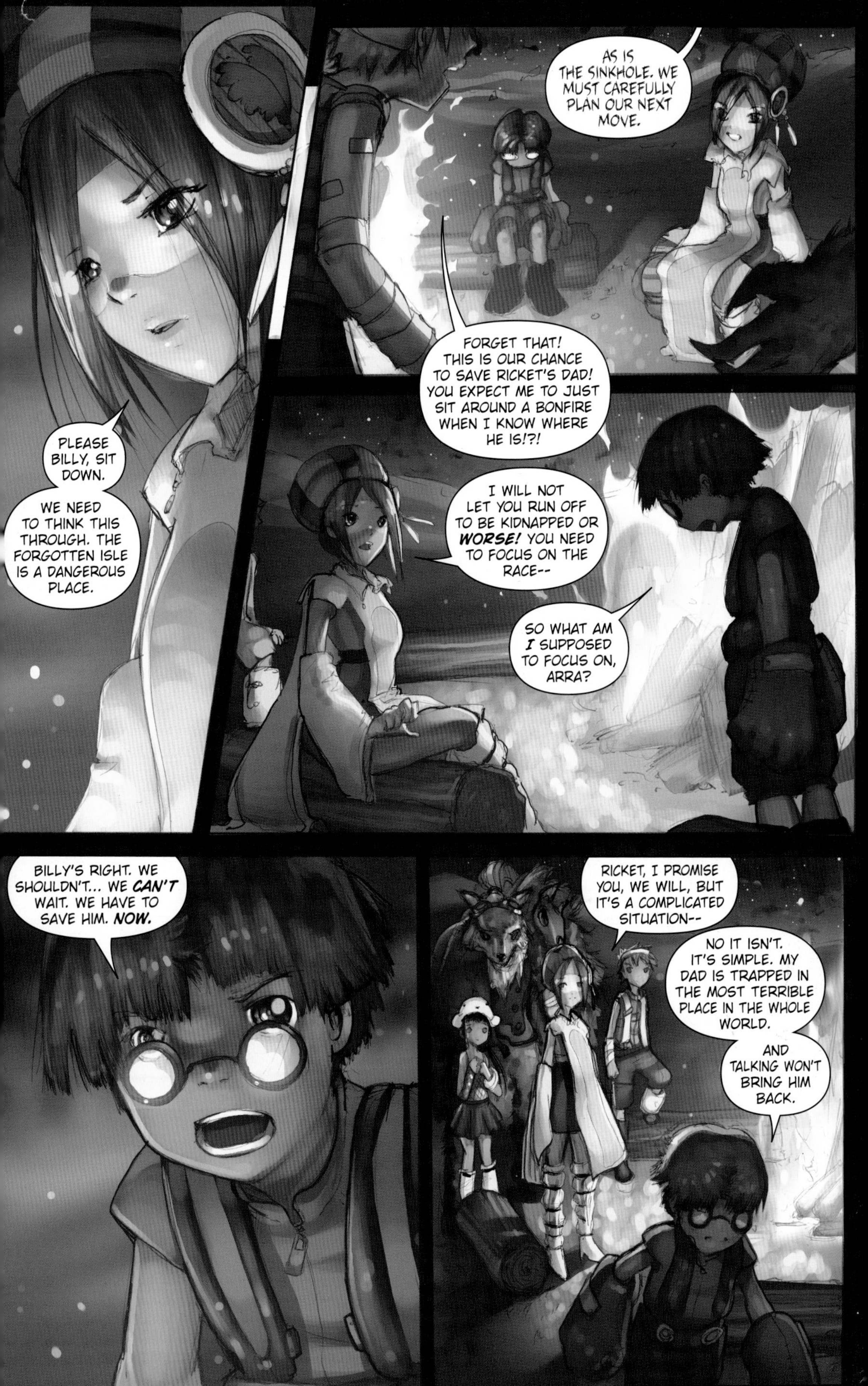
AS IS THE SINKHOLE. WE MUST CAREFULLY PLAN OUR NEXT MOVE.
FORGET THAT! THIS IS OUR CHANCE TO SAVE RICKET'S DAD! YOU EXPECT ME TO JUST SIT AROUND A BONFIRE WHEN I KNOW WHERE HE IS!?!
PLEASE BILLY, SIT DOWN.
WE NEED TO THINK THIS THROUGH. THE FORGOTTEN ISLE IS A DANGEROUS PLACE.
I WILL NOT LET YOU RUN OFF TO BE KIDNAPPED OR WORSE! YOU NEED TO FOCUS ON THE RACE--
SO WHAT AM I SUPPOSED TO FOCUS ON, ARRA?
BILLY'S RIGHT. WE SHOULDN'T... WE CAN'T WAIT. WE HAVE TO SAVE HIM. NOW.
RICKET, I PROMISE YOU, WE WILL, BUT IT'S A COMPLICATED SITUATION--
NO IT ISN'T. IT'S SIMPLE. MY DAD IS TRAPPED IN THE MOST TERRIBLE PLACE IN THE WHOLE WORLD.
AND TALKING WON'T BRING HIM BACK.

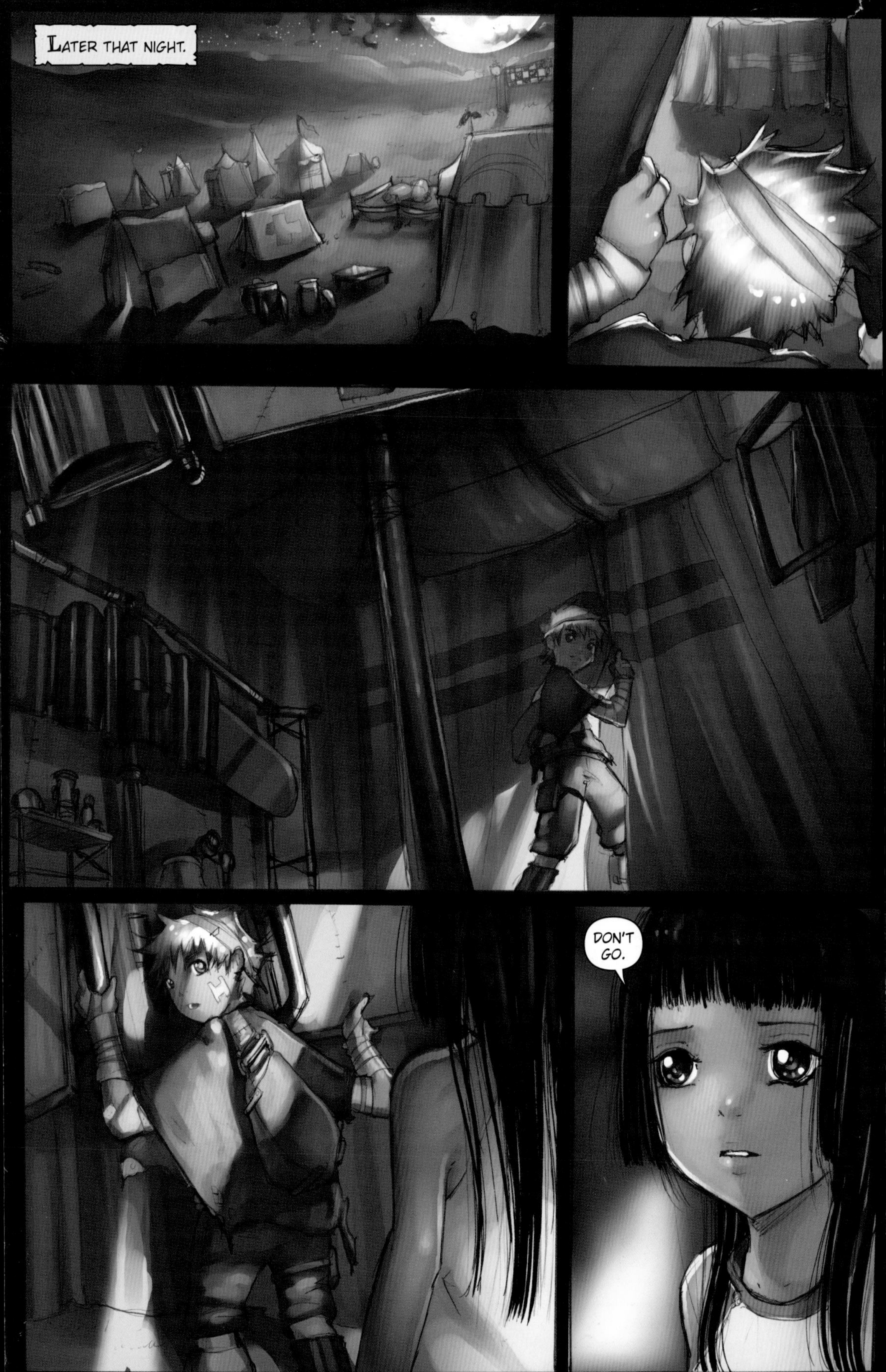
LATER THAT NIGHT.
DON'T GO.

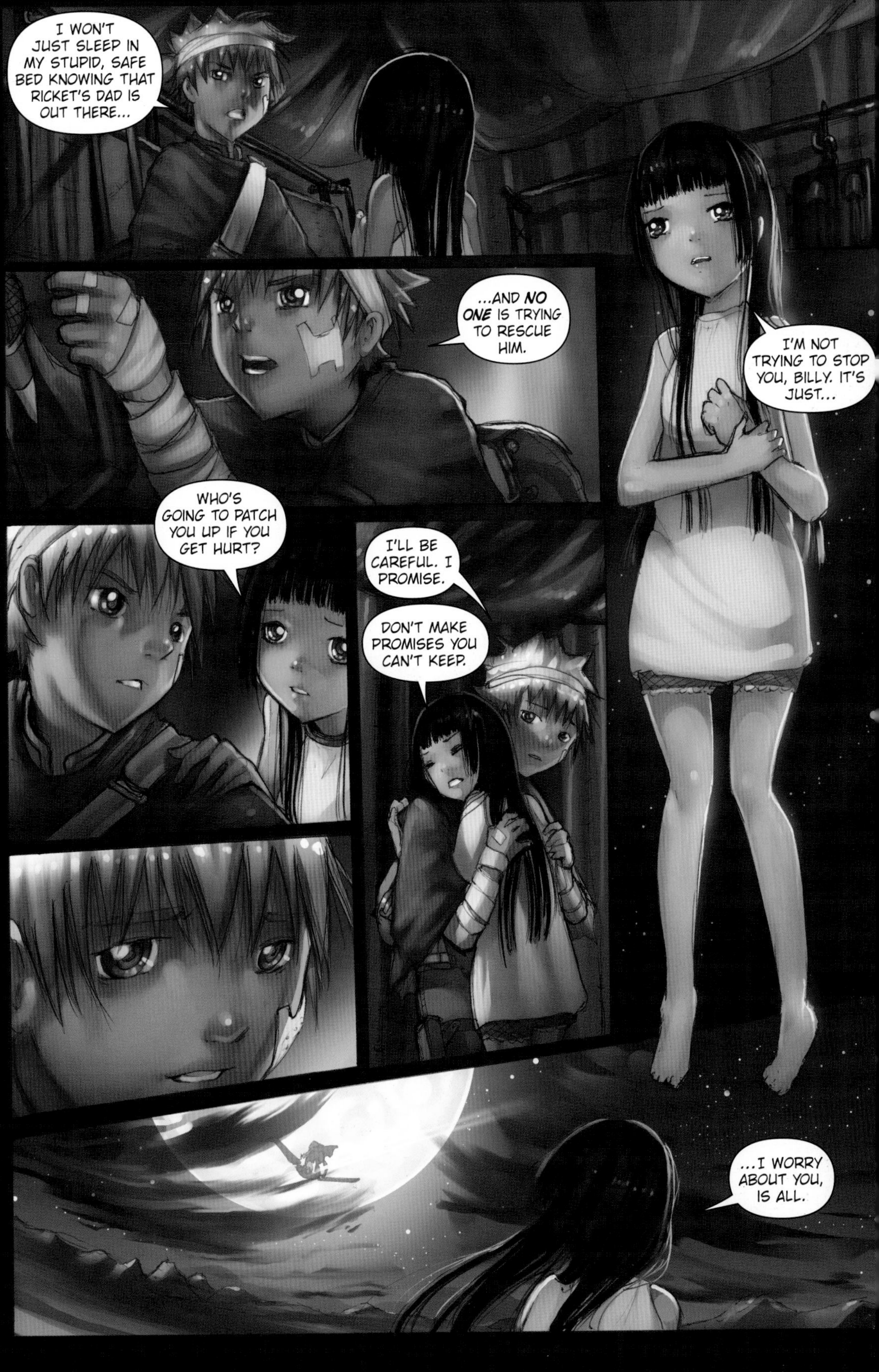
I WON'T JUST SLEEP IN MY STUPID, SAFE BED KNOWING THAT RICKET'S DAD IS OUT THERE...
...AND ***NO ONE*** IS TRYING TO RESCUE HIM.
I'M NOT TRYING TO STOP YOU, BILLY. IT'S JUST...
WHO'S GOING TO PATCH YOU UP IF YOU GET HURT?
I'LL BE CAREFUL. I PROMISE.
DON'T MAKE PROMISES YOU CAN'T KEEP.
...I WORRY ABOUT YOU, IS ALL.

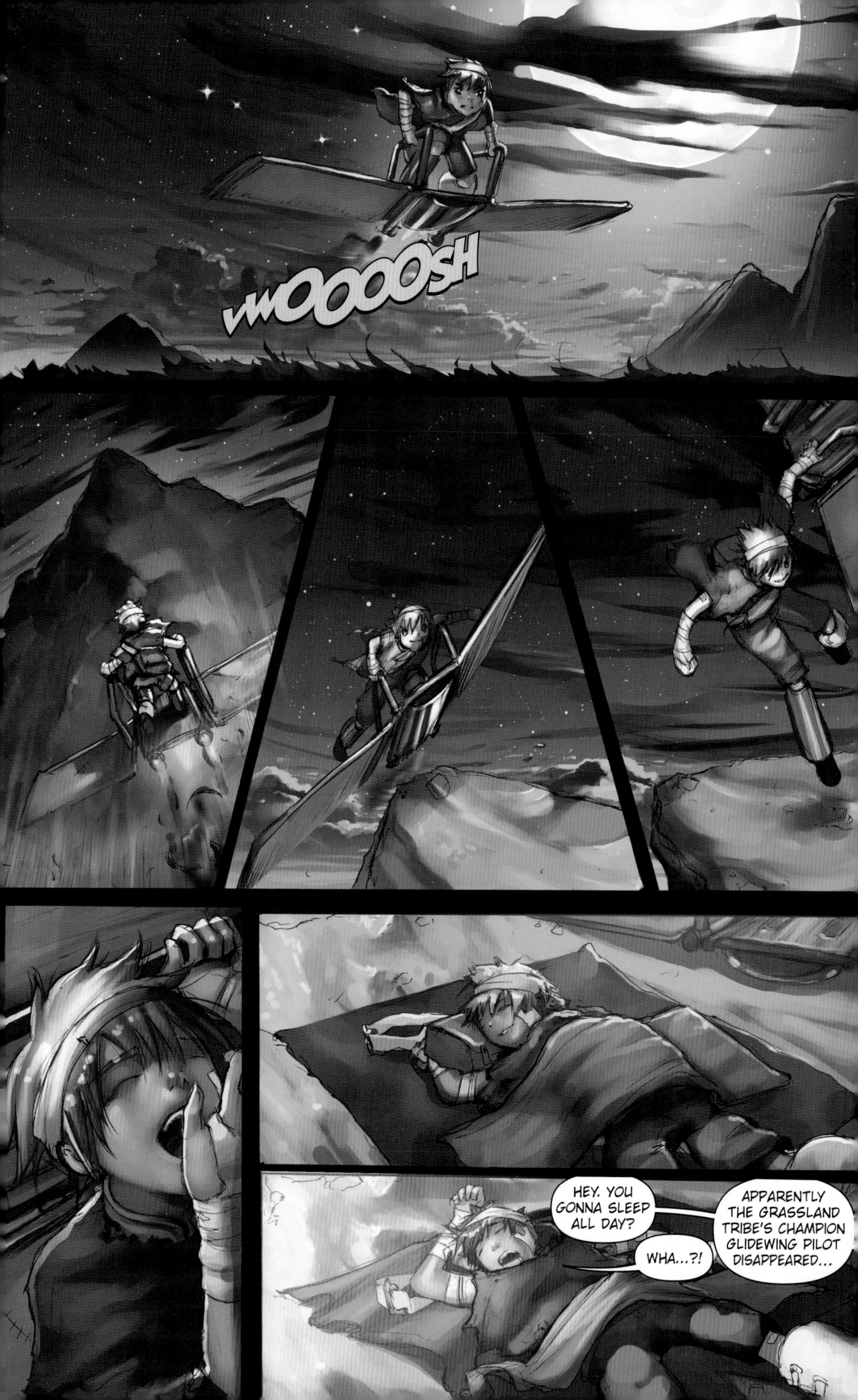
VWOOOOSH
HEY. YOU GONNA SLEEP ALL DAY?
WHA...?!
APPARENTLY THE GRASSLAND TRIBE'S CHAMPION GLIDEWING PILOT DISAPPEARED...

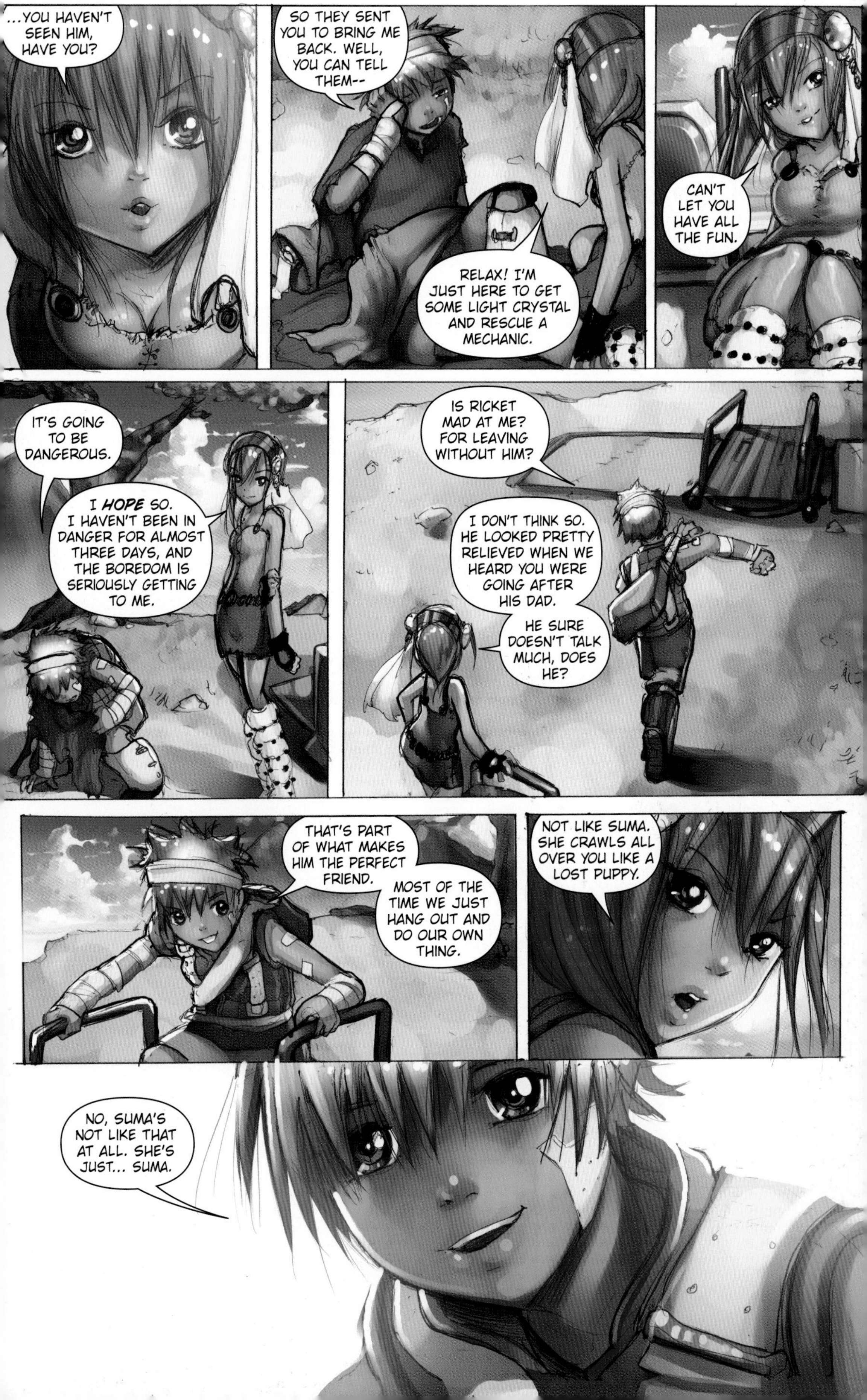
...YOU HAVEN'T SEEN HIM, HAVE YOU?
SO THEY SENT YOU TO BRING ME BACK. WELL, YOU CAN TELL THEM--
RELAX! I'M JUST HERE TO GET SOME LIGHT CRYSTAL AND RESCUE A MECHANIC.
CAN'T LET YOU HAVE ALL THE FUN.
IT'S GOING TO BE DANGEROUS.
I *HOPE* SO. I HAVEN'T BEEN IN DANGER FOR ALMOST THREE DAYS, AND THE BOREDOM IS SERIOUSLY GETTING TO ME.
IS RICKET MAD AT ME? FOR LEAVING WITHOUT HIM?
I DON'T THINK SO. HE LOOKED PRETTY RELIEVED WHEN WE HEARD YOU WERE GOING AFTER HIS DAD.
HE SURE DOESN'T TALK MUCH, DOES HE?
THAT'S PART OF WHAT MAKES HIM THE PERFECT FRIEND.
MOST OF THE TIME WE JUST HANG OUT AND DO OUR OWN THING.
NOT LIKE SUMA. SHE CRAWLS ALL OVER YOU LIKE A LOST PUPPY.
NO, SUMA'S NOT LIKE THAT AT ALL. SHE'S JUST... SUMA.

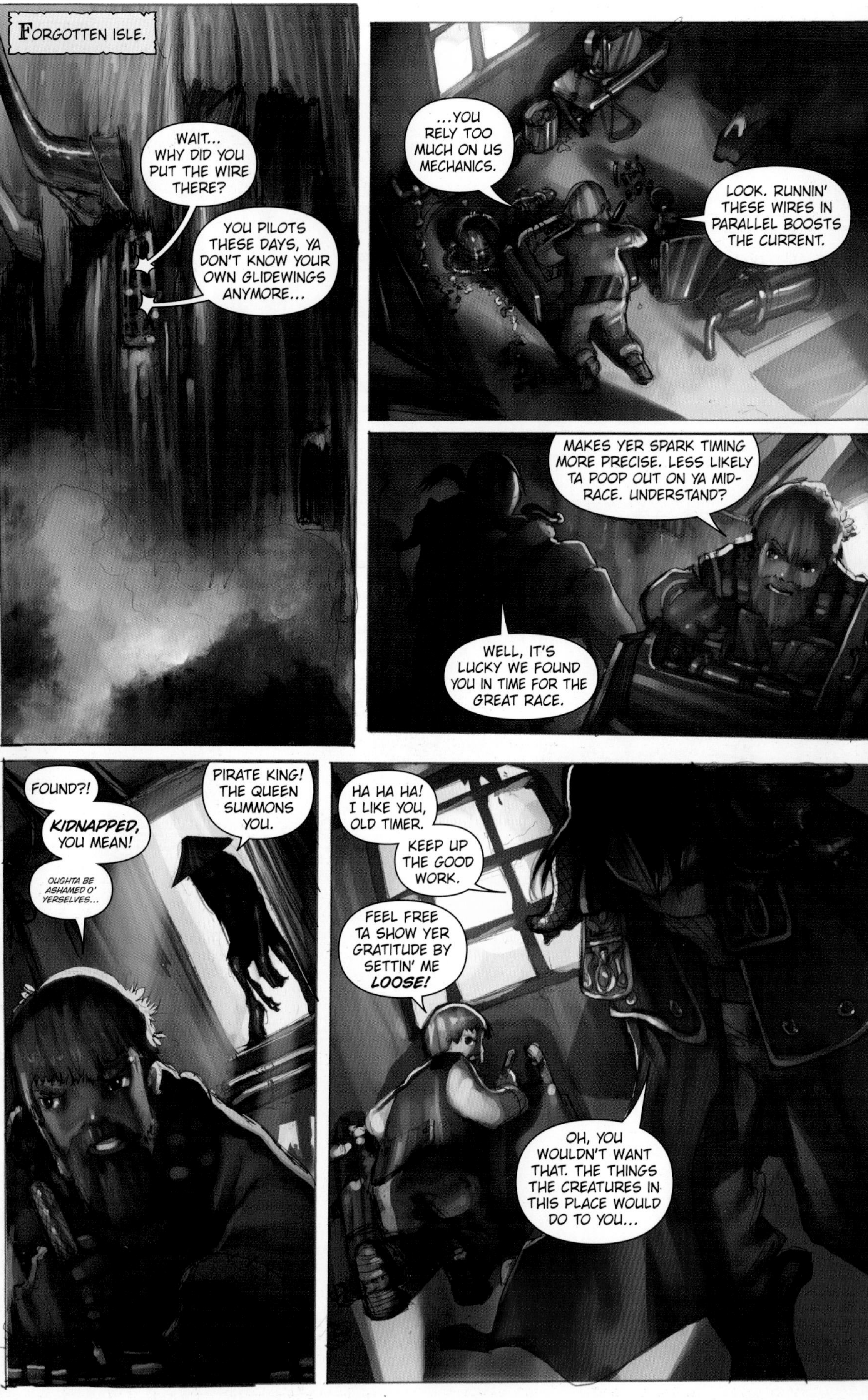
FORGOTTEN ISLE.
WAIT... WHY DID YOU PUT THE WIRE THERE?
YOU PILOTS THESE DAYS, YA DON'T KNOW YOUR OWN GLIDEWINGS ANYMORE...
...YOU RELY TOO MUCH ON US MECHANICS.
LOOK. RUNNIN' THESE WIRES IN PARALLEL BOOSTS THE CURRENT.
MAKES YER SPARK TIMING MORE PRECISE. LESS LIKELY TA POOP OUT ON YA MID-RACE. UNDERSTAND?
WELL, IT'S LUCKY WE FOUND YOU IN TIME FOR THE GREAT RACE.
FOUND?!
KIDNAPPED, YOU MEAN!
OUGHTA BE ASHAMED O' YERSELVES...
PIRATE KING! THE QUEEN SUMMONS YOU.
HA HA HA! I LIKE YOU, OLD TIMER.
KEEP UP THE GOOD WORK.
FEEL FREE TA SHOW YER GRATITUDE BY SETTIN' ME LOOSE!
OH, YOU WOULDN'T WANT THAT. THE THINGS THE CREATURES IN THIS PLACE WOULD DO TO YOU...

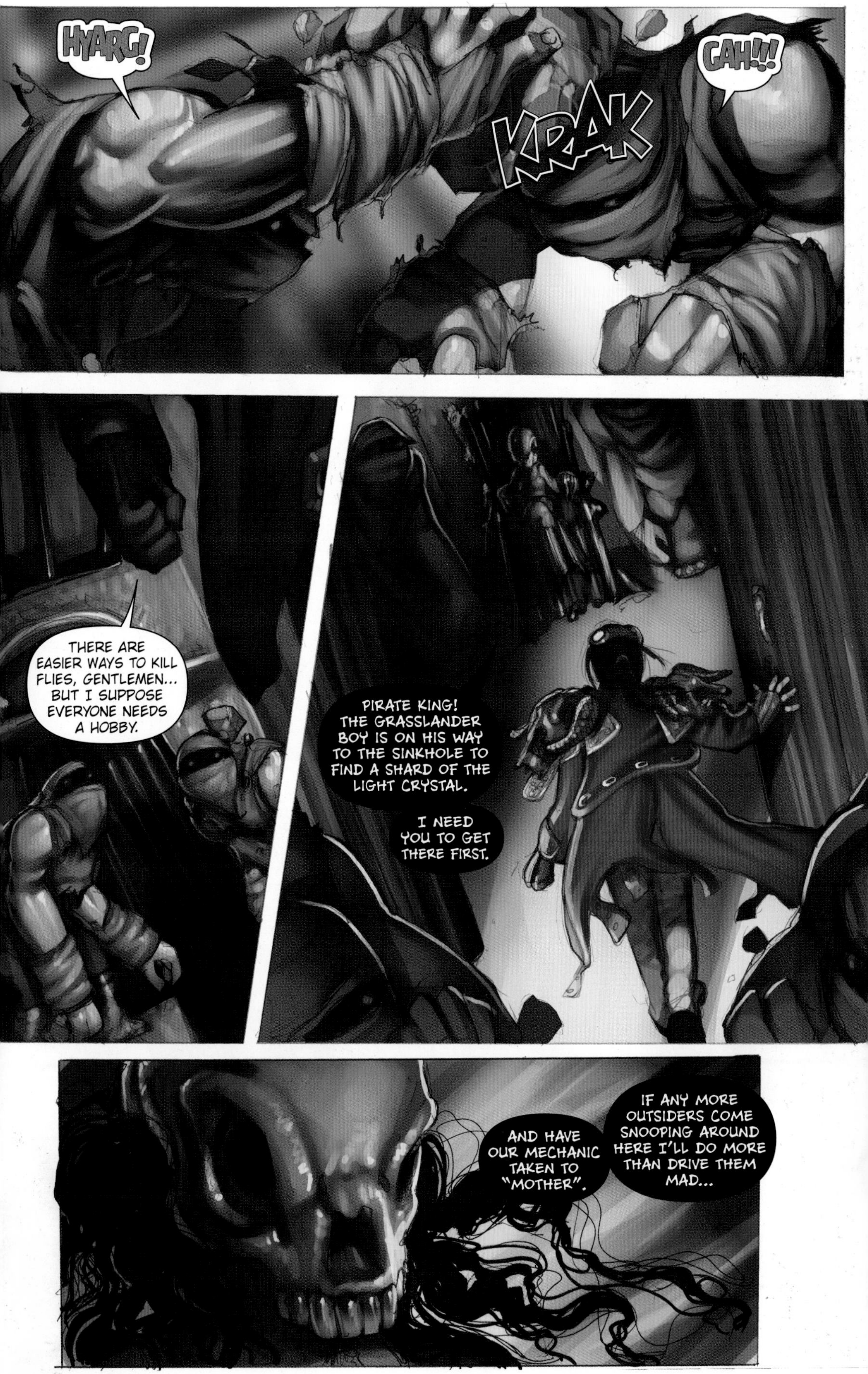
HYARG!
KRAK
GAH!!!
THERE ARE EASIER WAYS TO KILL FLIES, GENTLEMEN... BUT I SUPPOSE EVERYONE NEEDS A HOBBY.
PIRATE KING! THE GRASSLANDER BOY IS ON HIS WAY TO THE SINKHOLE TO FIND A SHARD OF THE LIGHT CRYSTAL.
I NEED YOU TO GET THERE FIRST.
AND HAVE OUR MECHANIC TAKEN TO "MOTHER".
IF ANY MORE OUTSIDERS COME SNOOPING AROUND HERE I'LL DO MORE THAN DRIVE THEM MAD...

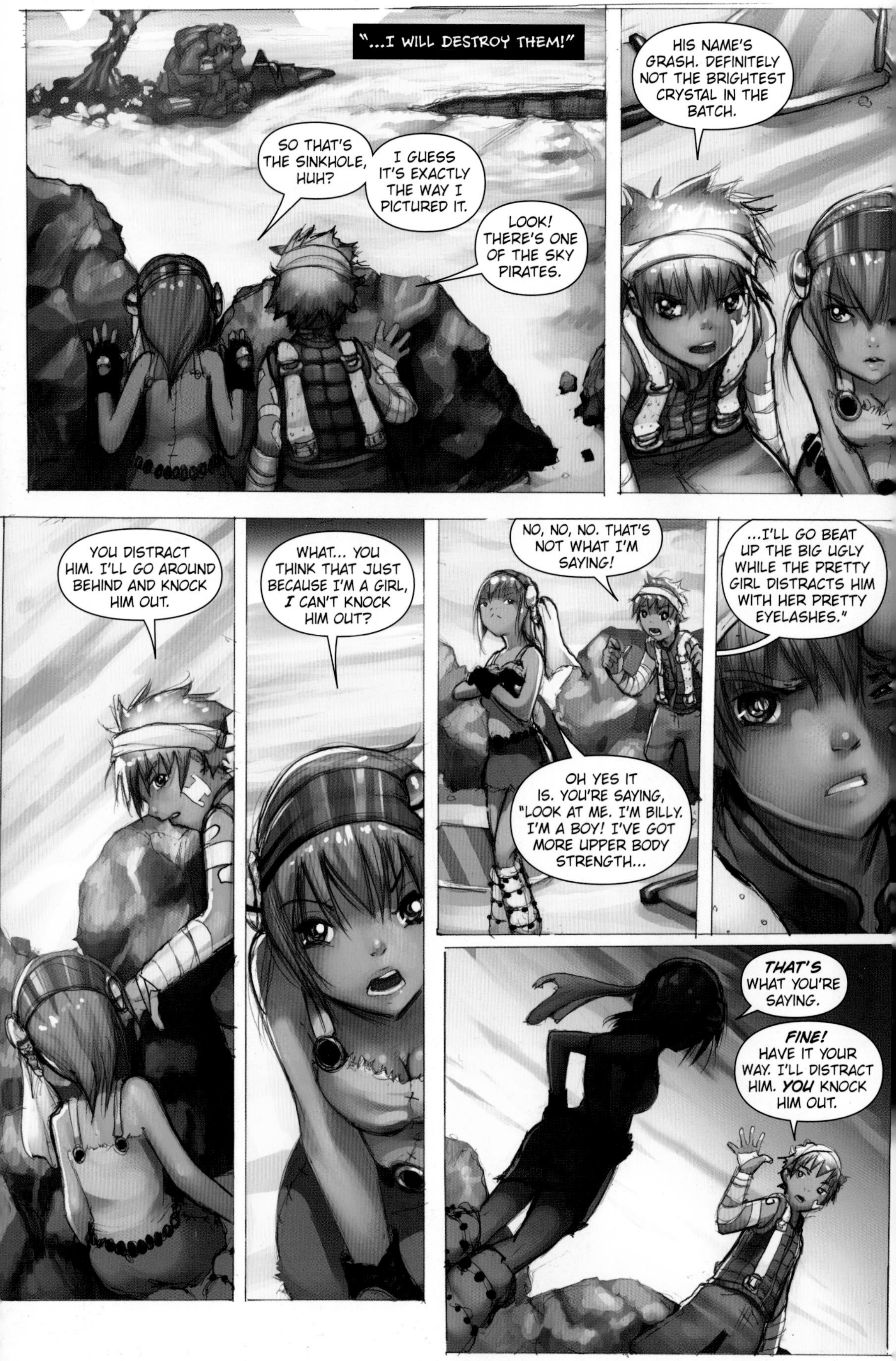
"...I WILL DESTROY THEM!"
SO THAT'S THE SINKHOLE, HUH?
I GUESS IT'S EXACTLY THE WAY I PICTURED IT.
LOOK! THERE'S ONE OF THE SKY PIRATES.
HIS NAME'S GRASH. DEFINITELY NOT THE BRIGHTEST CRYSTAL IN THE BATCH.
YOU DISTRACT HIM. I'LL GO AROUND BEHIND AND KNOCK HIM OUT.
WHAT... YOU THINK THAT JUST BECAUSE I'M A GIRL, I CAN'T KNOCK HIM OUT?
NO, NO, NO. THAT'S NOT WHAT I'M SAYING!
OH YES IT IS. YOU'RE SAYING, "LOOK AT ME. I'M BILLY. I'M A BOY! I'VE GOT MORE UPPER BODY STRENGTH...
...I'LL GO BEAT UP THE BIG UGLY WHILE THE PRETTY GIRL DISTRACTS HIM WITH HER PRETTY EYELASHES."
THAT'S WHAT YOU'RE SAYING.
FINE! HAVE IT YOUR WAY. I'LL DISTRACT HIM. YOU KNOCK HIM OUT.

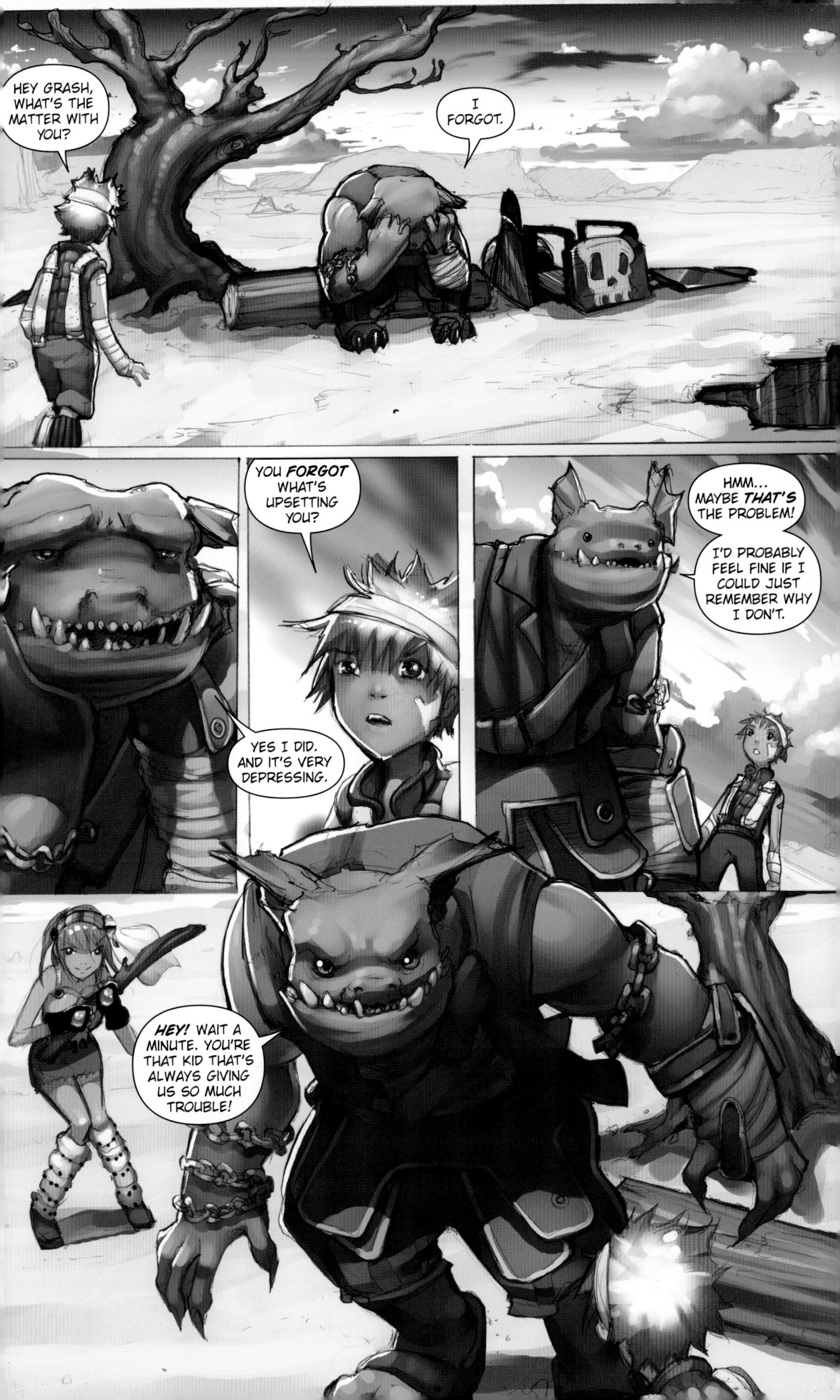
HEY GRASH, WHAT'S THE MATTER WITH YOU?
I FORGOT.
YOU *FORGOT* WHAT'S UPSETTING YOU?
YES I DID. AND IT'S VERY DEPRESSING.
HMM... MAYBE *THAT'S* THE PROBLEM!
I'D PROBABLY FEEL FINE IF I COULD JUST REMEMBER WHY I DON'T.
HEY! WAIT A MINUTE. YOU'RE THAT KID THAT'S ALWAYS GIVING US SO MUCH TROUBLE!

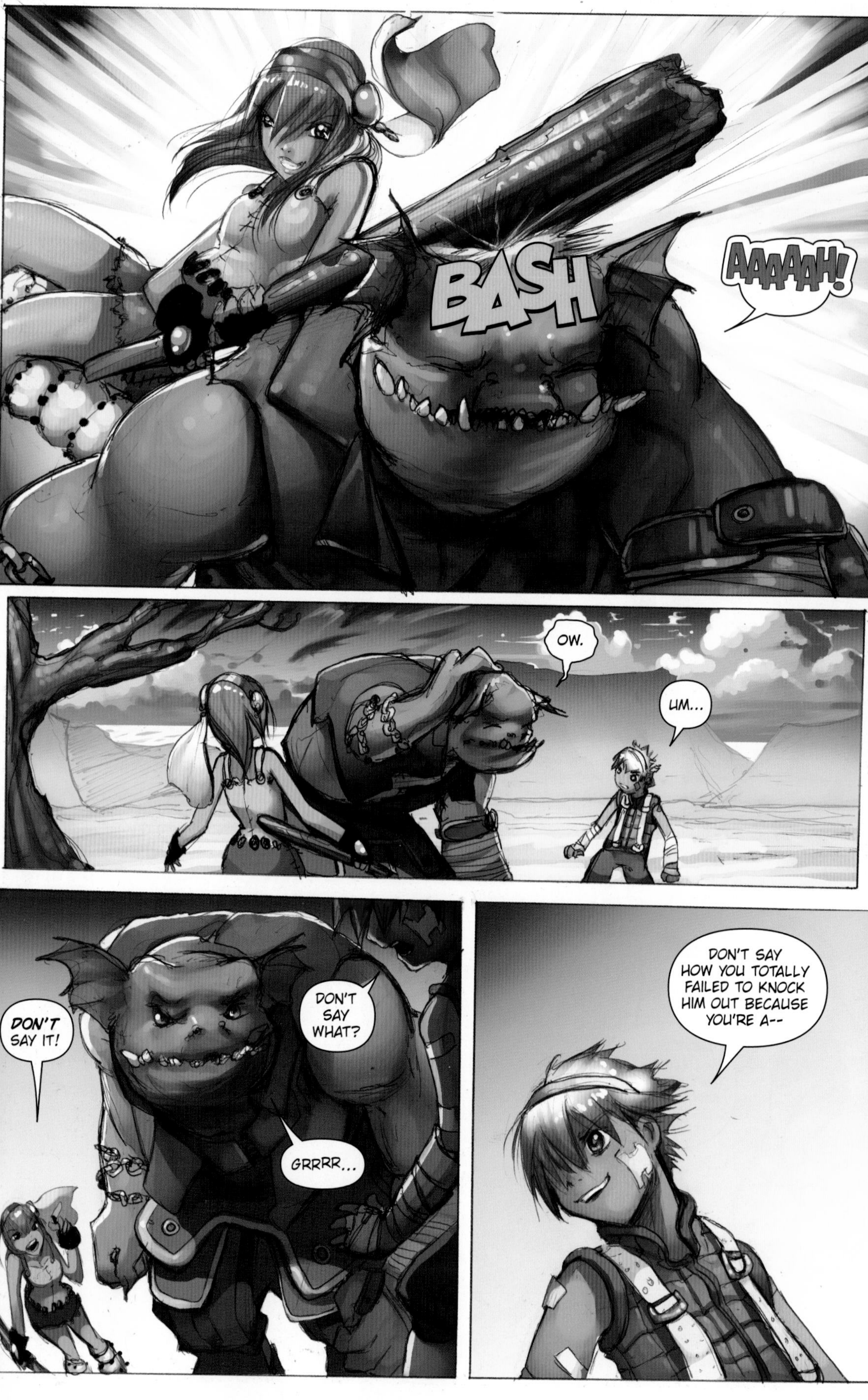
BASH
AAAAAH!
OW.
UM...
DON'T SAY IT!
DON'T SAY WHAT?
GRRRR...
DON'T SAY HOW YOU TOTALLY FAILED TO KNOCK HIM OUT BECAUSE YOU'RE A--

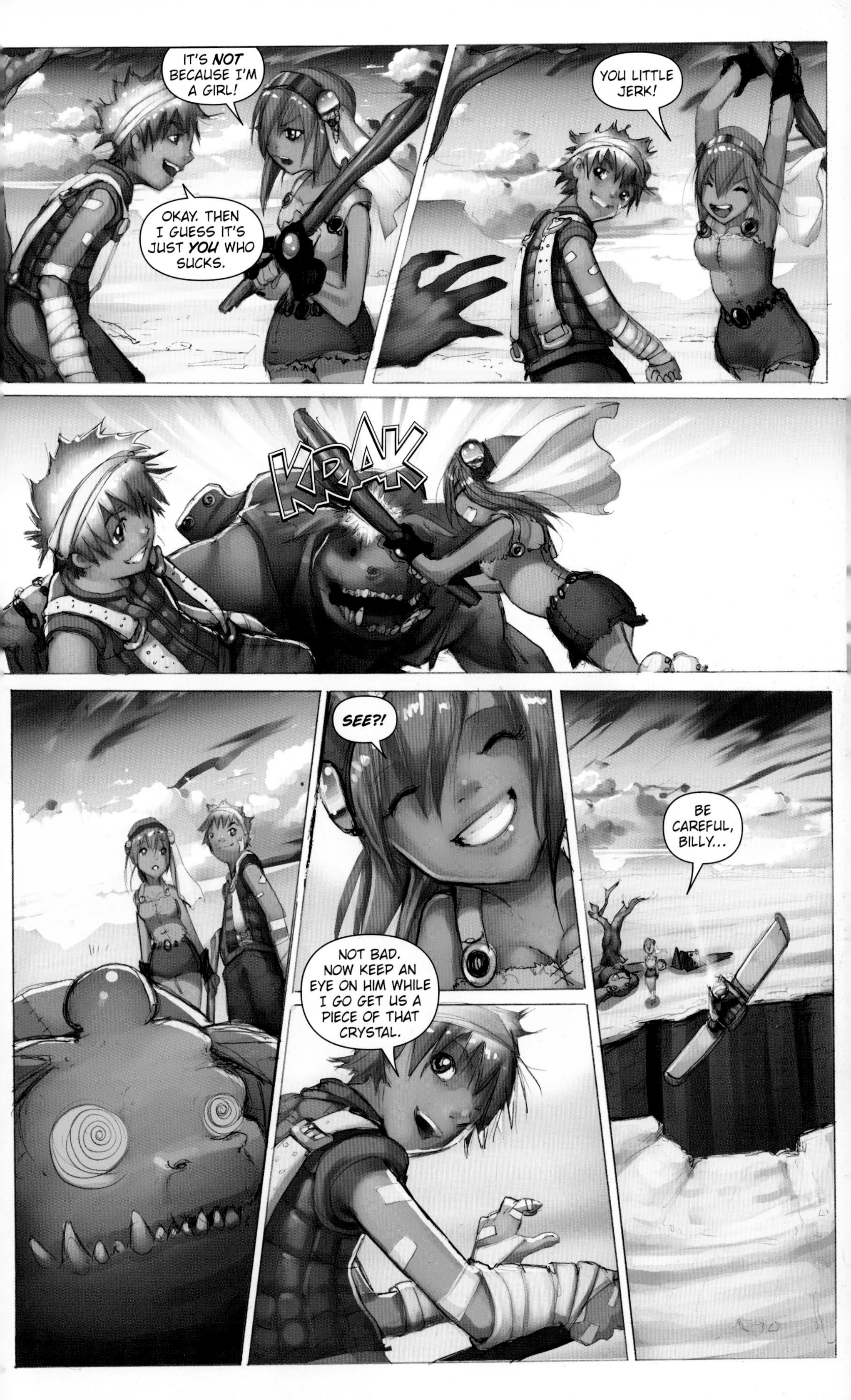

IT'S **NOT** BECAUSE I'M A GIRL!
OKAY. THEN I GUESS IT'S JUST **YOU** WHO SUCKS.
YOU LITTLE JERK!
KRAAK
SEE?!
NOT BAD. NOW KEEP AN EYE ON HIM WHILE I GO GET US A PIECE OF THAT CRYSTAL.
BE CAREFUL, BILLY...

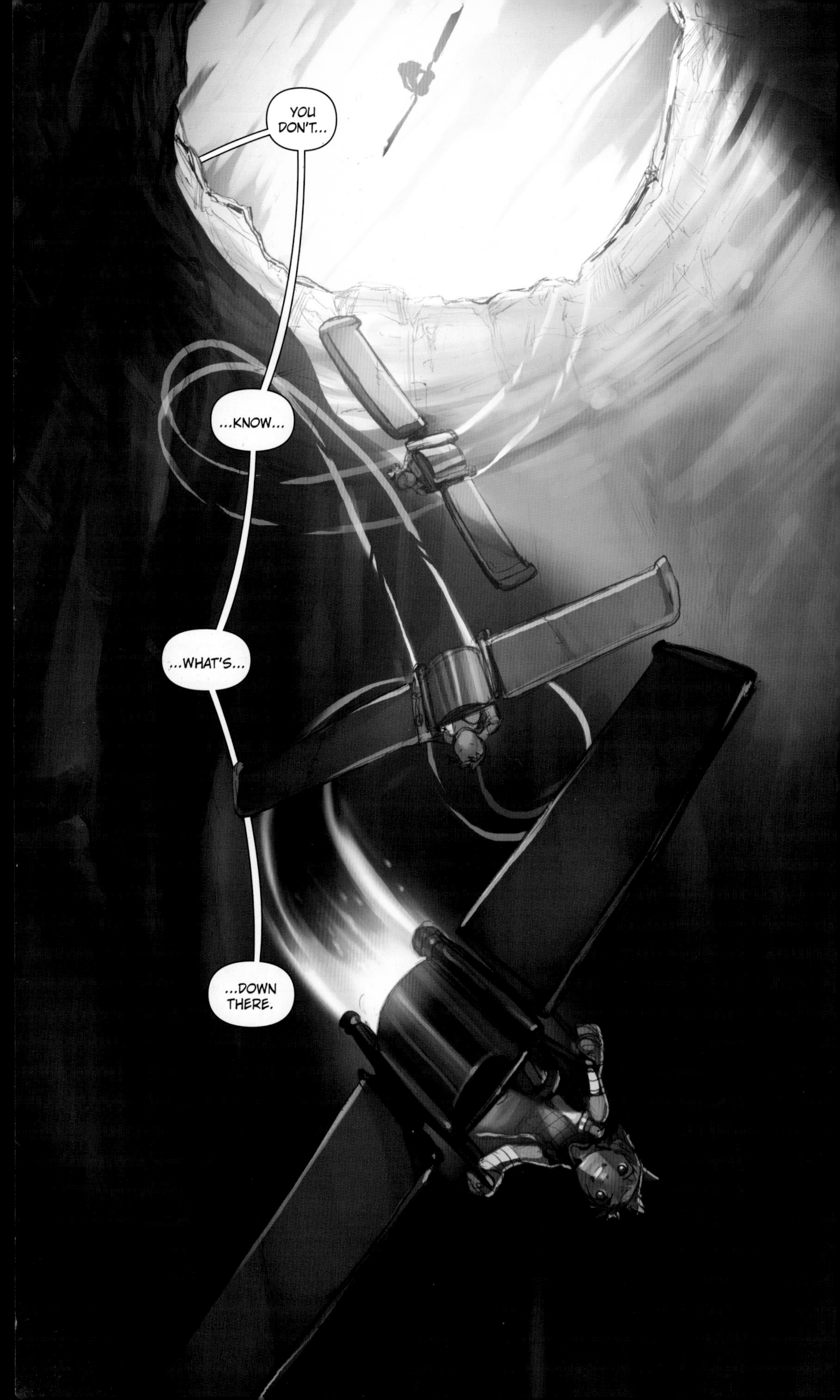
YOU DON'T...
...KNOW...
...WHAT'S...
...DOWN THERE.

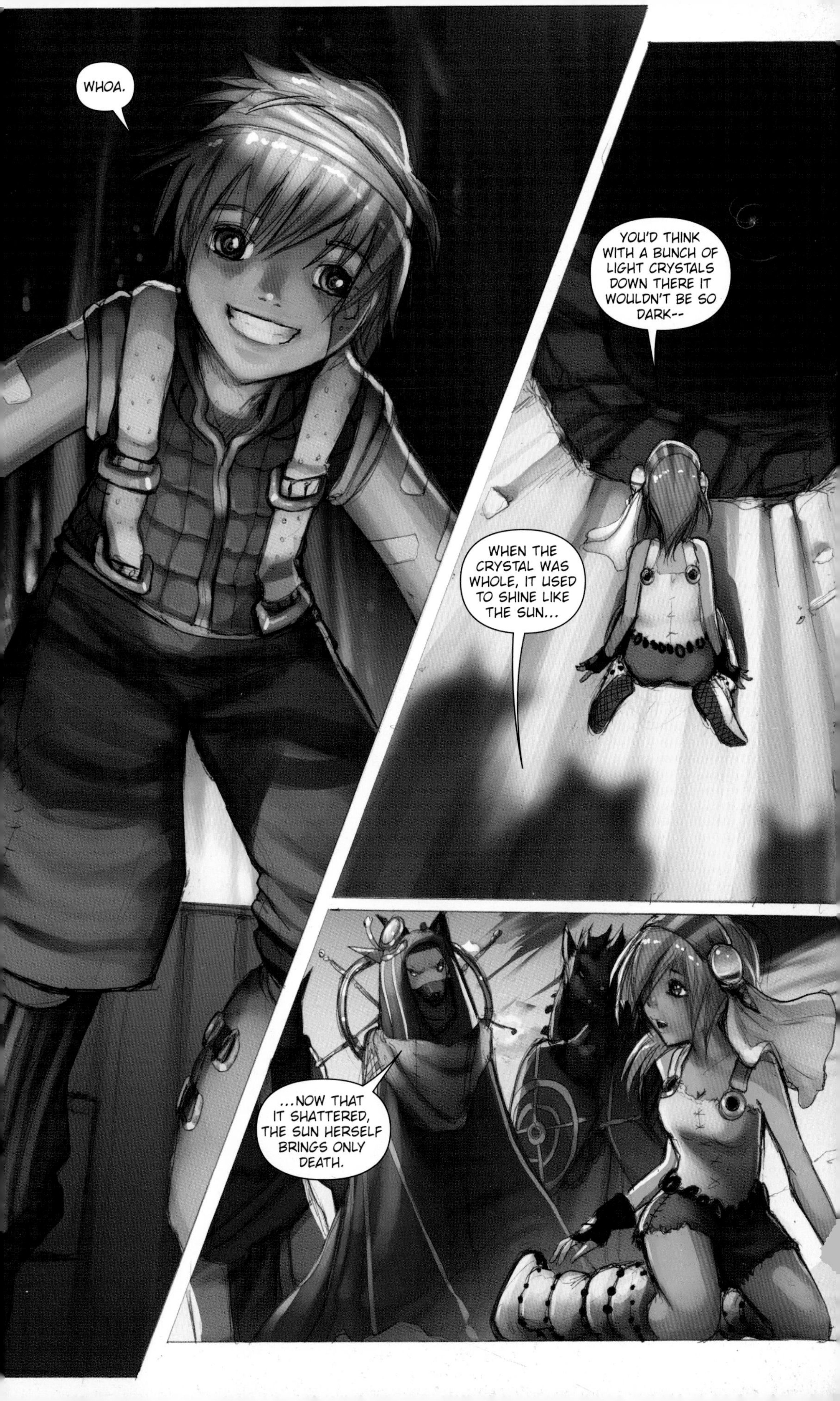
WHOA.
YOU'D THINK WITH A BUNCH OF LIGHT CRYSTALS DOWN THERE IT WOULDN'T BE SO DARK--
WHEN THE CRYSTAL WAS WHOLE, IT USED TO SHINE LIKE THE SUN...
...NOW THAT IT SHATTERED, THE SUN HERSELF BRINGS ONLY DEATH.

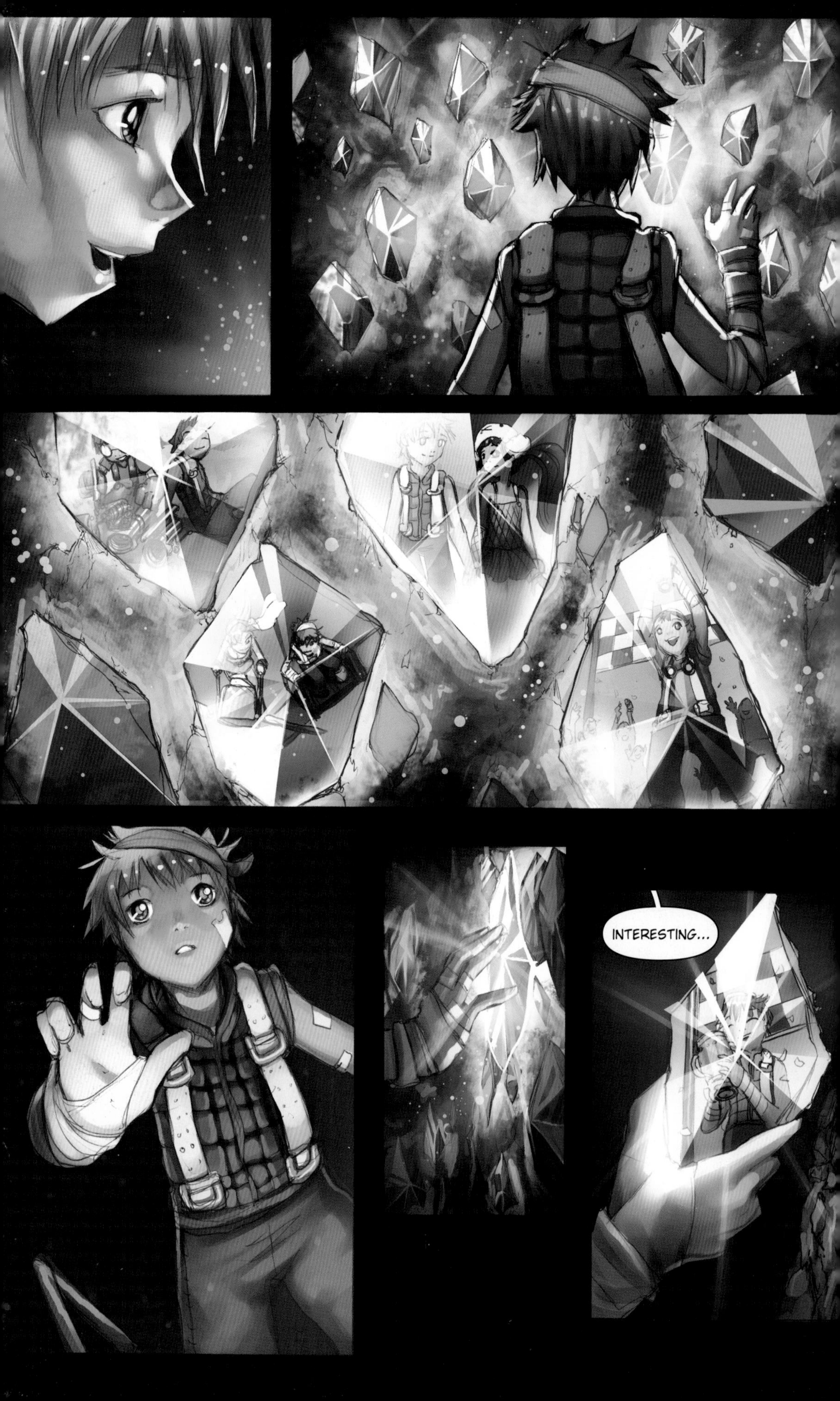
INTERESTING...

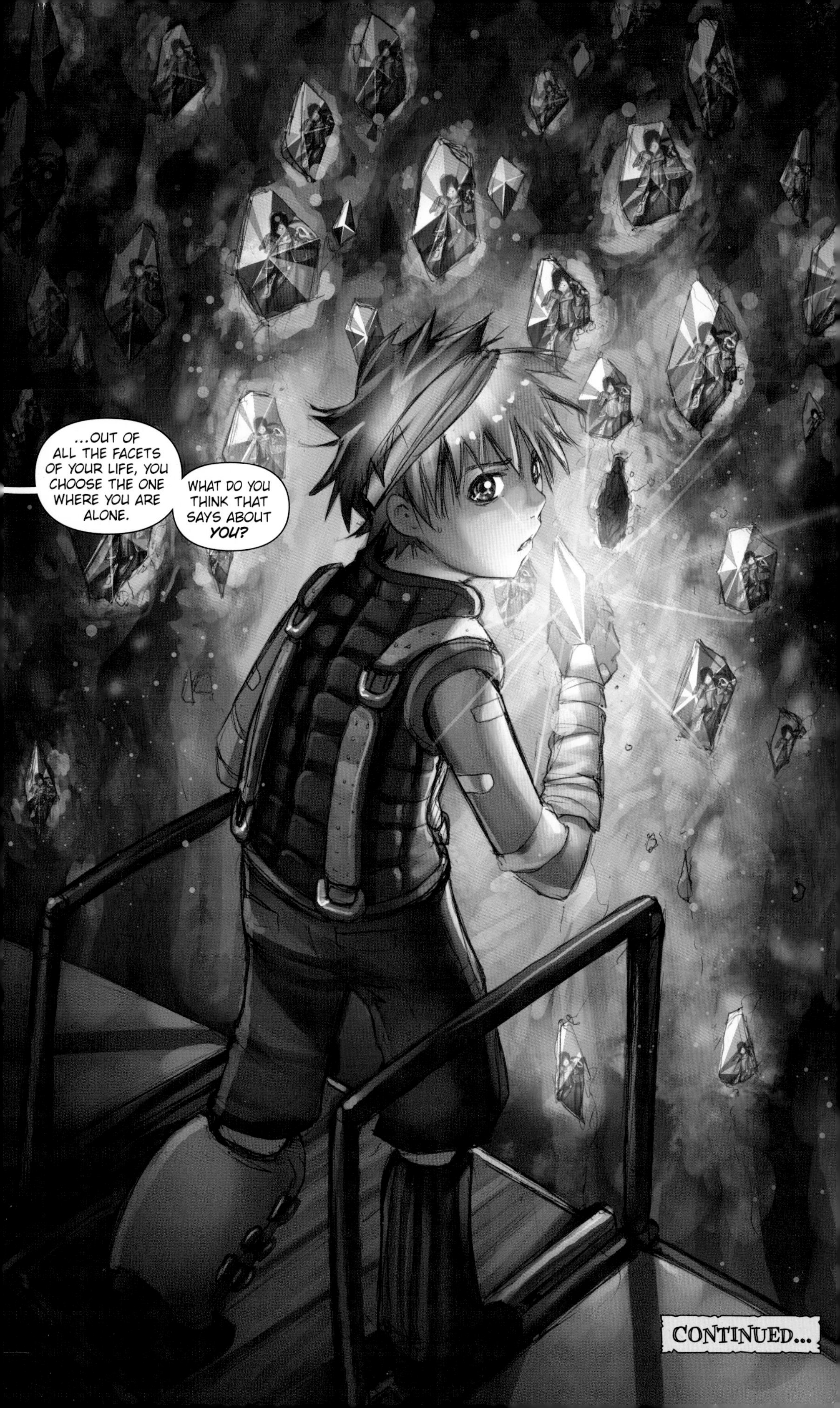
...OUT OF ALL THE FACETS OF YOUR LIFE, YOU CHOOSE THE ONE WHERE YOU ARE ALONE.
WHAT DO YOU THINK THAT SAYS ABOUT YOU?
CONTINUED...

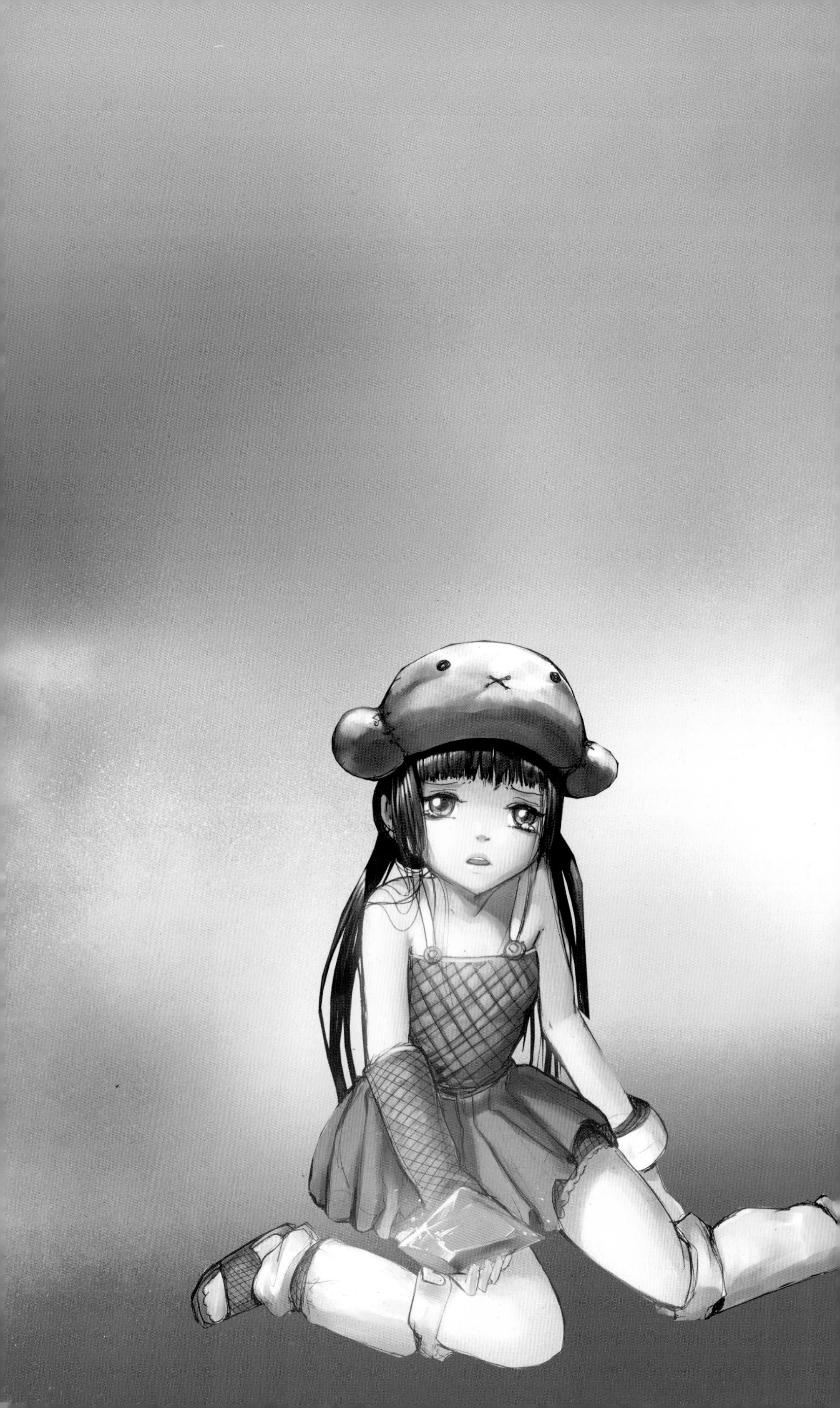

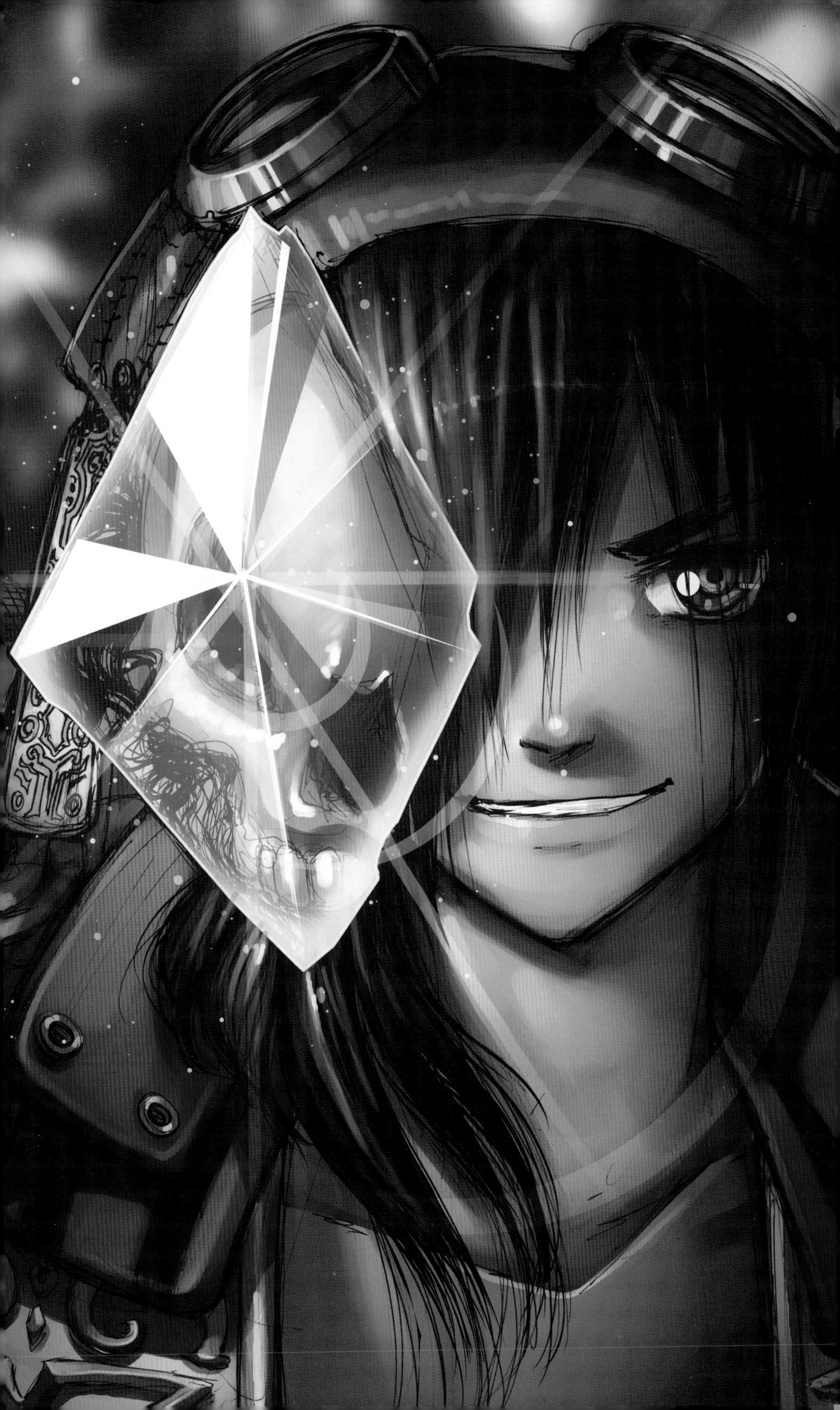

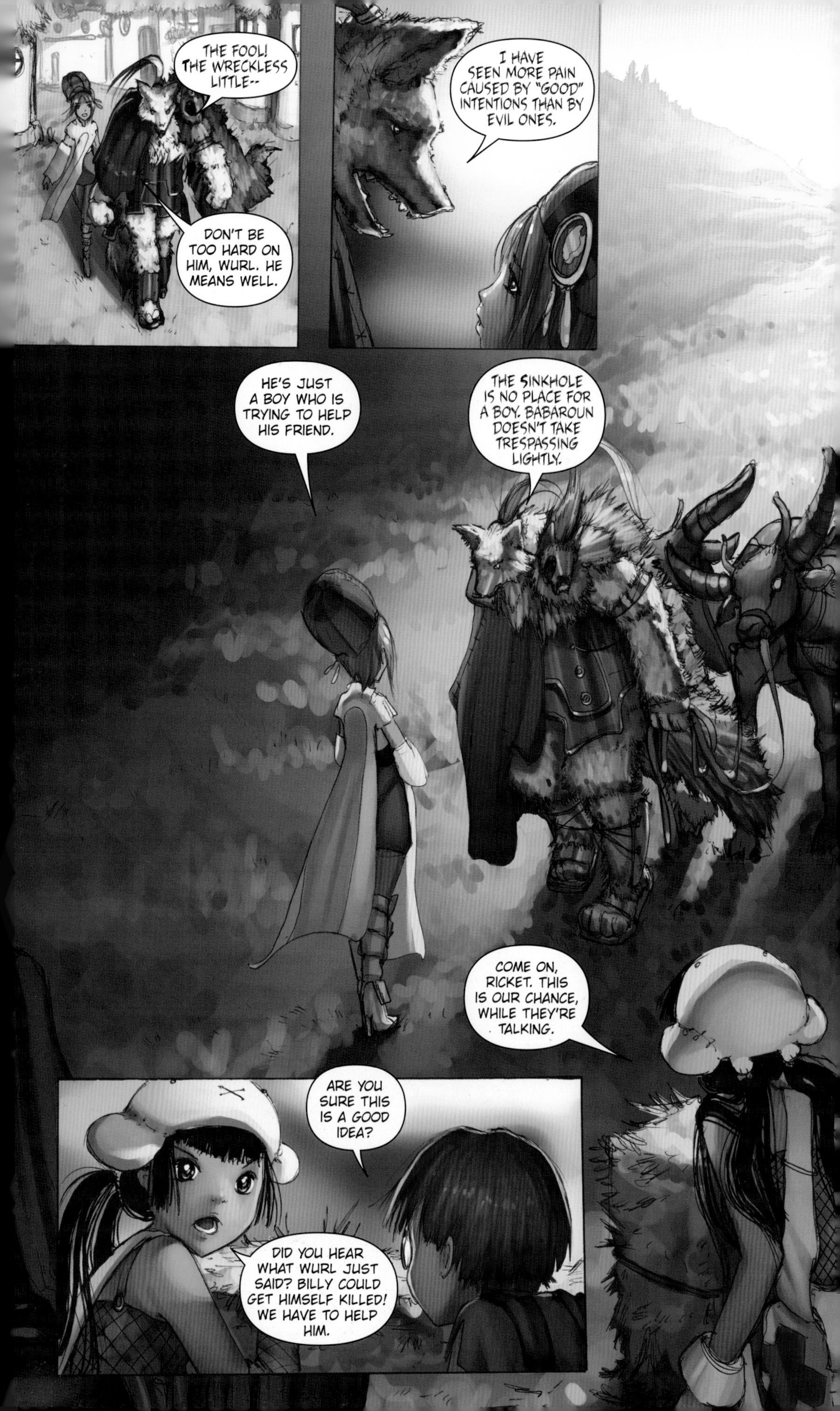
THE FOOL! THE WRECKLESS LITTLE--
DON'T BE TOO HARD ON HIM, WURL. HE MEANS WELL.
I HAVE SEEN MORE PAIN CAUSED BY "GOOD" INTENTIONS THAN BY EVIL ONES.
HE'S JUST A BOY WHO IS TRYING TO HELP HIS FRIEND.
THE SINKHOLE IS NO PLACE FOR A BOY. BABAROUN DOESN'T TAKE TRESPASSING LIGHTLY.
COME ON, RICKET. THIS IS OUR CHANCE, WHILE THEY'RE TALKING.
ARE YOU SURE THIS IS A GOOD IDEA?
DID YOU HEAR WHAT WURL JUST SAID? BILLY COULD GET HIMSELF KILLED! WE HAVE TO HELP HIM.

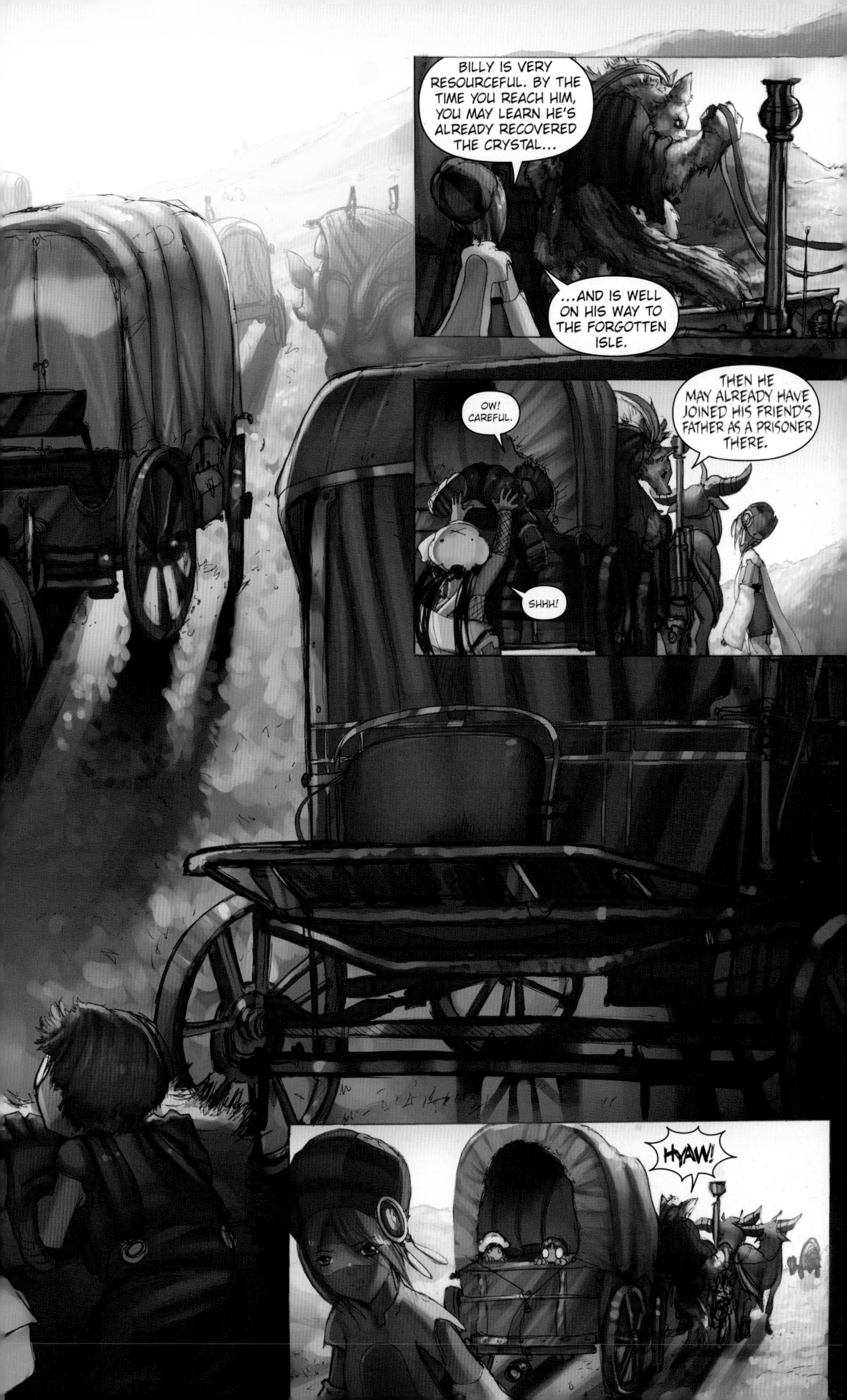
BILLY IS VERY RESOURCEFUL. BY THE TIME YOU REACH HIM, YOU MAY LEARN HE'S ALREADY RECOVERED THE CRYSTAL...
...AND IS WELL ON HIS WAY TO THE FORGOTTEN ISLE.
OW! CAREFUL.
THEN HE MAY ALREADY HAVE JOINED HIS FRIEND'S FATHER AS A PRISONER THERE.
SHHH!
HYAW!

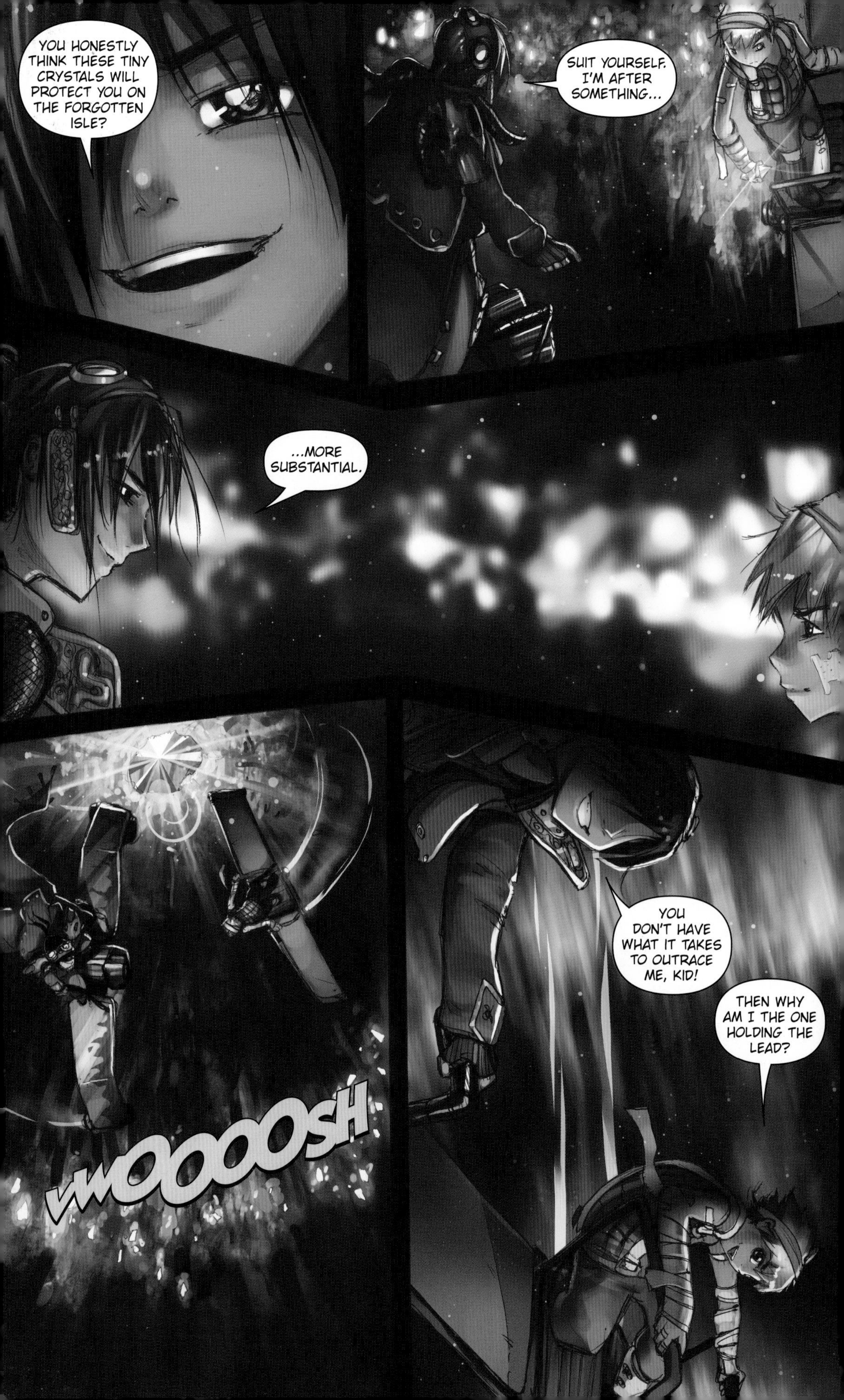
YOU HONESTLY THINK THESE TINY CRYSTALS WILL PROTECT YOU ON THE FORGOTTEN ISLE?
SUIT YOURSELF. I'M AFTER SOMETHING...
...MORE SUBSTANTIAL.
VWOOOOOSH
YOU DON'T HAVE WHAT IT TAKES TO OUTRACE ME, KID!
THEN WHY AM I THE ONE HOLDING THE LEAD?

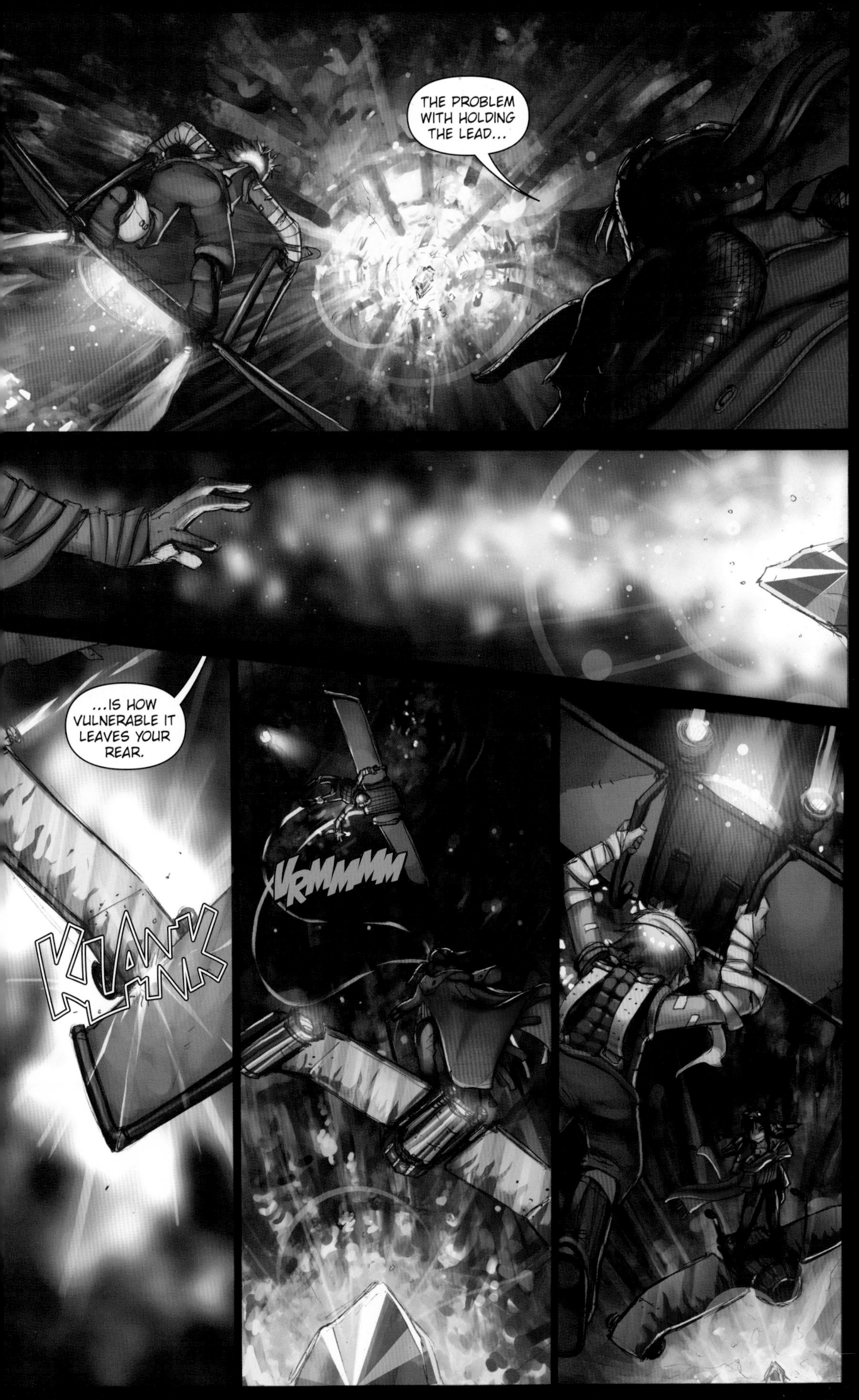
THE PROBLEM WITH HOLDING THE LEAD...
...IS HOW VULNERABLE IT LEAVES YOUR REAR.
KLANK
VRMMMM

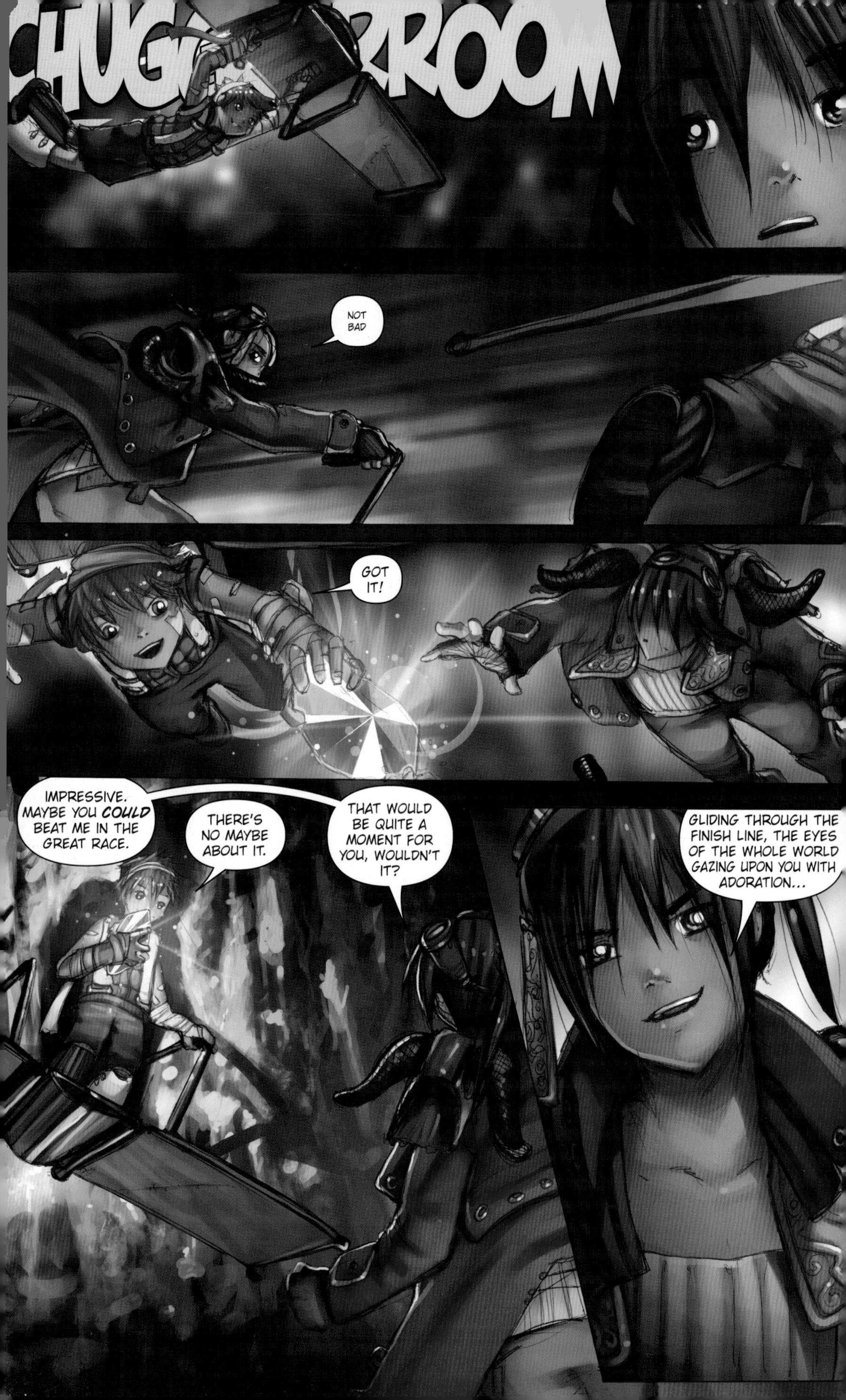
CHUG-BRROOM
NOT BAD
GOT IT!
IMPRESSIVE. MAYBE YOU *COULD* BEAT ME IN THE GREAT RACE.
THERE'S NO MAYBE ABOUT IT.
THAT WOULD BE QUITE A MOMENT FOR YOU, WOULDN'T IT?
GLIDING THROUGH THE FINISH LINE, THE EYES OF THE WHOLE WORLD GAZING UPON YOU WITH ADORATION...

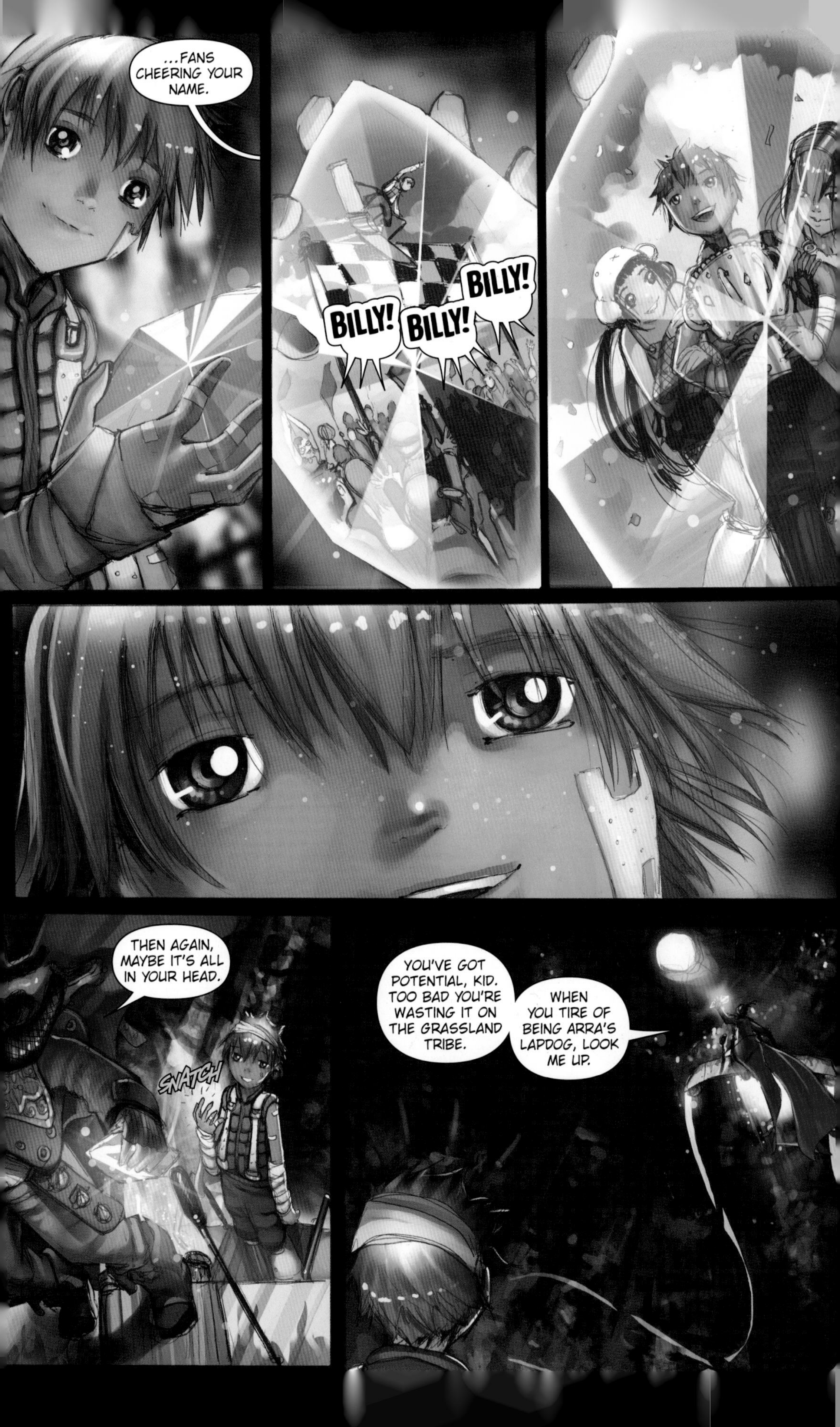
...FANS CHEERING YOUR NAME.
BILLY!
BILLY!
BILLY!
THEN AGAIN, MAYBE IT'S ALL IN YOUR HEAD.
SNATCH
YOU'VE GOT POTENTIAL, KID. TOO BAD YOU'RE WASTING IT ON THE GRASSLAND TRIBE.
WHEN YOU TIRE OF BEING ARRA'S LAPDOG, LOOK ME UP.

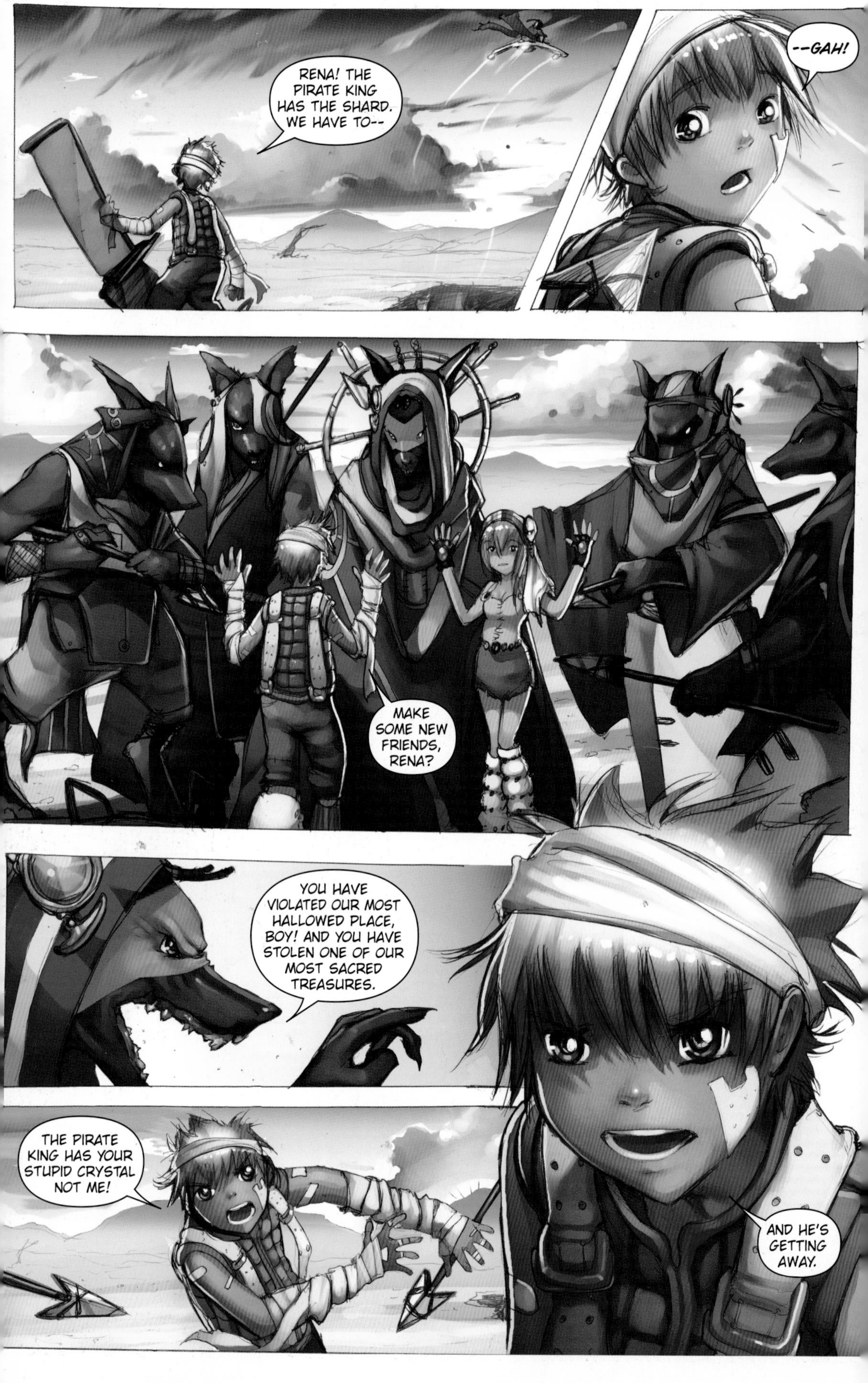
RENA! THE PIRATE KING HAS THE SHARD. WE HAVE TO--
--GAH!
MAKE SOME NEW FRIENDS, RENA?
YOU HAVE VIOLATED OUR MOST HALLOWED PLACE, BOY! AND YOU HAVE STOLEN ONE OF OUR MOST SACRED TREASURES.
THE PIRATE KING HAS YOUR STUPID CRYSTAL NOT ME!
AND HE'S GETTING AWAY.

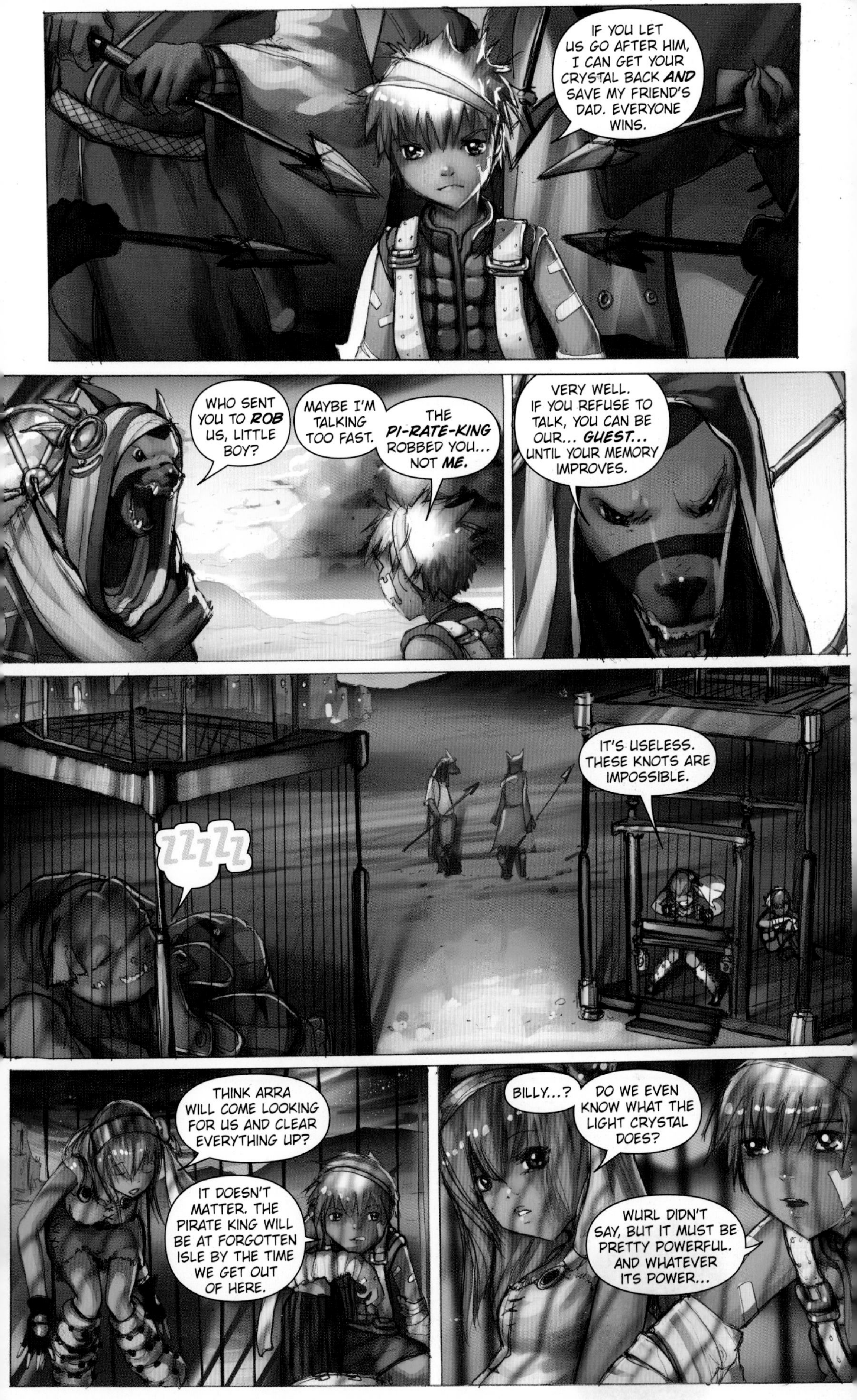
IF YOU LET US GO AFTER HIM, I CAN GET YOUR CRYSTAL BACK AND SAVE MY FRIEND'S DAD. EVERYONE WINS.
WHO SENT YOU TO ROB US, LITTLE BOY?
MAYBE I'M TALKING TOO FAST.
THE PI-RATE-KING ROBBED YOU... NOT ME.
VERY WELL. IF YOU REFUSE TO TALK, YOU CAN BE OUR... GUEST... UNTIL YOUR MEMORY IMPROVES.
ZZZZZ
IT'S USELESS. THESE KNOTS ARE IMPOSSIBLE.
THINK ARRA WILL COME LOOKING FOR US AND CLEAR EVERYTHING UP?
IT DOESN'T MATTER. THE PIRATE KING WILL BE AT FORGOTTEN ISLE BY THE TIME WE GET OUT OF HERE.
BILLY...?
DO WE EVEN KNOW WHAT THE LIGHT CRYSTAL DOES?
WURL DIDN'T SAY, BUT IT MUST BE PRETTY POWERFUL. AND WHATEVER ITS POWER...

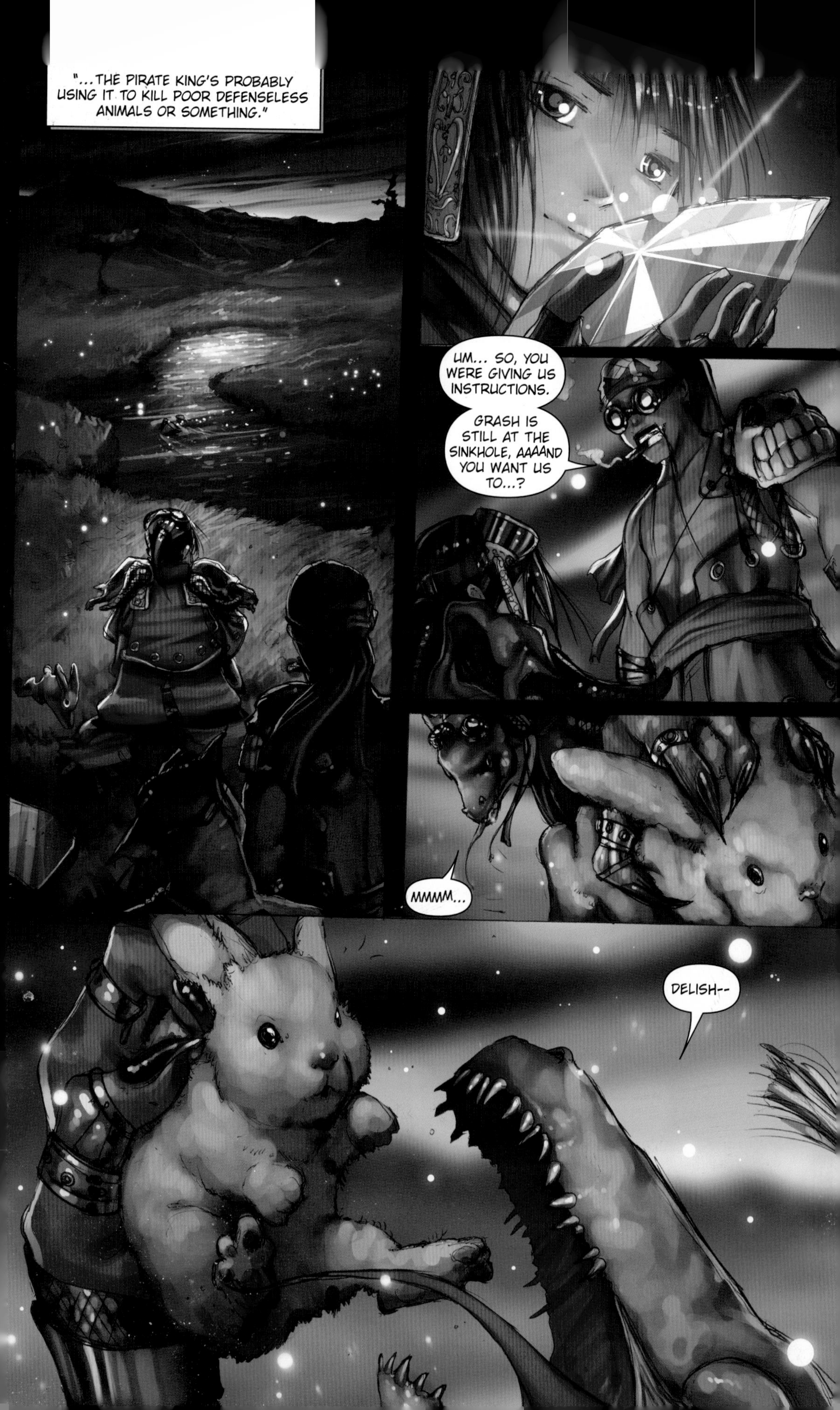
"...THE PIRATE KING'S PROBABLY USING IT TO KILL POOR DEFENSELESS ANIMALS OR SOMETHING."
UM... SO, YOU WERE GIVING US INSTRUCTIONS.
GRASH IS STILL AT THE SINKHOLE, AAAAND YOU WANT US TO...?
MMMM...
DELISH--

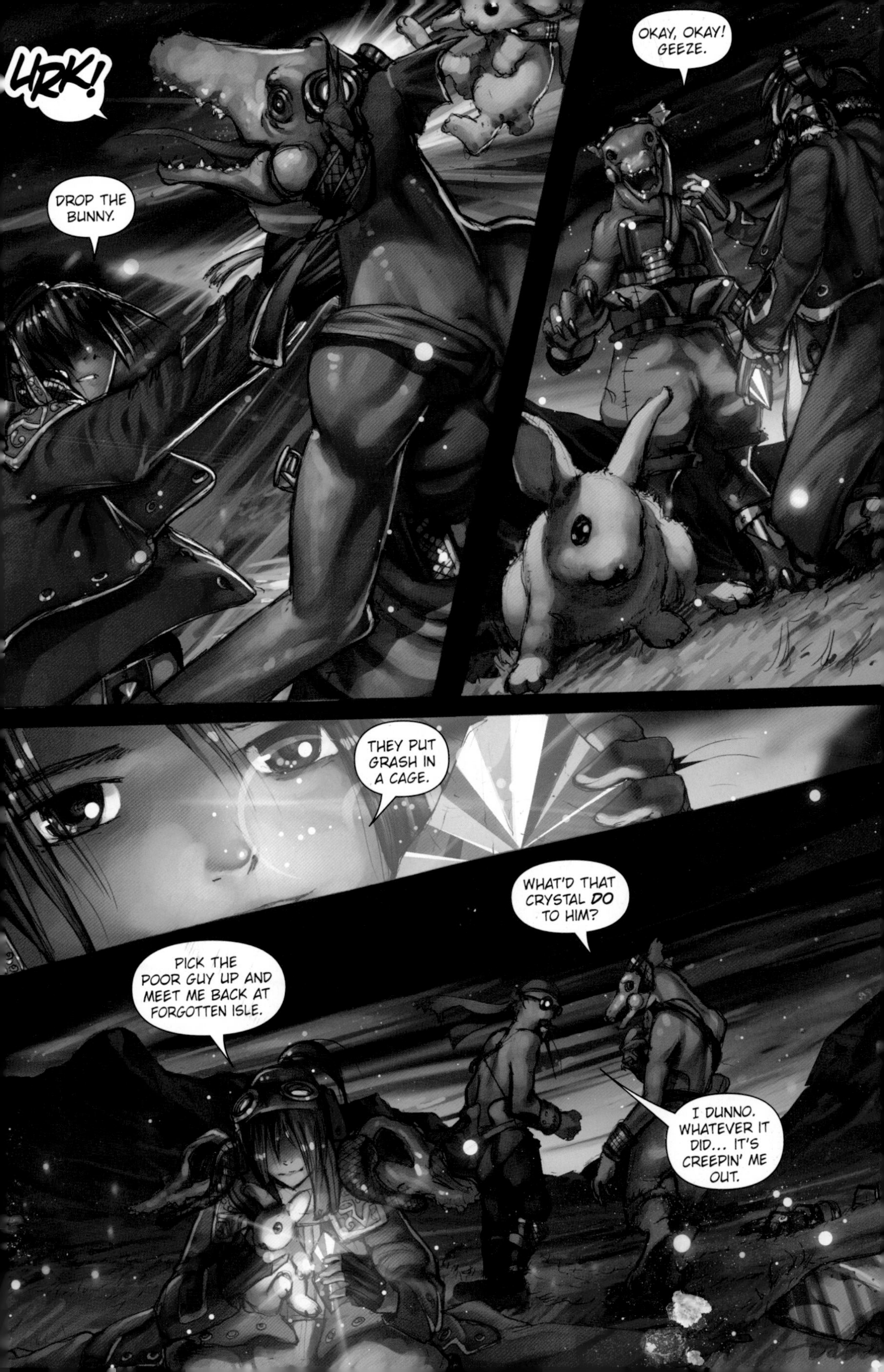
URK!
DROP THE BUNNY.
OKAY, OKAY! GEEZE.
THEY PUT GRASH IN A CAGE.
WHAT'D THAT CRYSTAL *DO* TO HIM?
PICK THE POOR GUY UP AND MEET ME BACK AT FORGOTTEN ISLE.
I DUNNO. WHATEVER IT DID... IT'S CREEPIN' ME OUT.

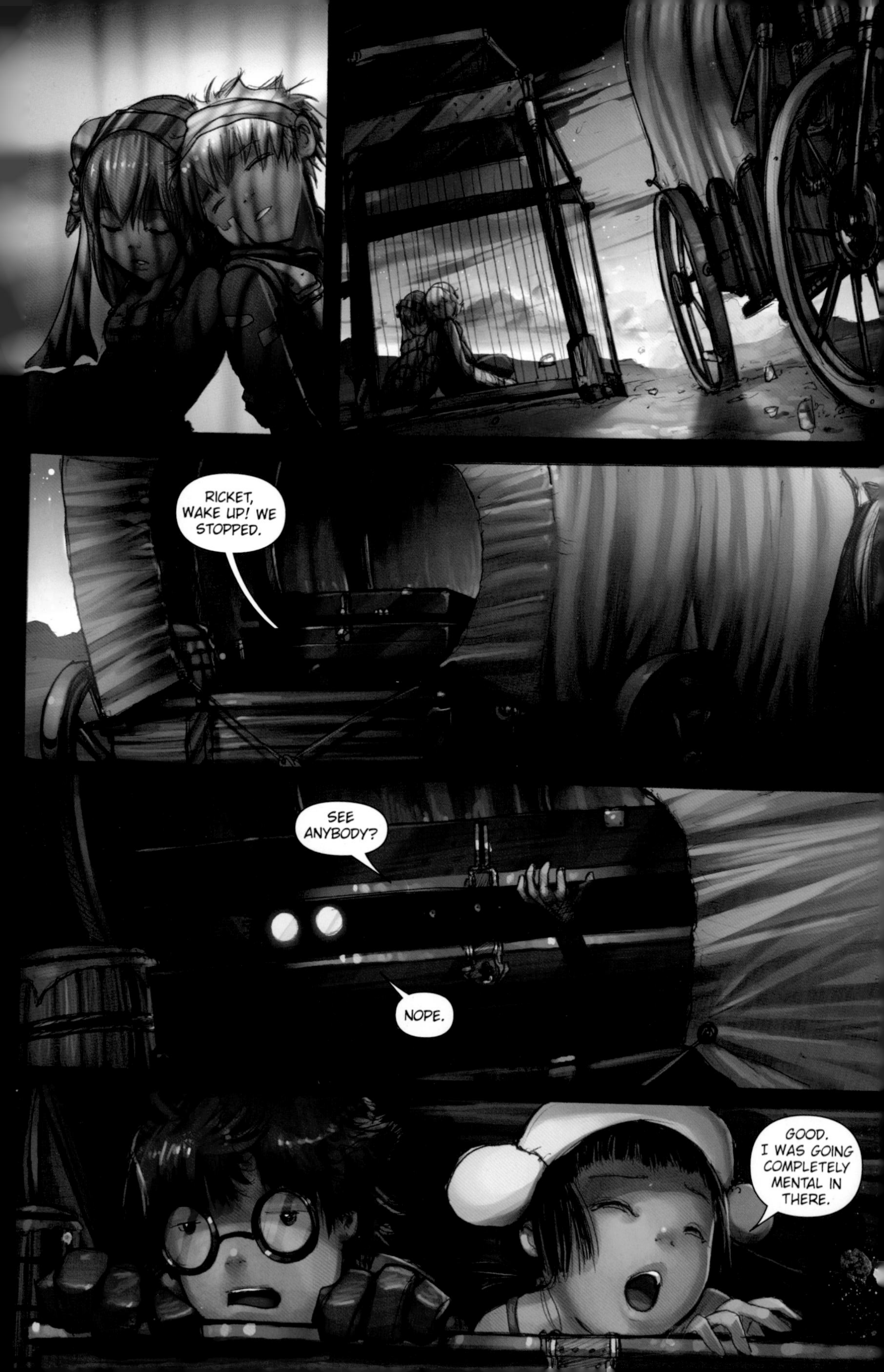
RICKET, WAKE UP! WE STOPPED.
SEE ANYBODY?
NOPE.
GOOD. I WAS GOING COMPLETELY MENTAL IN THERE.

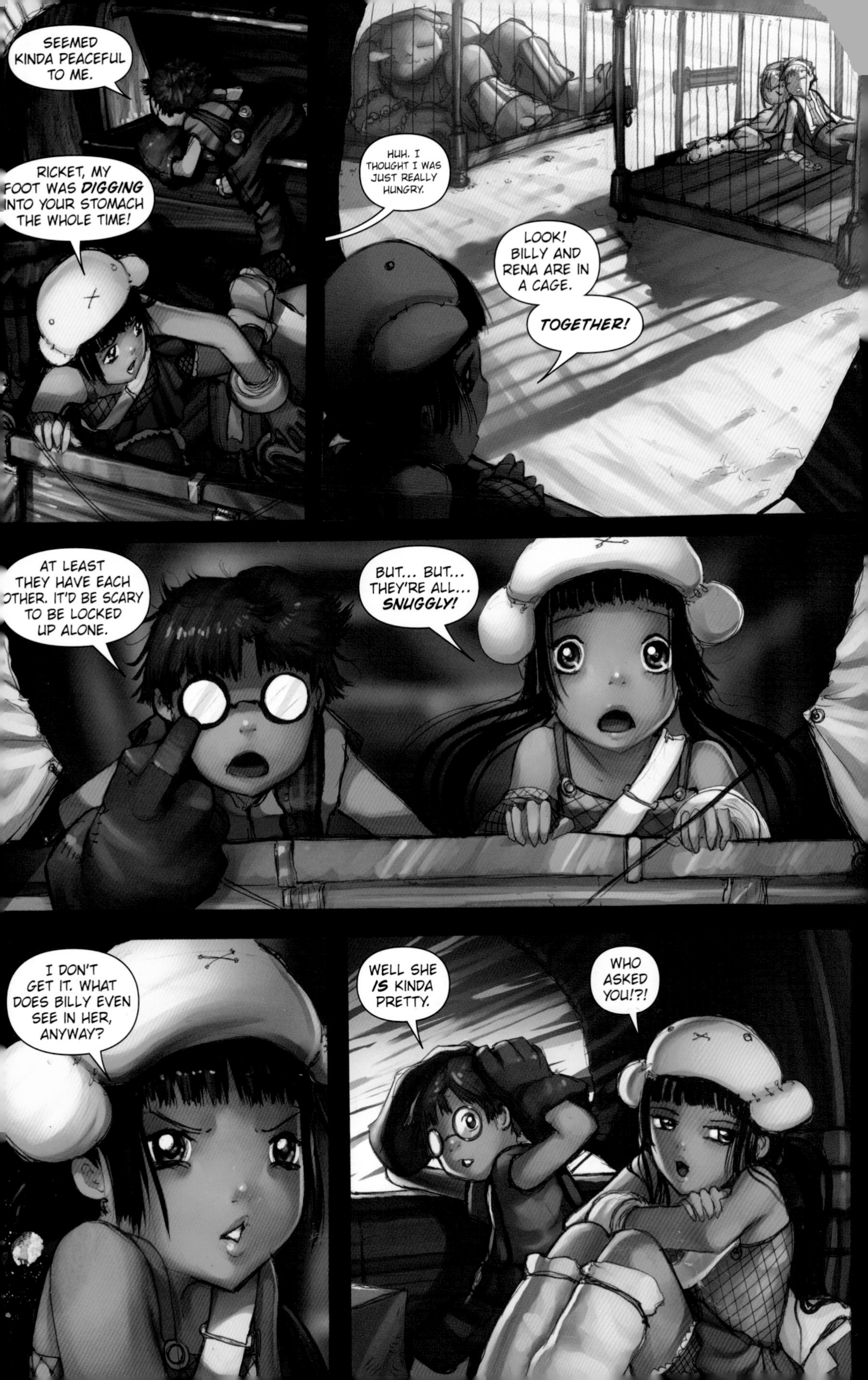
SEEMED KINDA PEACEFUL TO ME.
RICKET, MY FOOT WAS DIGGING INTO YOUR STOMACH THE WHOLE TIME!
HUH. I THOUGHT I WAS JUST REALLY HUNGRY.
LOOK! BILLY AND RENA ARE IN A CAGE.
TOGETHER!
AT LEAST THEY HAVE EACH OTHER. IT'D BE SCARY TO BE LOCKED UP ALONE.
BUT... BUT... THEY'RE ALL... SNUGGLY!
I DON'T GET IT. WHAT DOES BILLY EVEN SEE IN HER, ANYWAY?
WELL SHE IS KINDA PRETTY.
WHO ASKED YOU!?!

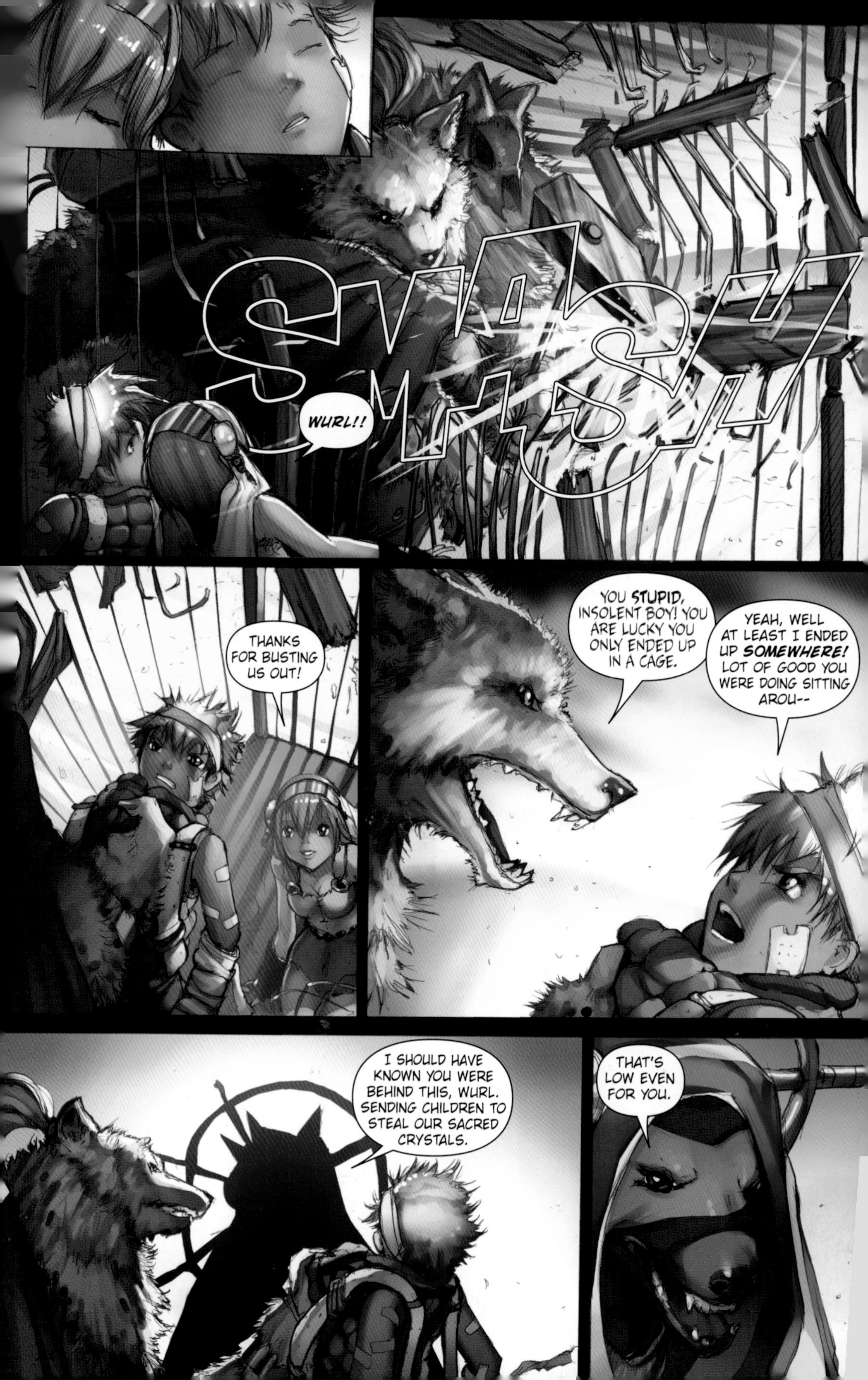
SMASH
WURL!!
THANKS FOR BUSTING US OUT!
YOU **STUPID,** INSOLENT BOY! YOU ARE LUCKY YOU ONLY ENDED UP IN A CAGE.
YEAH, WELL AT LEAST I ENDED UP ***SOMEWHERE!*** LOT OF GOOD YOU WERE DOING SITTING AROU--
I SHOULD HAVE KNOWN YOU WERE BEHIND THIS, WURL. SENDING CHILDREN TO STEAL OUR SACRED CRYSTALS.
THAT'S LOW EVEN FOR YOU.

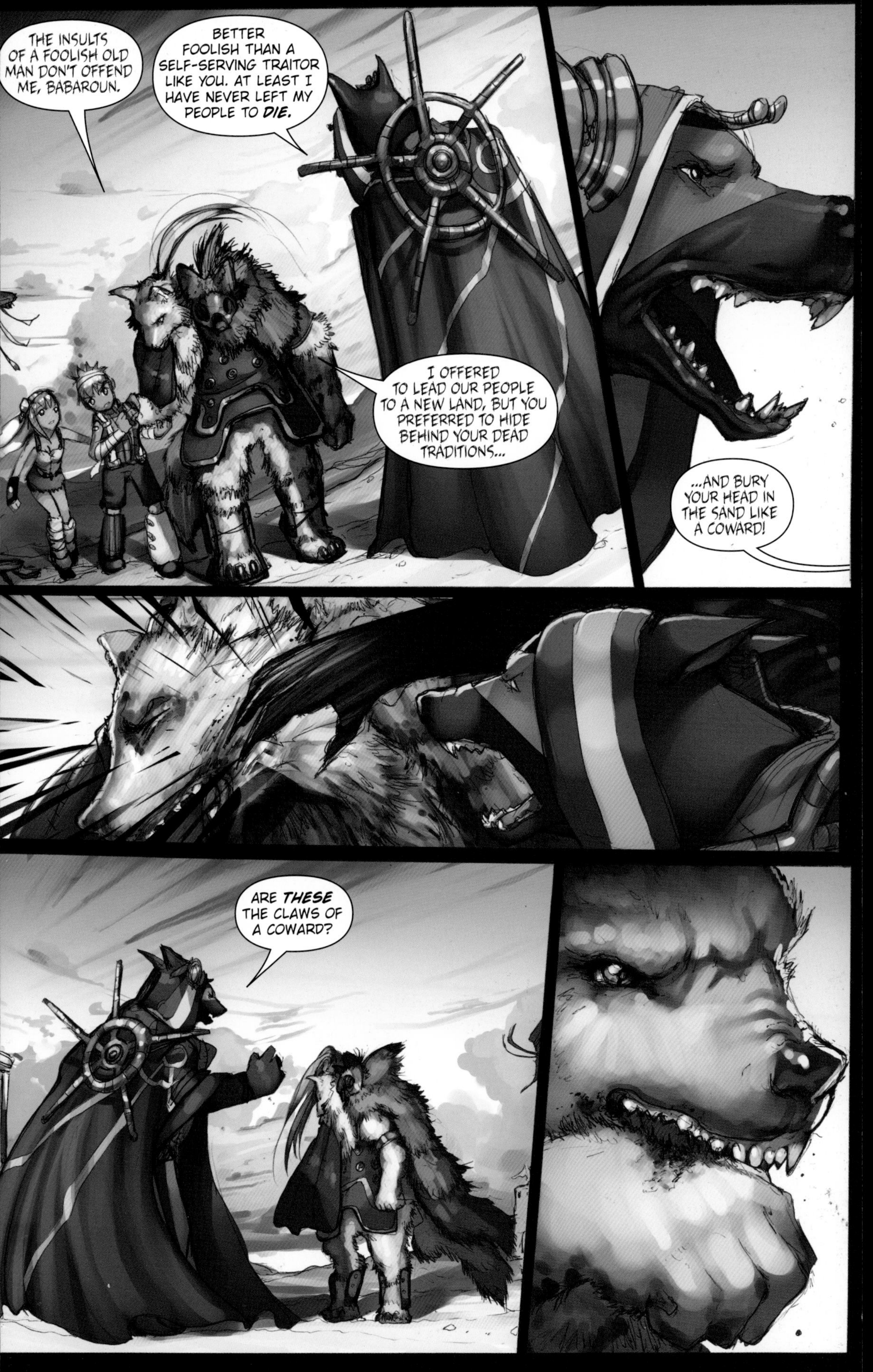
THE INSULTS OF A FOOLISH OLD MAN DON'T OFFEND ME, BABAROUN.
BETTER FOOLISH THAN A SELF-SERVING TRAITOR LIKE YOU. AT LEAST I HAVE NEVER LEFT MY PEOPLE TO ***DIE.***
I OFFERED TO LEAD OUR PEOPLE TO A NEW LAND, BUT YOU PREFERRED TO HIDE BEHIND YOUR DEAD TRADITIONS...
...AND BURY YOUR HEAD IN THE SAND LIKE A COWARD!
ARE ***THESE*** THE CLAWS OF A COWARD?

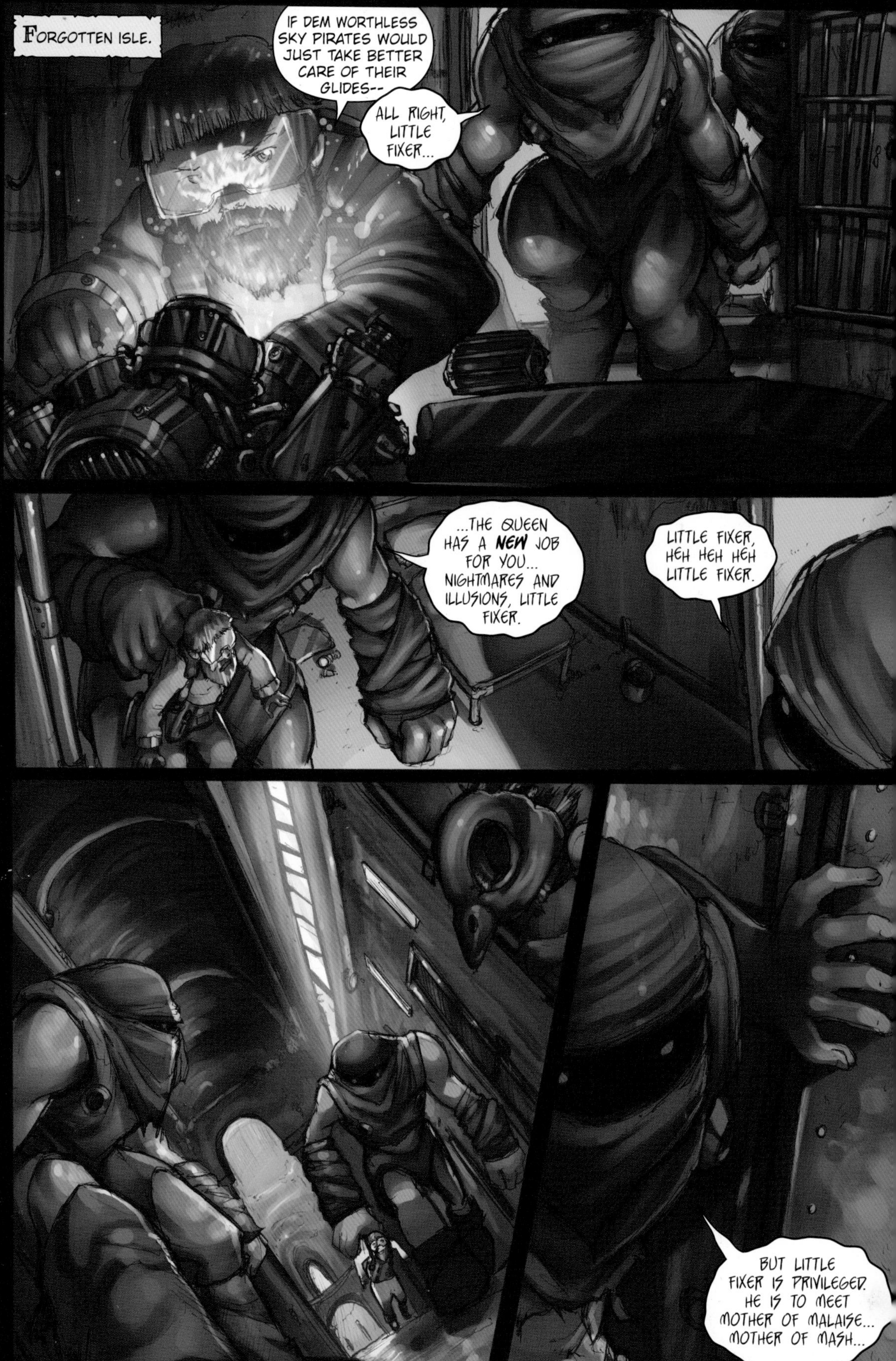

FORGOTTEN ISLE.
IF DEM WORTHLESS SKY PIRATES WOULD JUST TAKE BETTER CARE OF THEIR GLIDES--
ALL RIGHT, LITTLE FIXER...
...THE QUEEN HAS A NEW JOB FOR YOU... NIGHTMARES AND ILLUSIONS, LITTLE FIXER.
LITTLE FIXER, HEH HEH HEH LITTLE FIXER.
BUT LITTLE FIXER IS PRIVILEGED. HE IS TO MEET MOTHER OF MALAISE... MOTHER OF MASH...

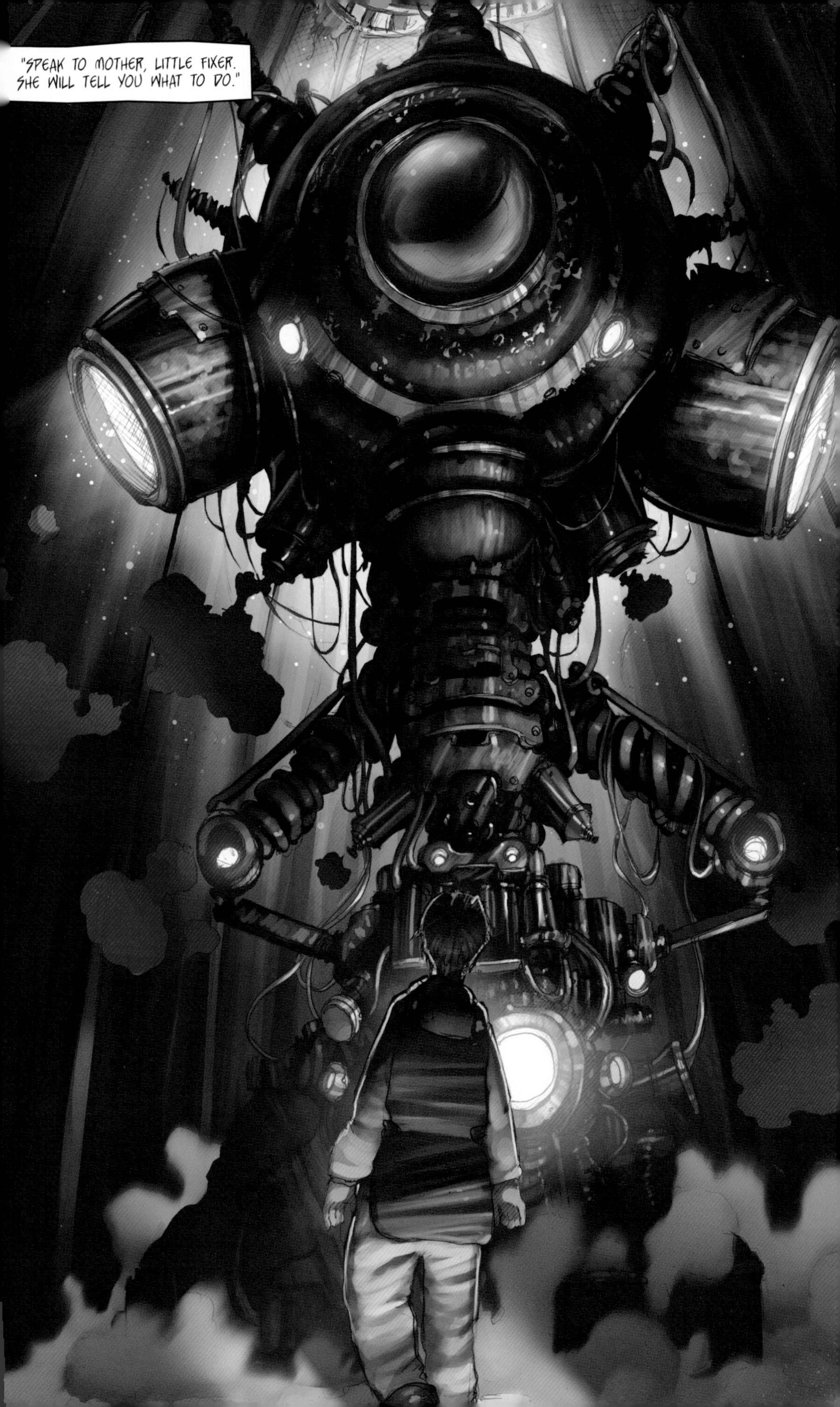
"SPEAK TO MOTHER, LITTLE FIXER. SHE WILL TELL YOU WHAT TO DO."

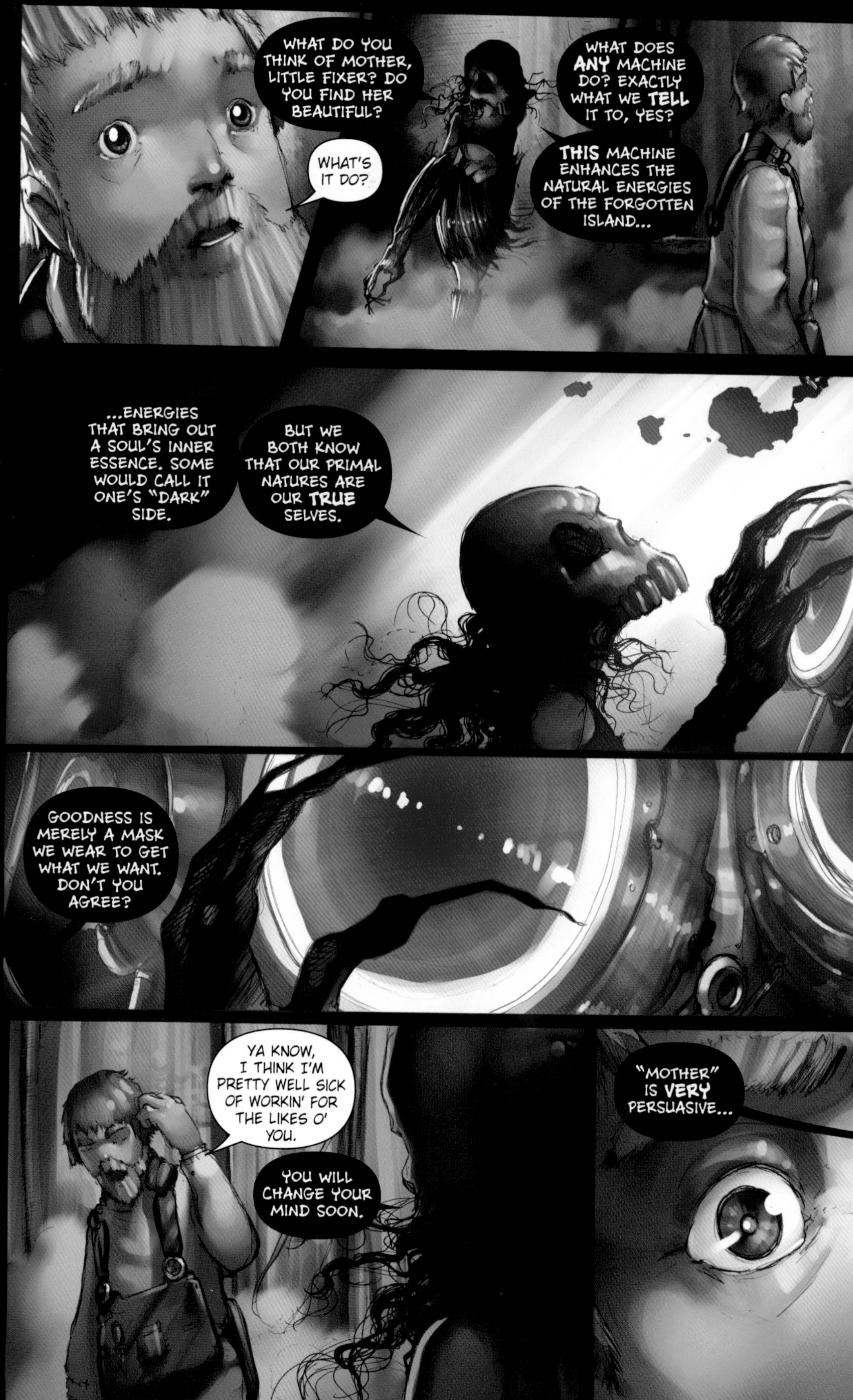
WHAT DO YOU THINK OF MOTHER, LITTLE FIXER? DO YOU FIND HER BEAUTIFUL?
WHAT'S IT DO?
WHAT DOES ANY MACHINE DO? EXACTLY WHAT WE TELL IT TO, YES?
THIS MACHINE ENHANCES THE NATURAL ENERGIES OF THE FORGOTTEN ISLAND...
...ENERGIES THAT BRING OUT A SOUL'S INNER ESSENCE. SOME WOULD CALL IT ONE'S "DARK" SIDE.
BUT WE BOTH KNOW THAT OUR PRIMAL NATURES ARE OUR TRUE SELVES.
GOODNESS IS MERELY A MASK WE WEAR TO GET WHAT WE WANT. DON'T YOU AGREE?
YA KNOW, I THINK I'M PRETTY WELL SICK OF WORKIN' FOR THE LIKES O' YOU.
YOU WILL CHANGE YOUR MIND SOON.
"MOTHER" IS VERY PERSUASIVE...

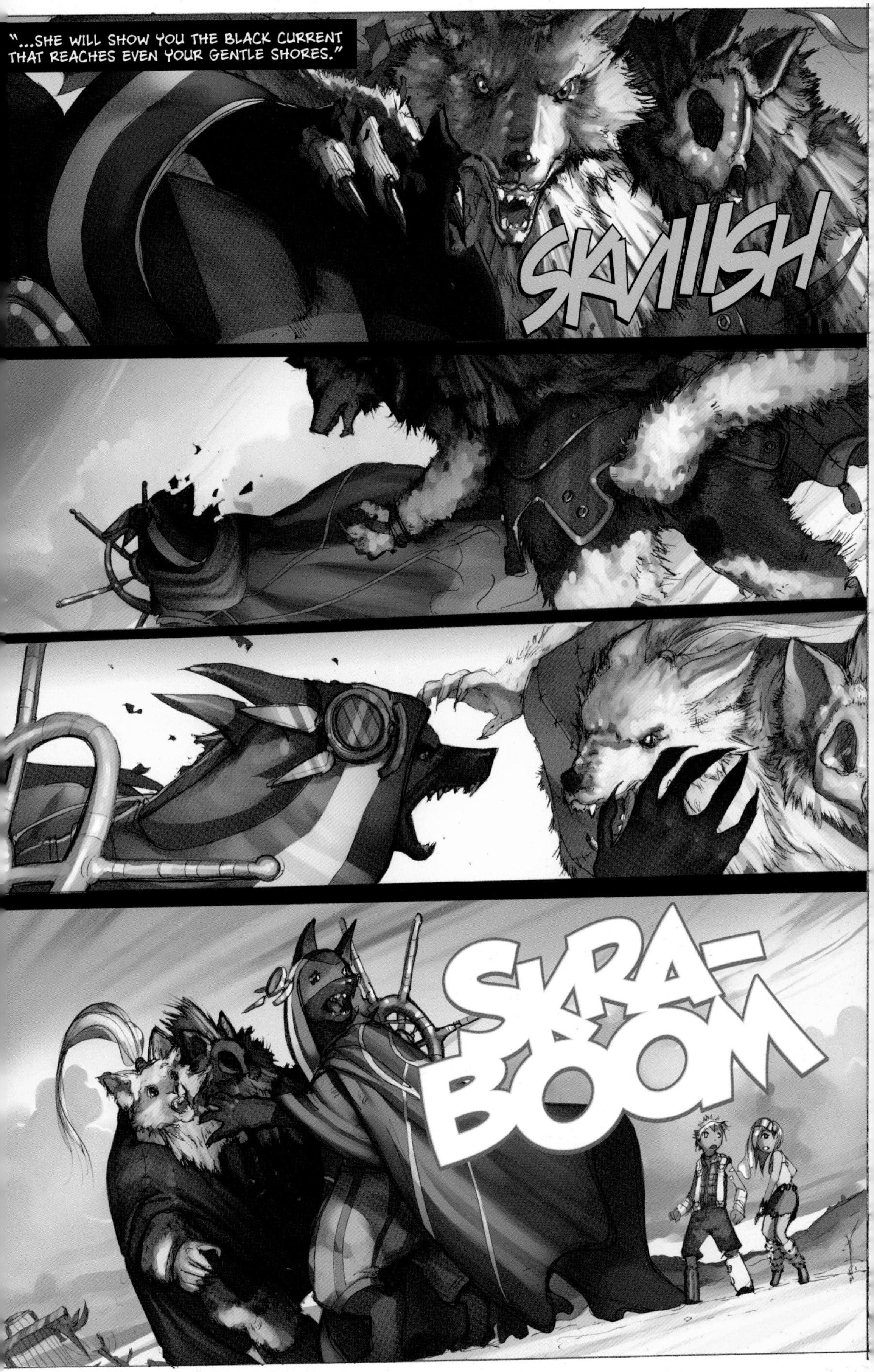
"...SHE WILL SHOW YOU THE BLACK CURRENT
THAT REACHES EVEN YOUR GENTLE SHORES."
SKVIISH
SKRA-
BOOM

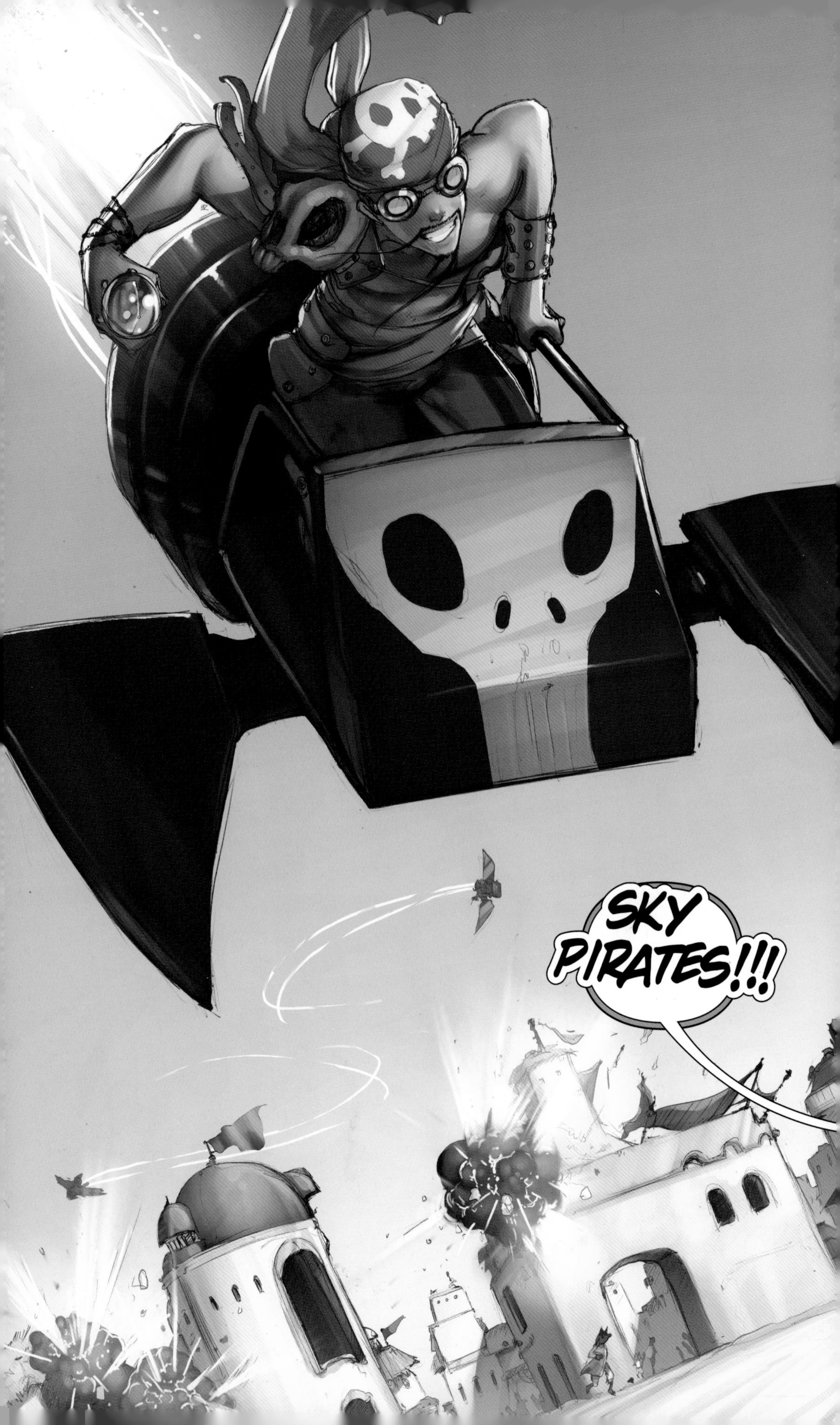
SKY PIRATES!!!

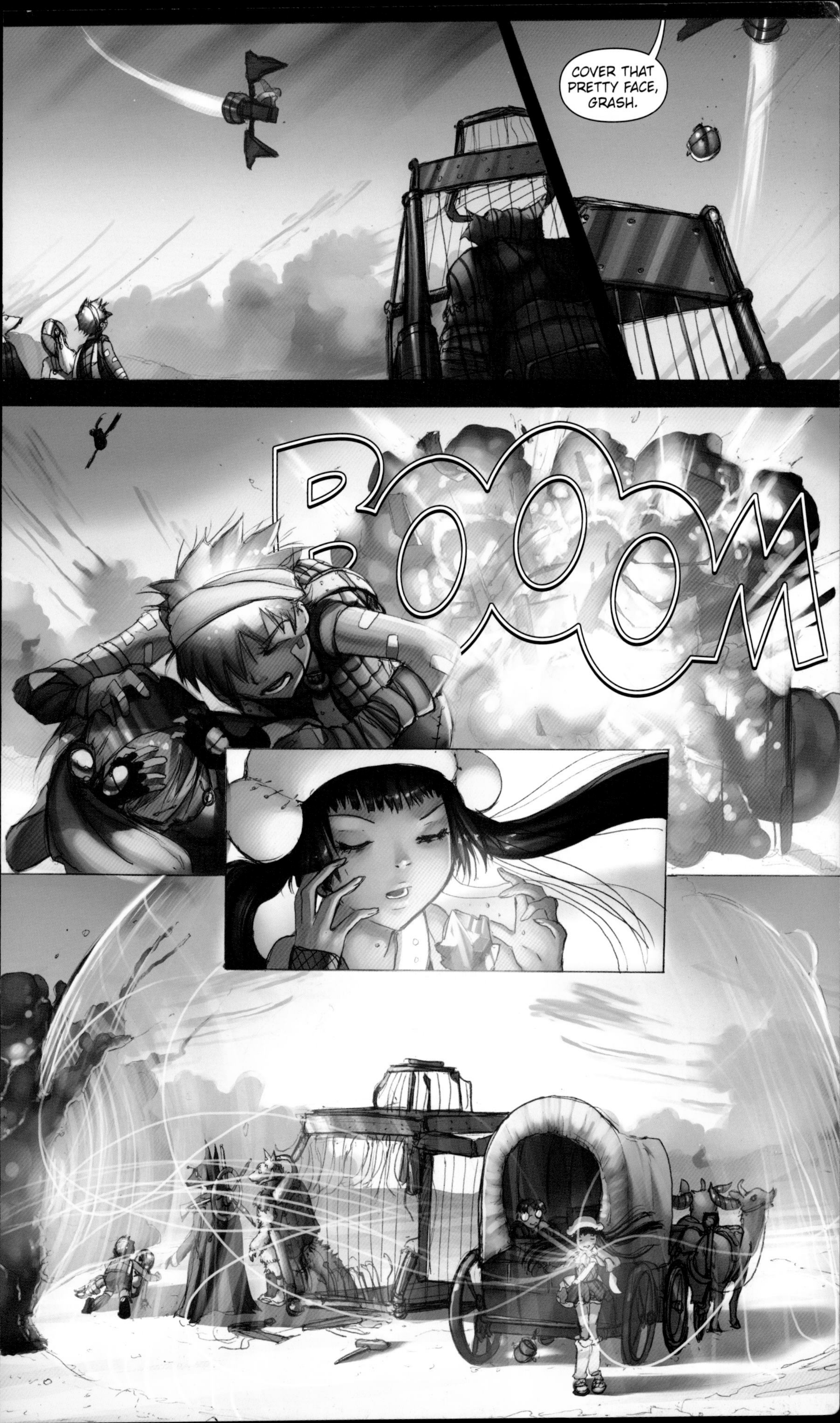
COVER THAT PRETTY FACE, GRASH.
BOOOOM

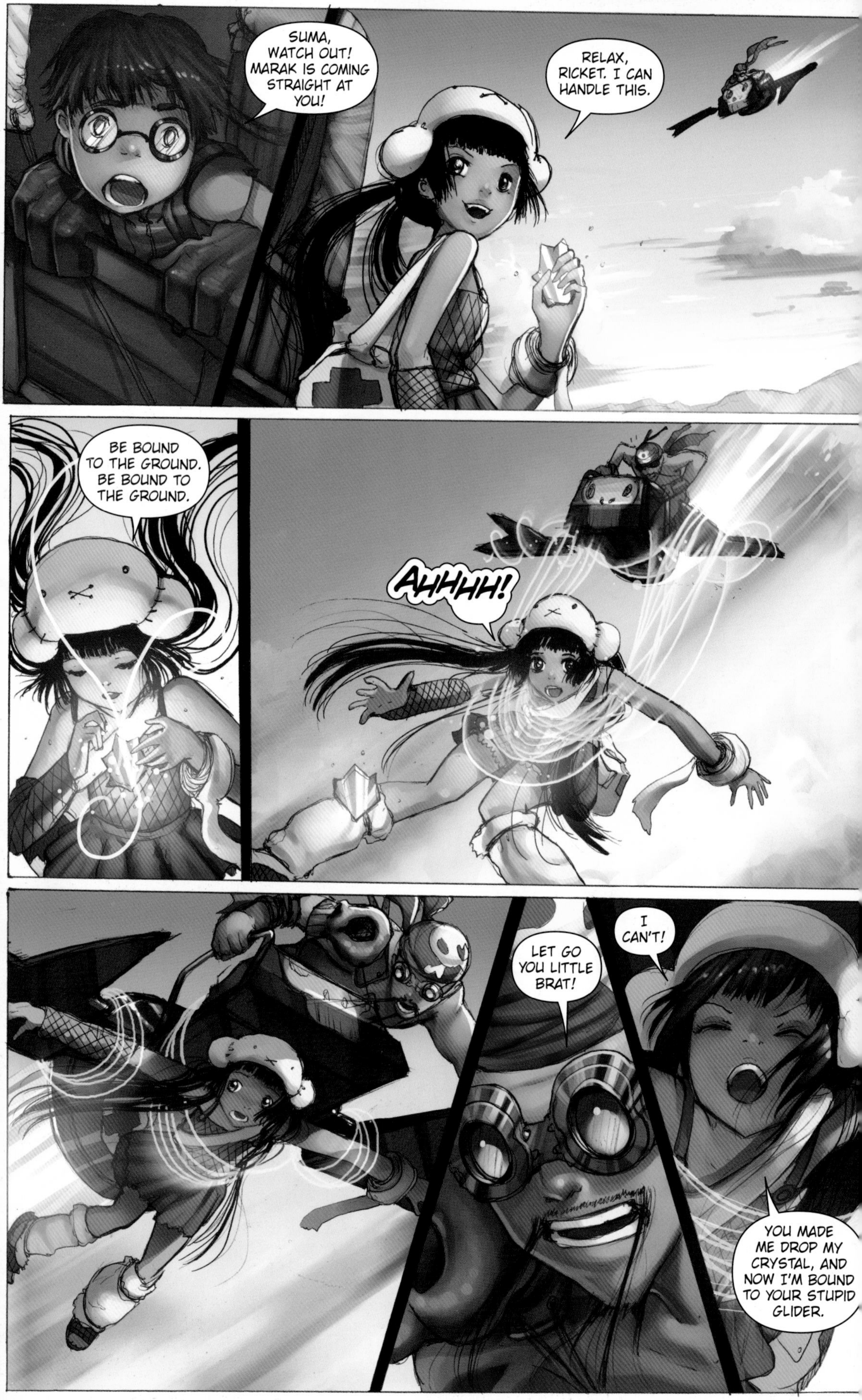
SUMA, WATCH OUT! MARAK IS COMING STRAIGHT AT YOU!
RELAX, RICKET. I CAN HANDLE THIS.
BE BOUND TO THE GROUND. BE BOUND TO THE GROUND.
AHHHH!
LET GO YOU LITTLE BRAT!
I CAN'T!
YOU MADE ME DROP MY CRYSTAL, AND NOW I'M BOUND TO YOUR STUPID GLIDER.

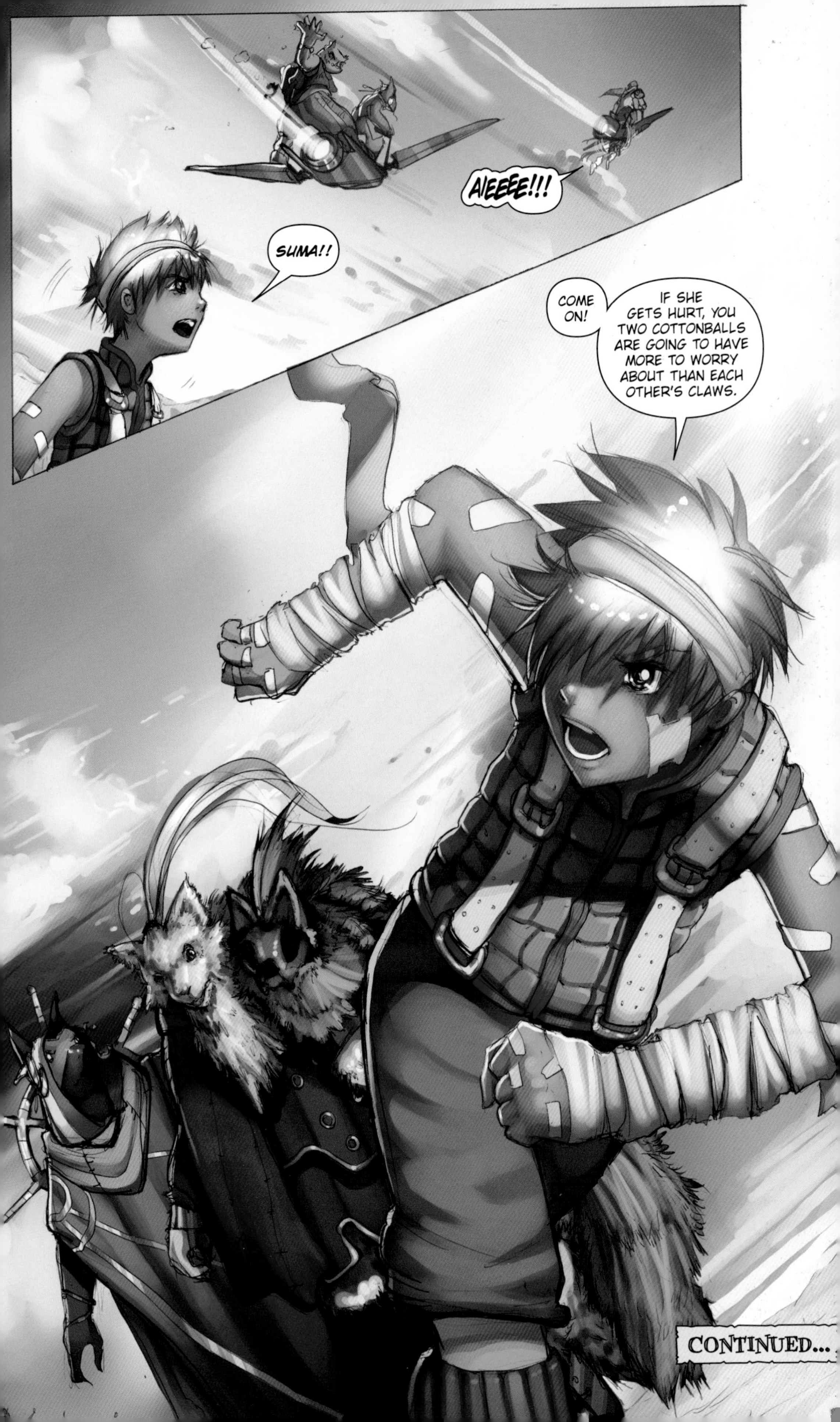
AIEEEE!!!
SUMA!!
COME ON!
IF SHE GETS HURT, YOU TWO COTTONBALLS ARE GOING TO HAVE MORE TO WORRY ABOUT THAN EACH OTHER'S CLAWS.
CONTINUED...

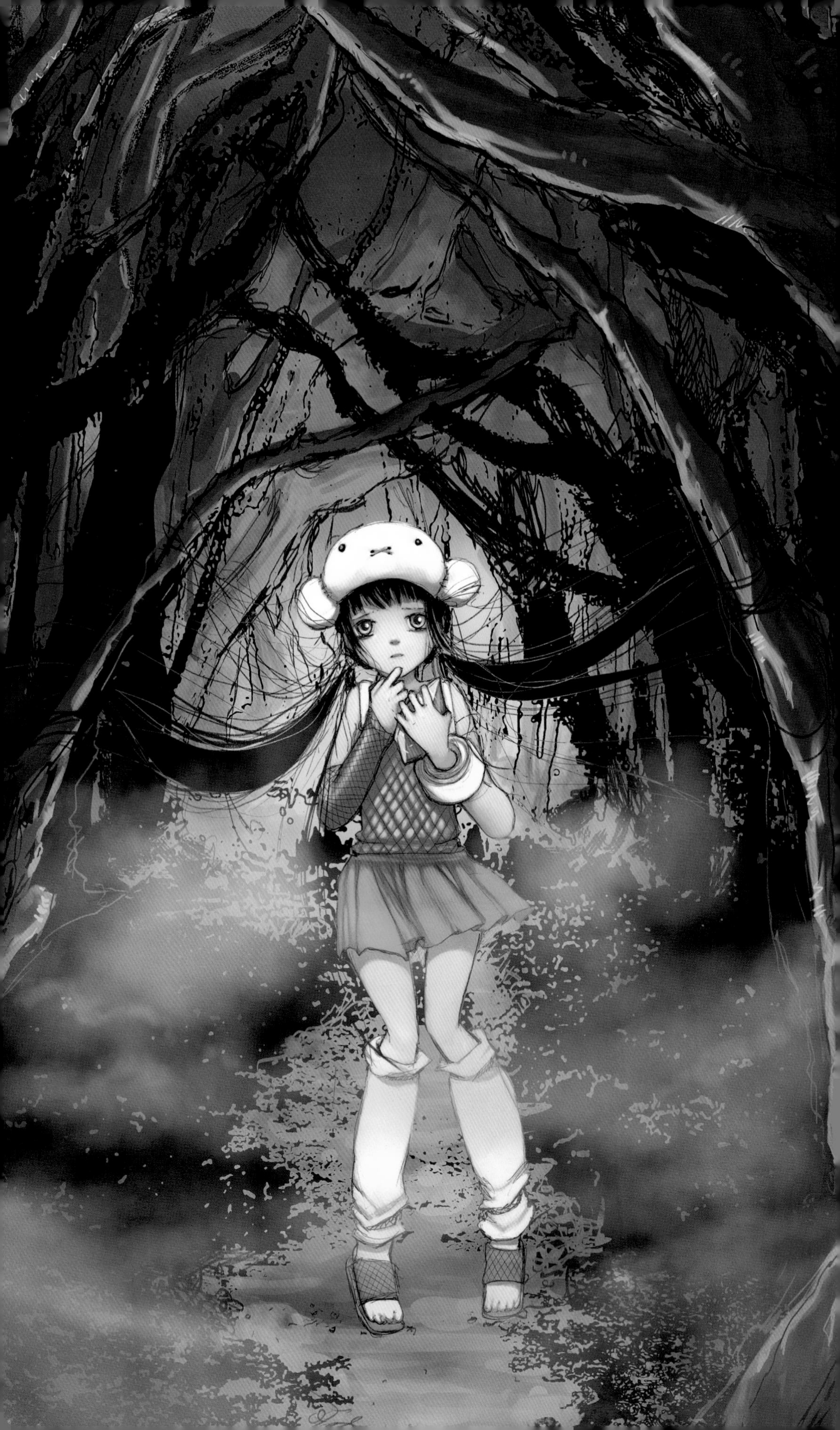

TURN THIS GLIDER AROUND BEFORE I MELT YOUR MUSTACHE WITH THIS FIRE CRYSTAL! OR SMASH YOUR BRAIN TO BITS WITH MY ROCK CRYSTAL! OR TURN YOU INTO A FISH WITH...

WURL, I NEED A GLIDEWING *NOW!*

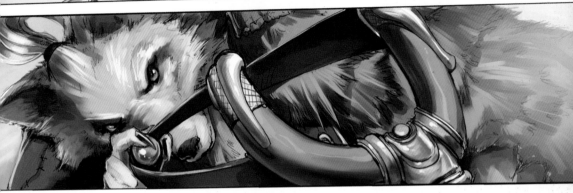

THWOK

AAAAAH!

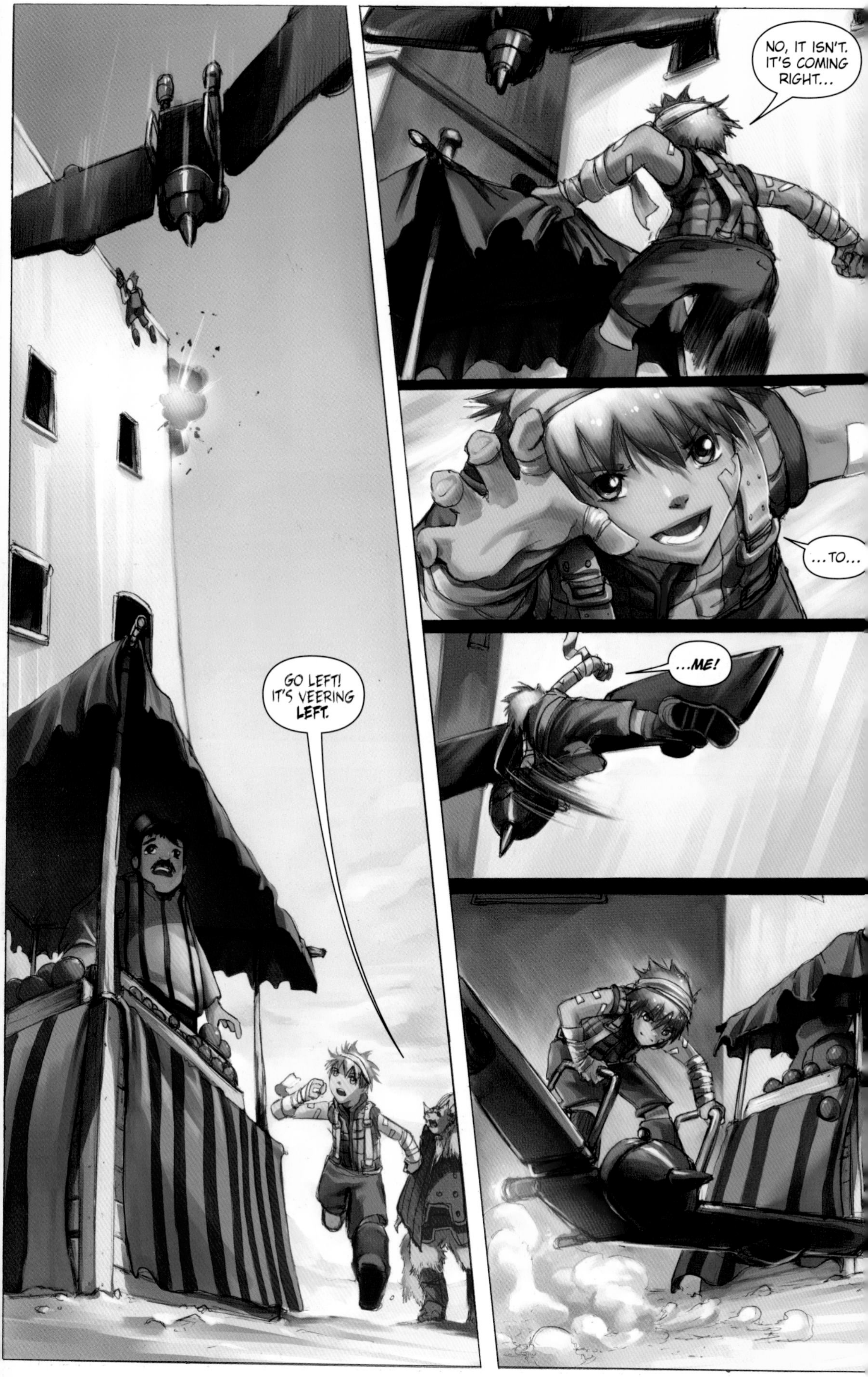
GO LEFT! IT'S VEERING LEFT.
NO, IT ISN'T. IT'S COMING RIGHT...
...TO...
...ME!

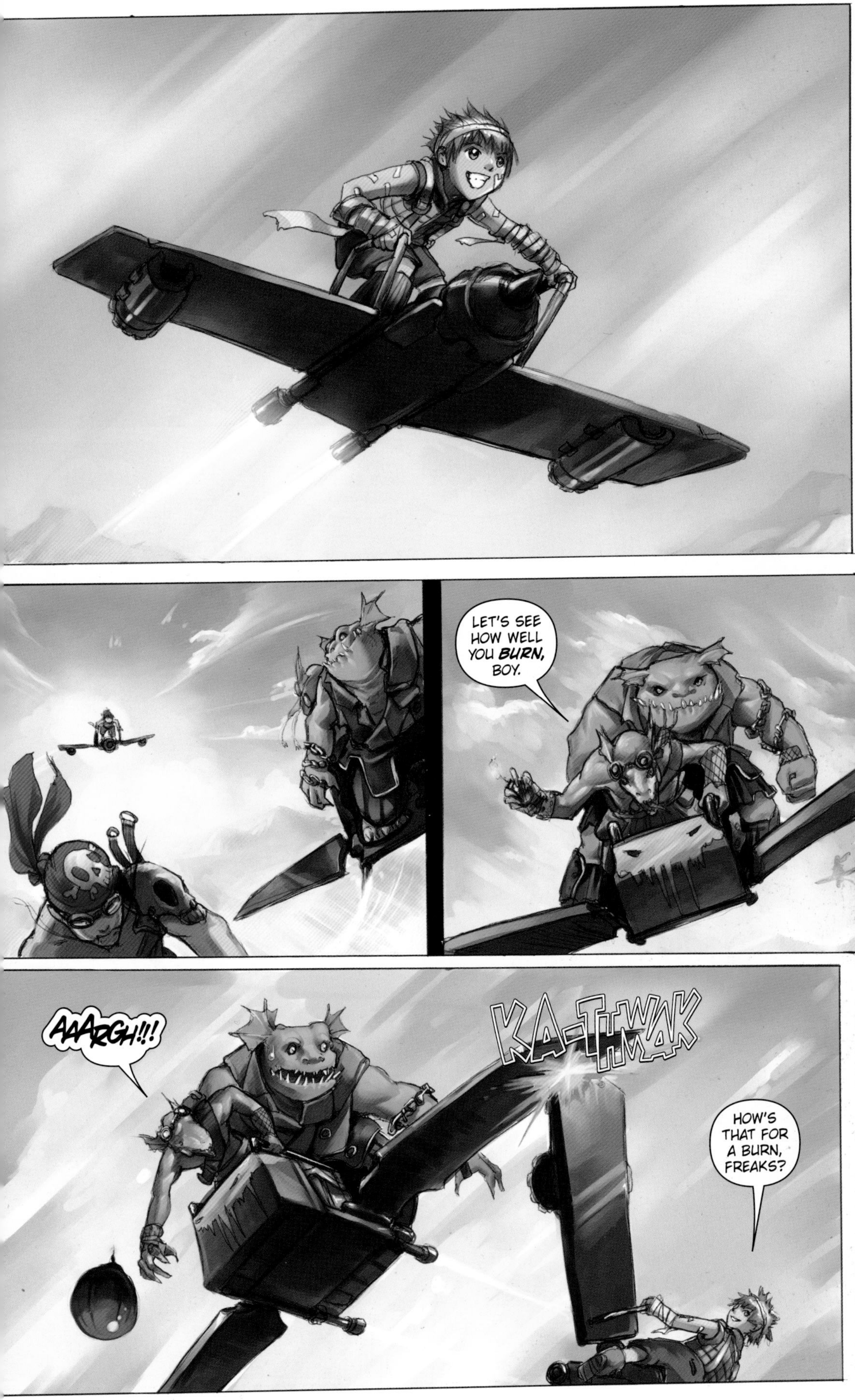
LET'S SEE HOW WELL YOU BURN, BOY.
AAARGH!!!
KA-THWAK
HOW'S THAT FOR A BURN, FREAKS?

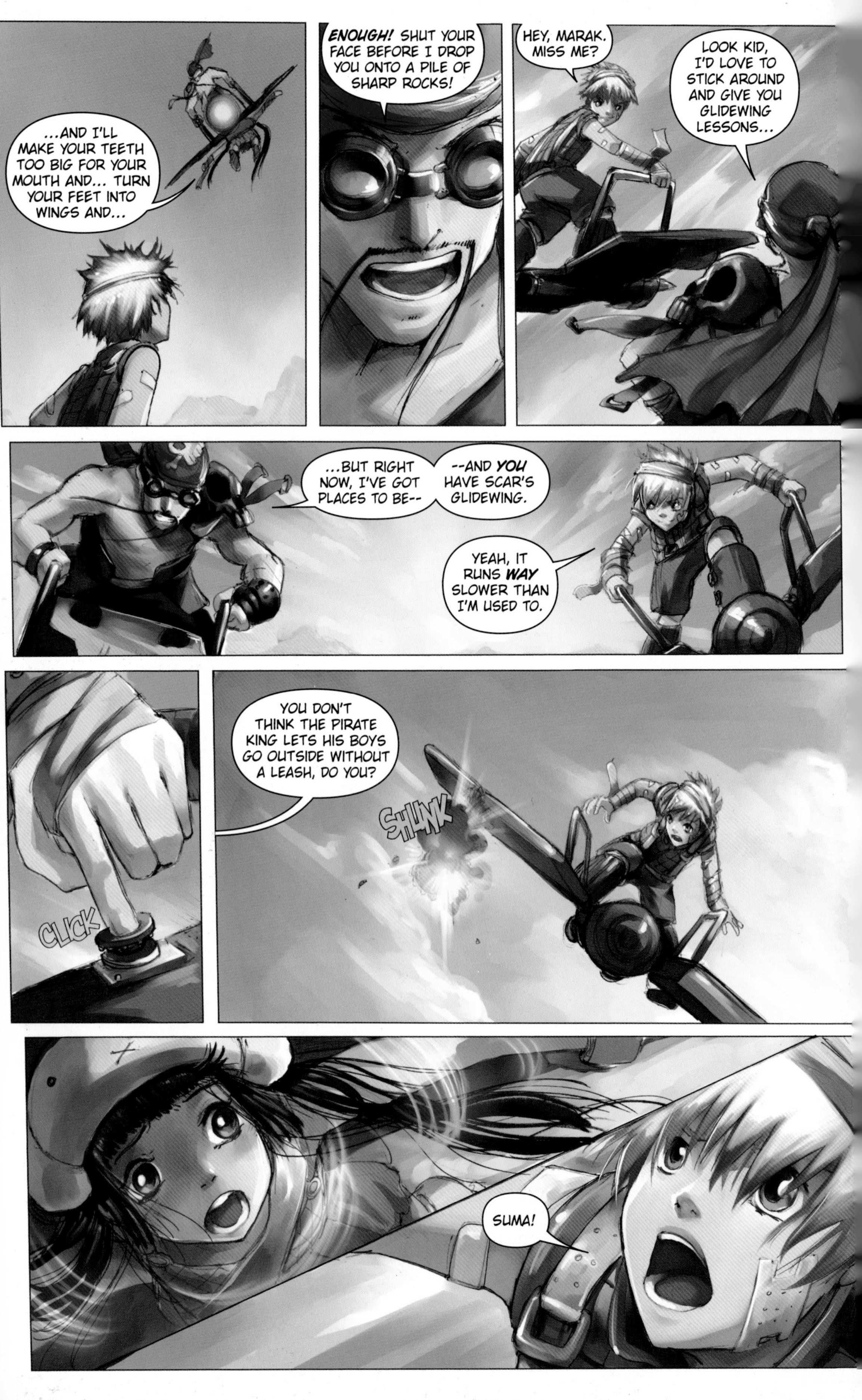

...AND I'LL MAKE YOUR TEETH TOO BIG FOR YOUR MOUTH AND... TURN YOUR FEET INTO WINGS AND...
ENOUGH! SHUT YOUR FACE BEFORE I DROP YOU ONTO A PILE OF SHARP ROCKS!
HEY, MARAK. MISS ME?
LOOK KID, I'D LOVE TO STICK AROUND AND GIVE YOU GLIDEWING LESSONS...
...BUT RIGHT NOW, I'VE GOT PLACES TO BE--
--AND YOU HAVE SCAR'S GLIDEWING.
YEAH, IT RUNS WAY SLOWER THAN I'M USED TO.
CLICK
YOU DON'T THINK THE PIRATE KING LETS HIS BOYS GO OUTSIDE WITHOUT A LEASH, DO YOU?
SHUNK
SUMA!

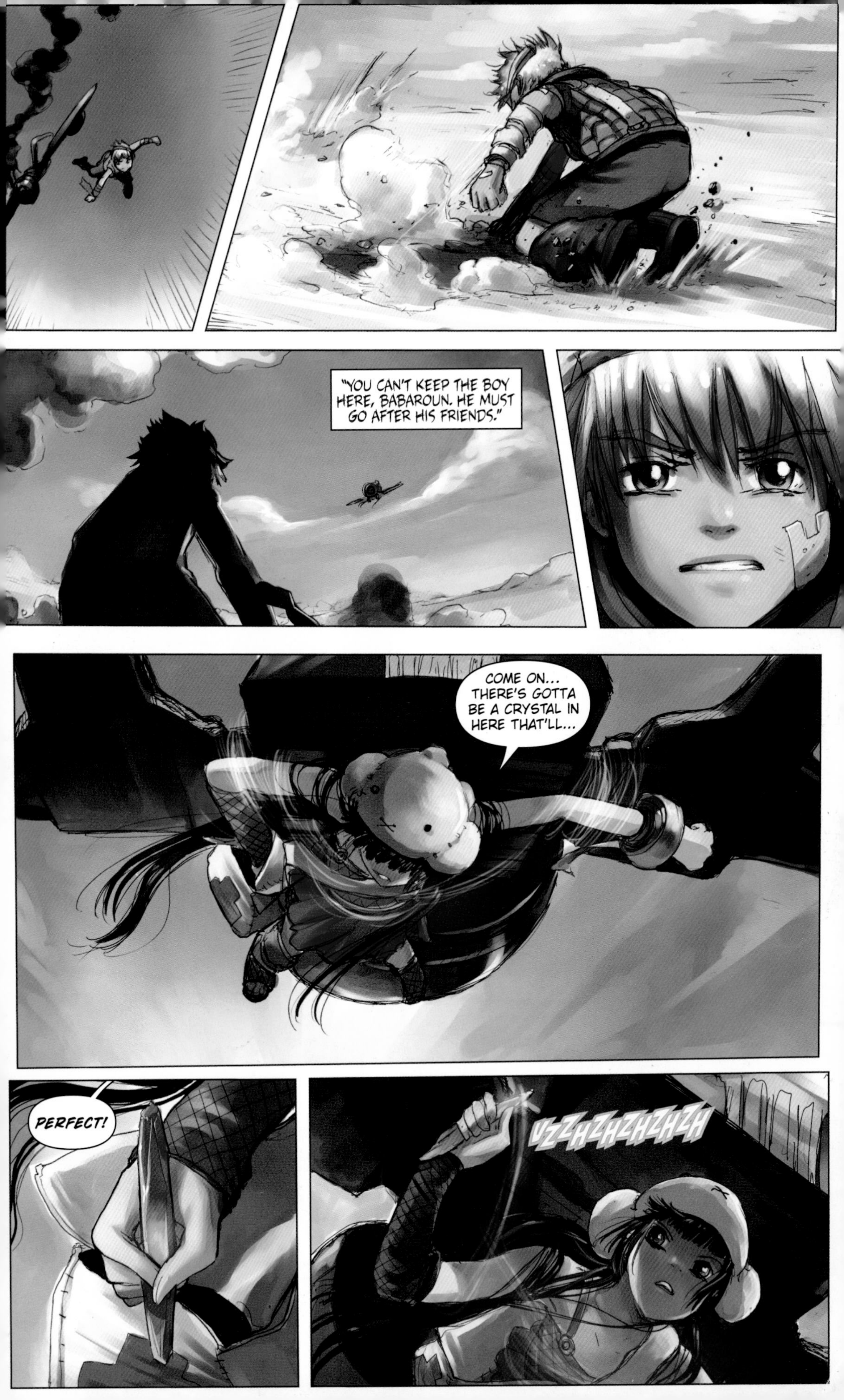
"YOU CAN'T KEEP THE BOY HERE, BABAROUN. HE MUST GO AFTER HIS FRIENDS."
COME ON... THERE'S GOTTA BE A CRYSTAL IN HERE THAT'LL...
PERFECT!
VZZHZHZHZHZH

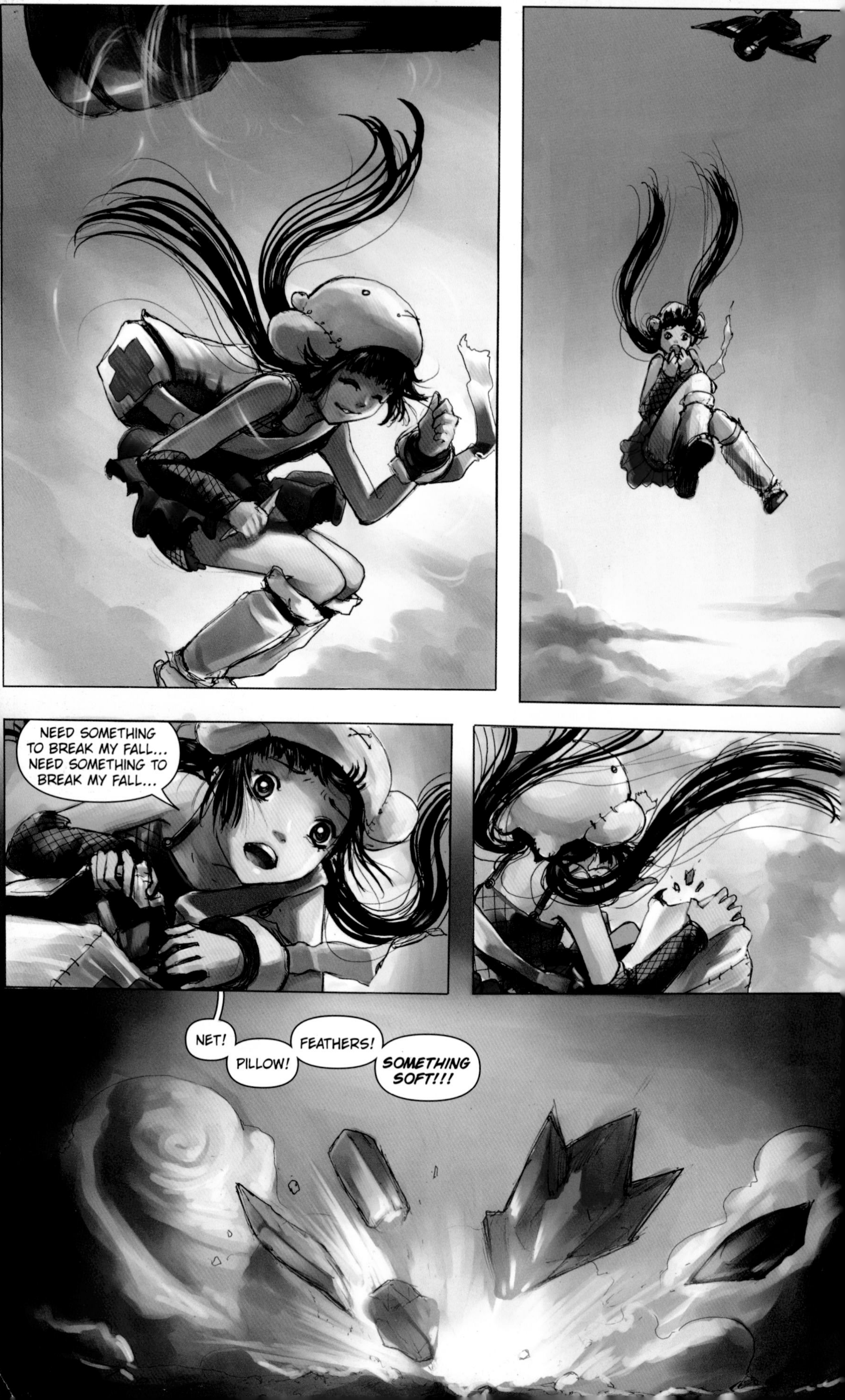
NEED SOMETHING TO BREAK MY FALL... NEED SOMETHING TO BREAK MY FALL...
NET!
PILLOW!
FEATHERS!
SOMETHING SOFT!!!

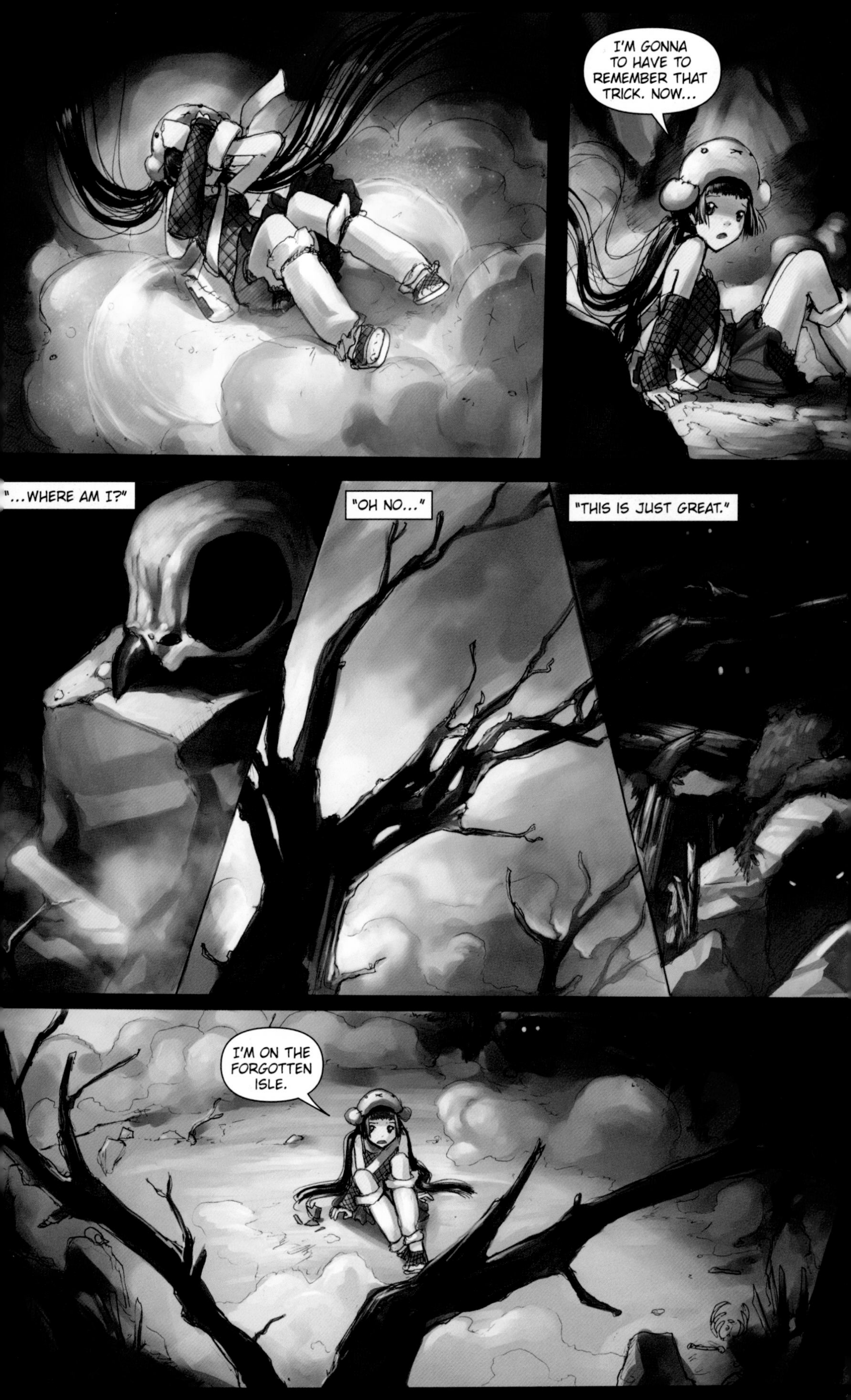
I'M GONNA TO HAVE TO REMEMBER THAT TRICK. NOW...
"...WHERE AM I?"
"OH NO..."
"THIS IS JUST GREAT."
I'M ON THE FORGOTTEN ISLE.

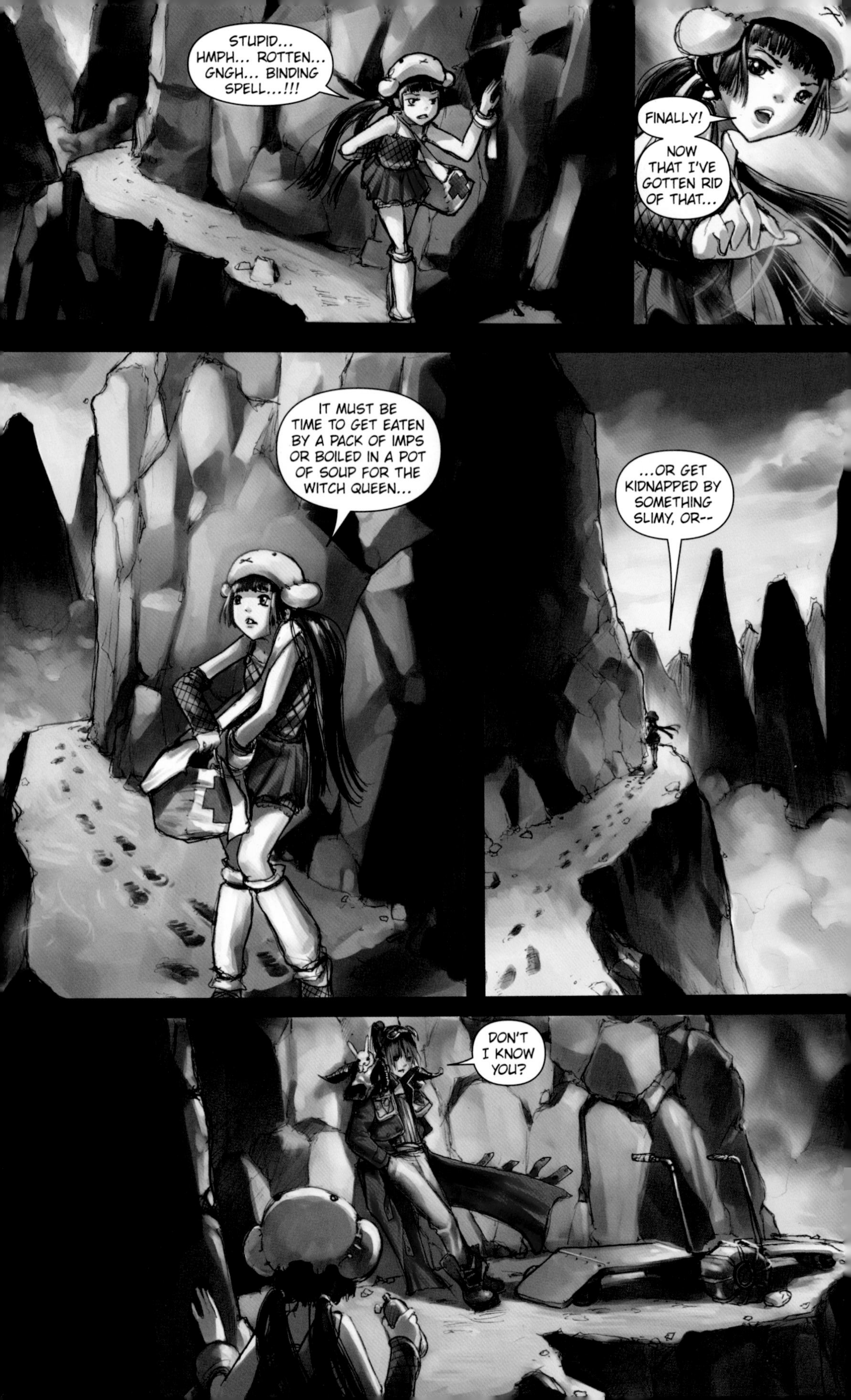
STUPID... HMPH... ROTTEN... GNGH... BINDING SPELL...!!!
FINALLY!
NOW THAT I'VE GOTTEN RID OF THAT...
IT MUST BE TIME TO GET EATEN BY A PACK OF IMPS OR BOILED IN A POT OF SOUP FOR THE WITCH QUEEN...
...OR GET KIDNAPPED BY SOMETHING SLIMY, OR--
DON'T I KNOW YOU?

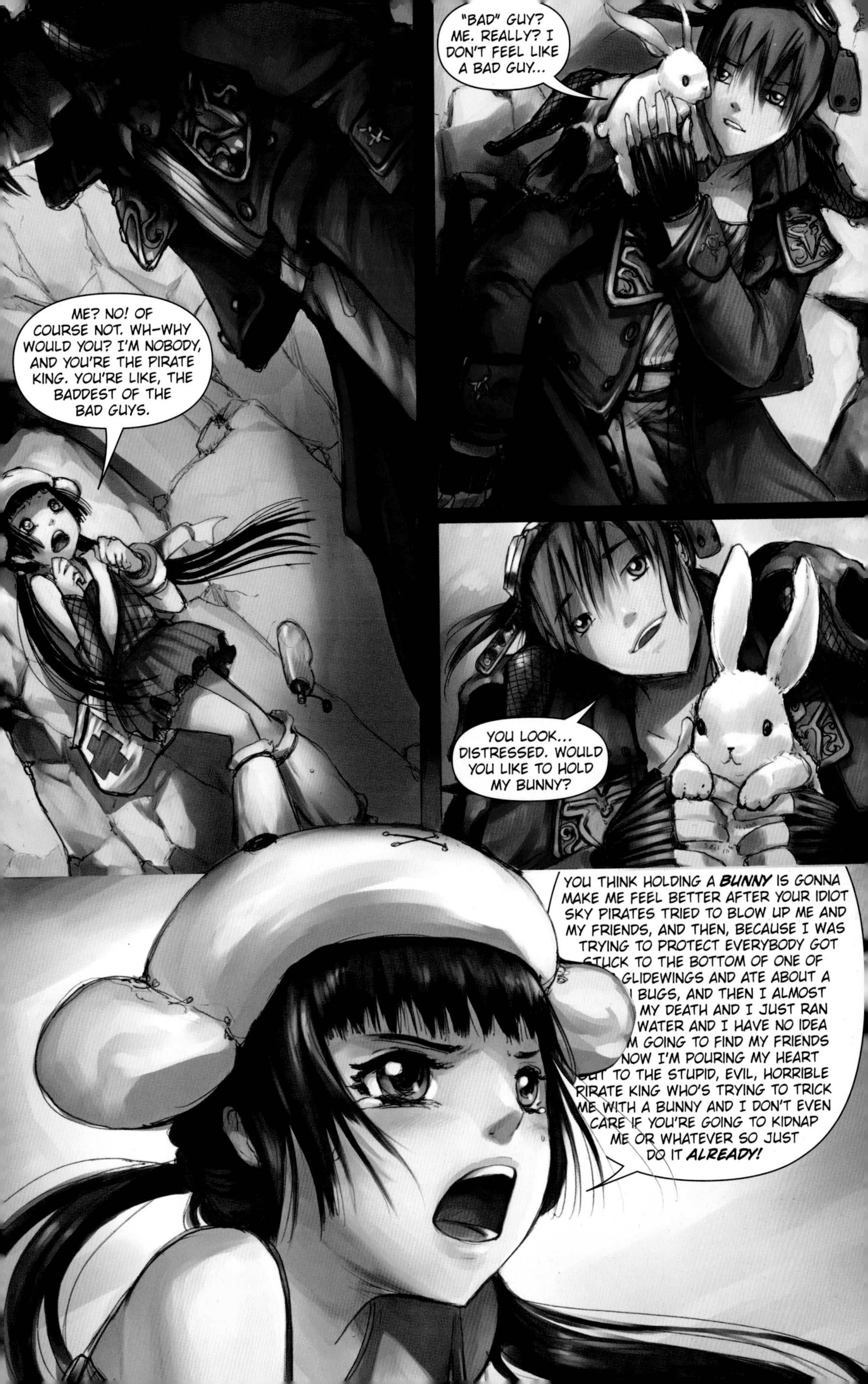

ME? NO! OF COURSE NOT. WH-WHY WOULD YOU? I'M NOBODY, AND YOU'RE THE PIRATE KING. YOU'RE LIKE, THE BADDEST OF THE BAD GUYS.
"BAD" GUY? ME. REALLY? I DON'T FEEL LIKE A BAD GUY...
YOU LOOK... DISTRESSED. WOULD YOU LIKE TO HOLD MY BUNNY?
YOU THINK HOLDING A ***BUNNY*** IS GONNA MAKE ME FEEL BETTER AFTER YOUR IDIOT SKY PIRATES TRIED TO BLOW UP ME AND MY FRIENDS, AND THEN, BECAUSE I WAS TRYING TO PROTECT EVERYBODY GOT STUCK TO THE BOTTOM OF ONE OF GLIDEWINGS AND ATE ABOUT A BUGS, AND THEN I ALMOST MY DEATH AND I JUST RAN WATER AND I HAVE NO IDEA M GOING TO FIND MY FRIENDS NOW I'M POURING MY HEART TO THE STUPID, EVIL, HORRIBLE PIRATE KING WHO'S TRYING TO TRICK ME WITH A BUNNY AND I DON'T EVEN CARE IF YOU'RE GOING TO KIDNAP ME OR WHATEVER SO JUST DO IT ***ALREADY!***

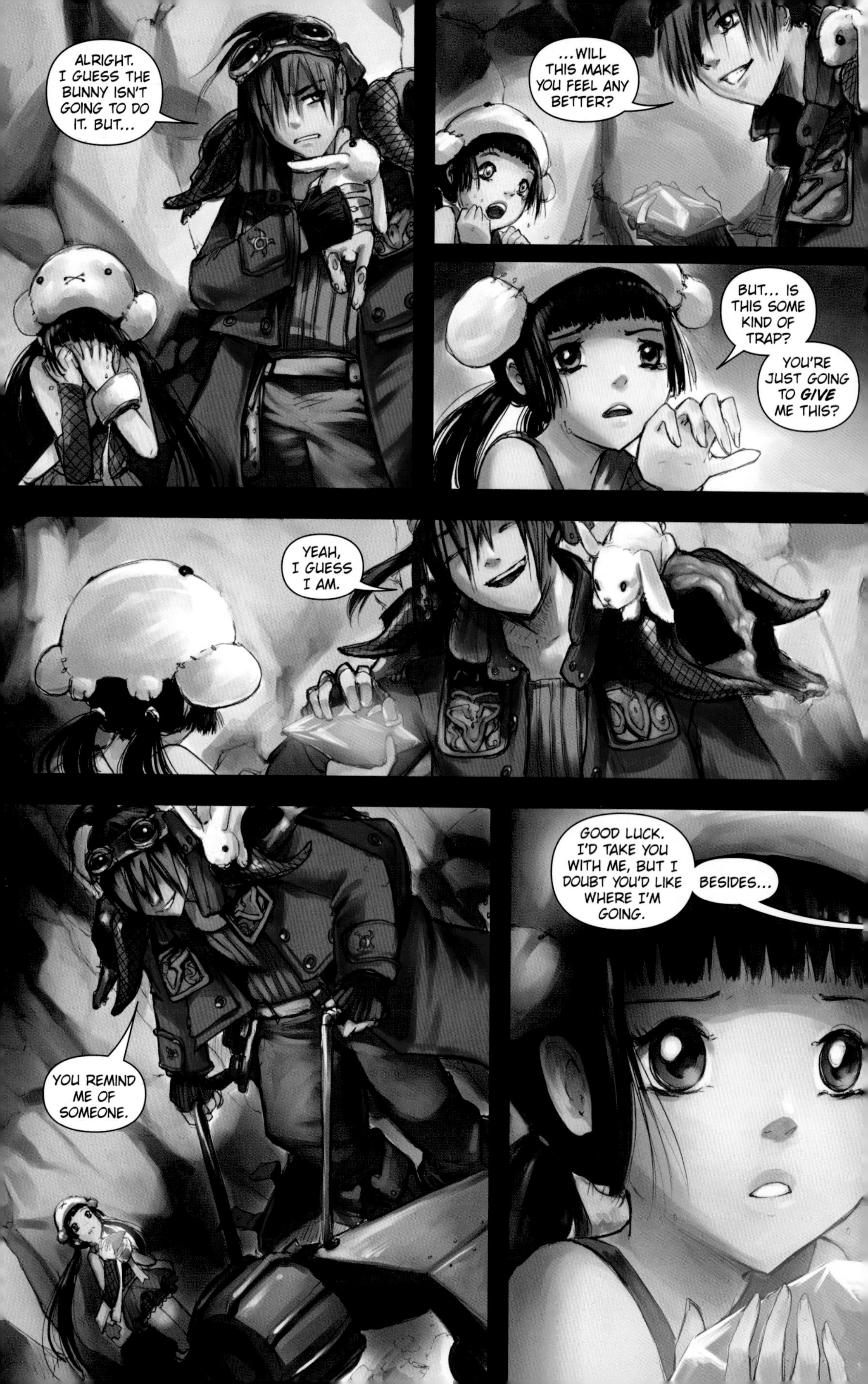
ALRIGHT. I GUESS THE BUNNY ISN'T GOING TO DO IT. BUT...
...WILL THIS MAKE YOU FEEL ANY BETTER?
BUT... IS THIS SOME KIND OF TRAP?
YOU'RE JUST GOING TO *GIVE* ME THIS?
YEAH, I GUESS I AM.
YOU REMIND ME OF SOMEONE.
GOOD LUCK. I'D TAKE YOU WITH ME, BUT I DOUBT YOU'D LIKE WHERE I'M GOING.
BESIDES...

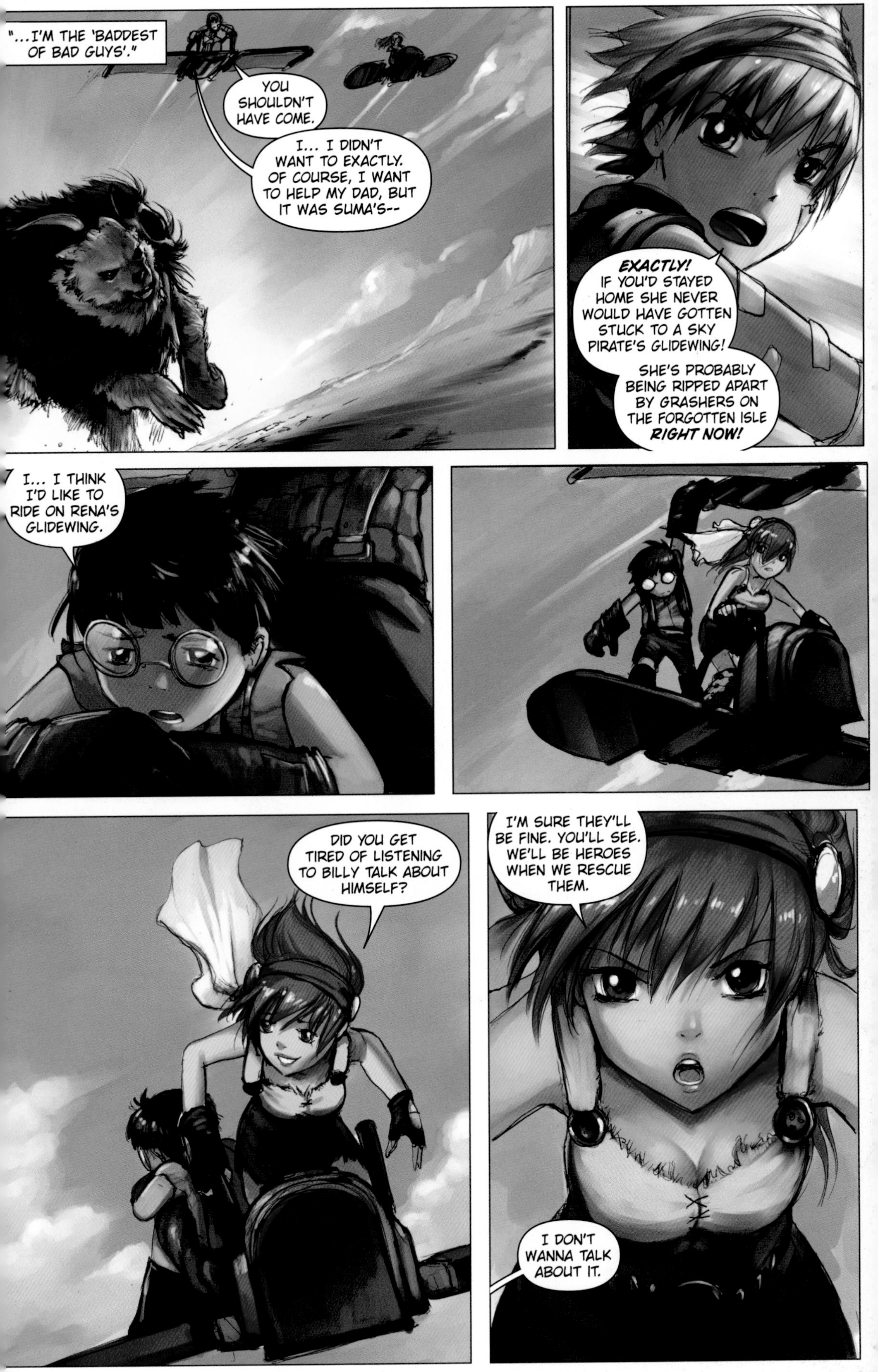
"...I'M THE 'BADDEST OF BAD GUYS'."
YOU SHOULDN'T HAVE COME.
I... I DIDN'T WANT TO EXACTLY. OF COURSE, I WANT TO HELP MY DAD, BUT IT WAS SUMA'S--
EXACTLY! IF YOU'D STAYED HOME SHE NEVER WOULD HAVE GOTTEN STUCK TO A SKY PIRATE'S GLIDEWING!
SHE'S PROBABLY BEING RIPPED APART BY GRASHERS ON THE FORGOTTEN ISLE RIGHT NOW!
I... I THINK I'D LIKE TO RIDE ON RENA'S GLIDEWING.
DID YOU GET TIRED OF LISTENING TO BILLY TALK ABOUT HIMSELF?
I'M SURE THEY'LL BE FINE. YOU'LL SEE. WE'LL BE HEROES WHEN WE RESCUE THEM.
I DON'T WANNA TALK ABOUT IT.

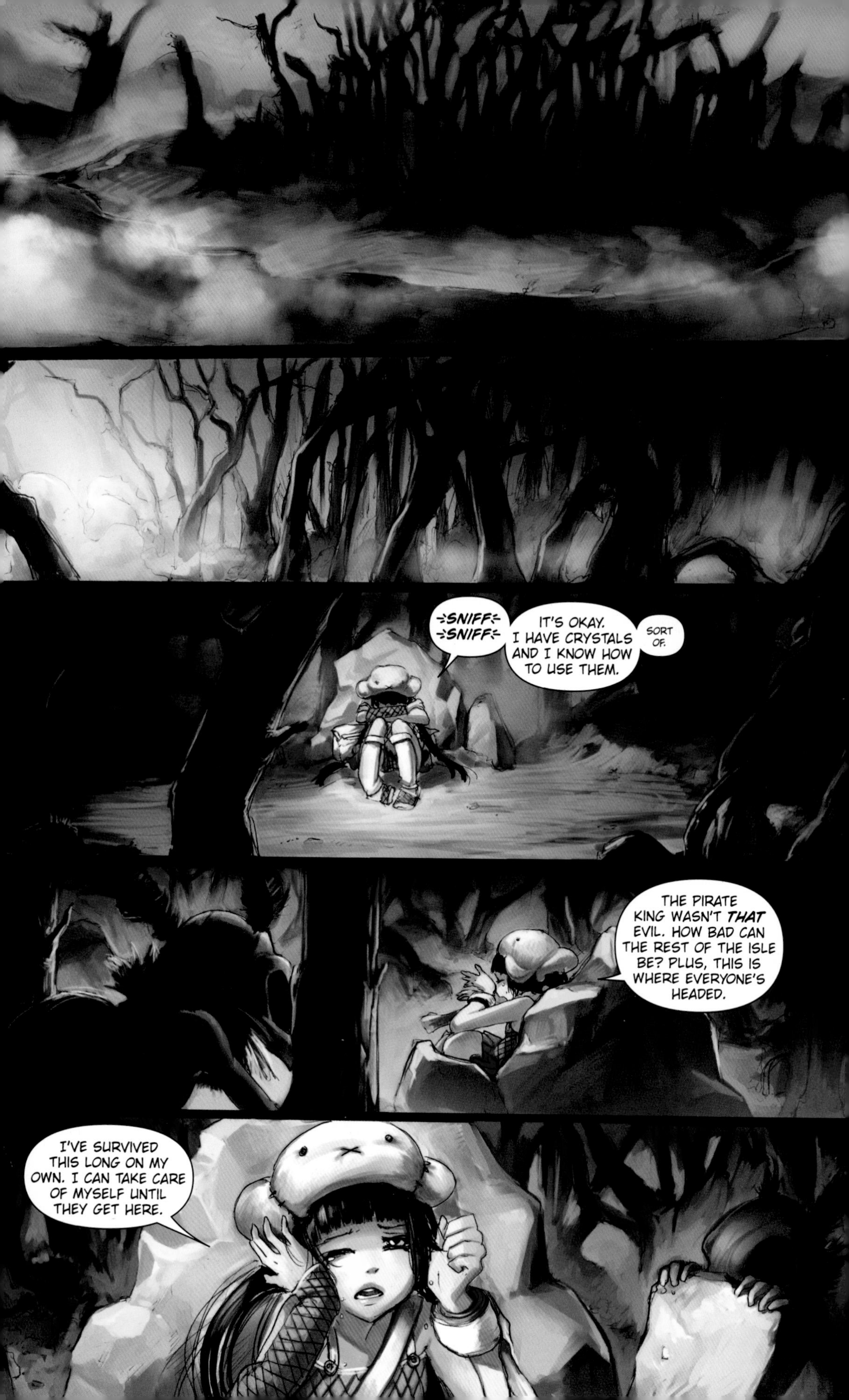
SNIFF SNIFF
IT'S OKAY. I HAVE CRYSTALS AND I KNOW HOW TO USE THEM.
SORT OF.
THE PIRATE KING WASN'T *THAT* EVIL. HOW BAD CAN THE REST OF THE ISLE BE? PLUS, THIS IS WHERE EVERYONE'S HEADED.
I'VE SURVIVED THIS LONG ON MY OWN. I CAN TAKE CARE OF MYSELF UNTIL THEY GET HERE.

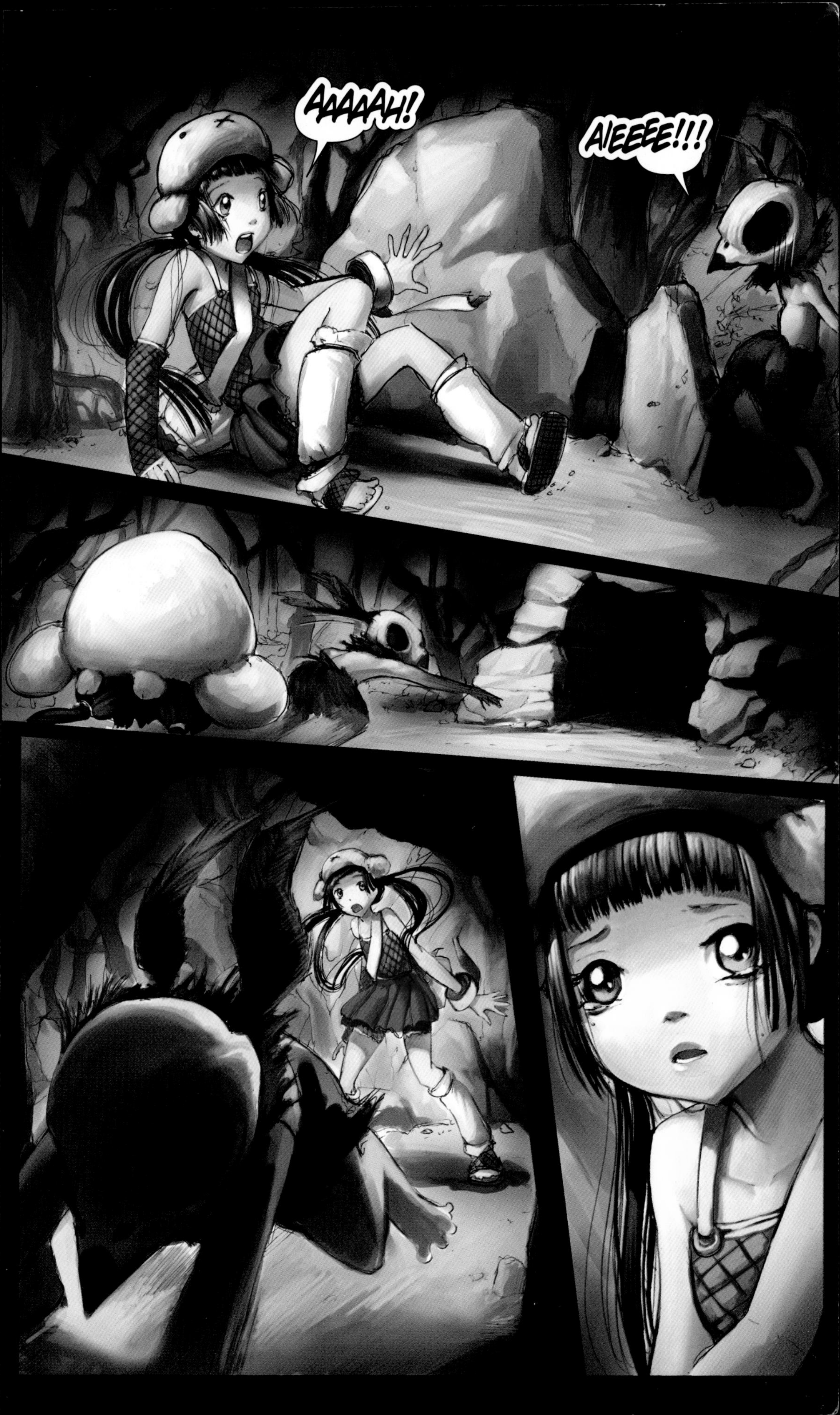
AAAAAH!
AIEEEE!!!

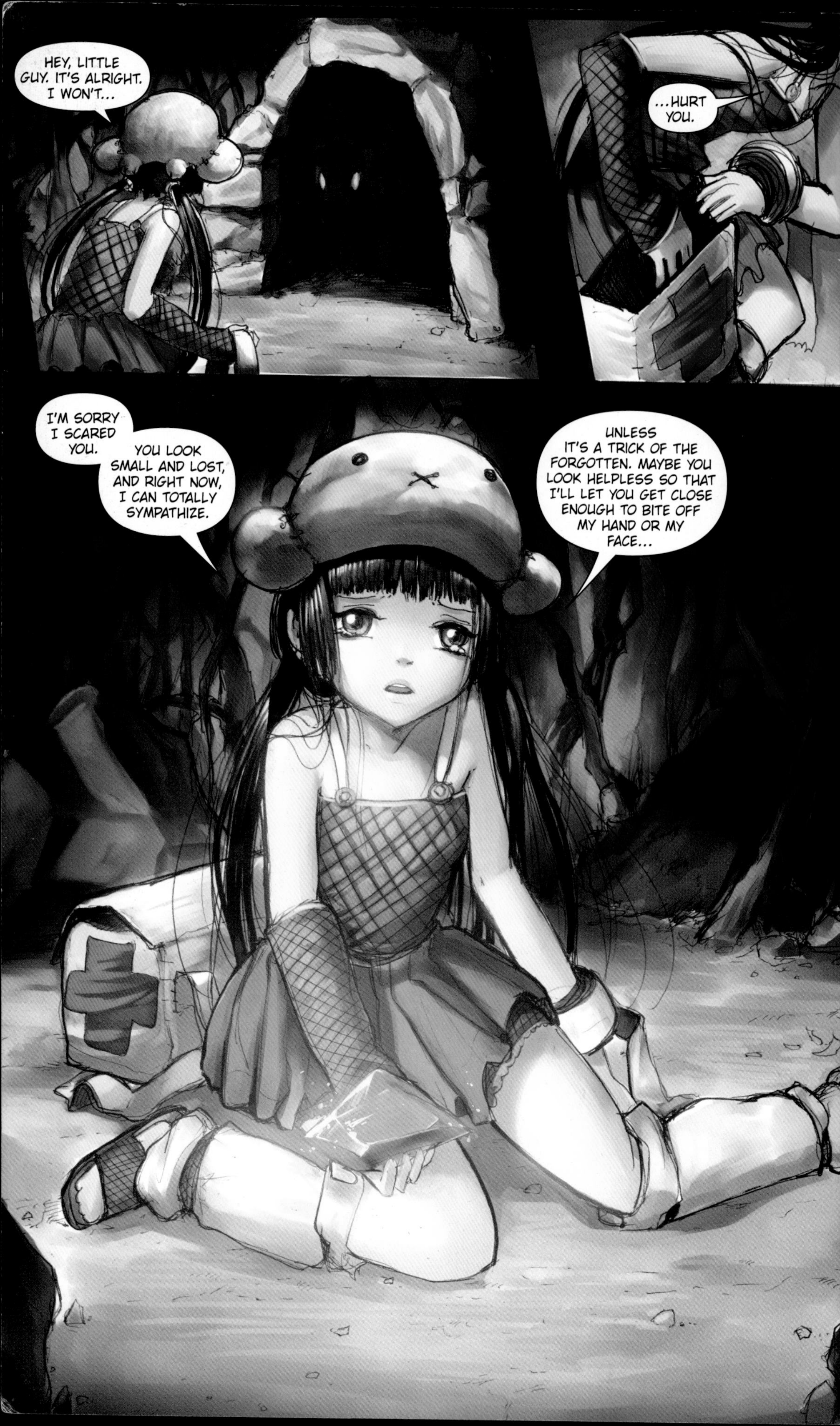
HEY, LITTLE GUY. IT'S ALRIGHT. I WON'T...
...HURT YOU.
I'M SORRY I SCARED YOU.
YOU LOOK SMALL AND LOST, AND RIGHT NOW, I CAN TOTALLY SYMPATHIZE.
UNLESS IT'S A TRICK OF THE FORGOTTEN. MAYBE YOU LOOK HELPLESS SO THAT I'LL LET YOU GET CLOSE ENOUGH TO BITE OFF MY HAND OR MY FACE...

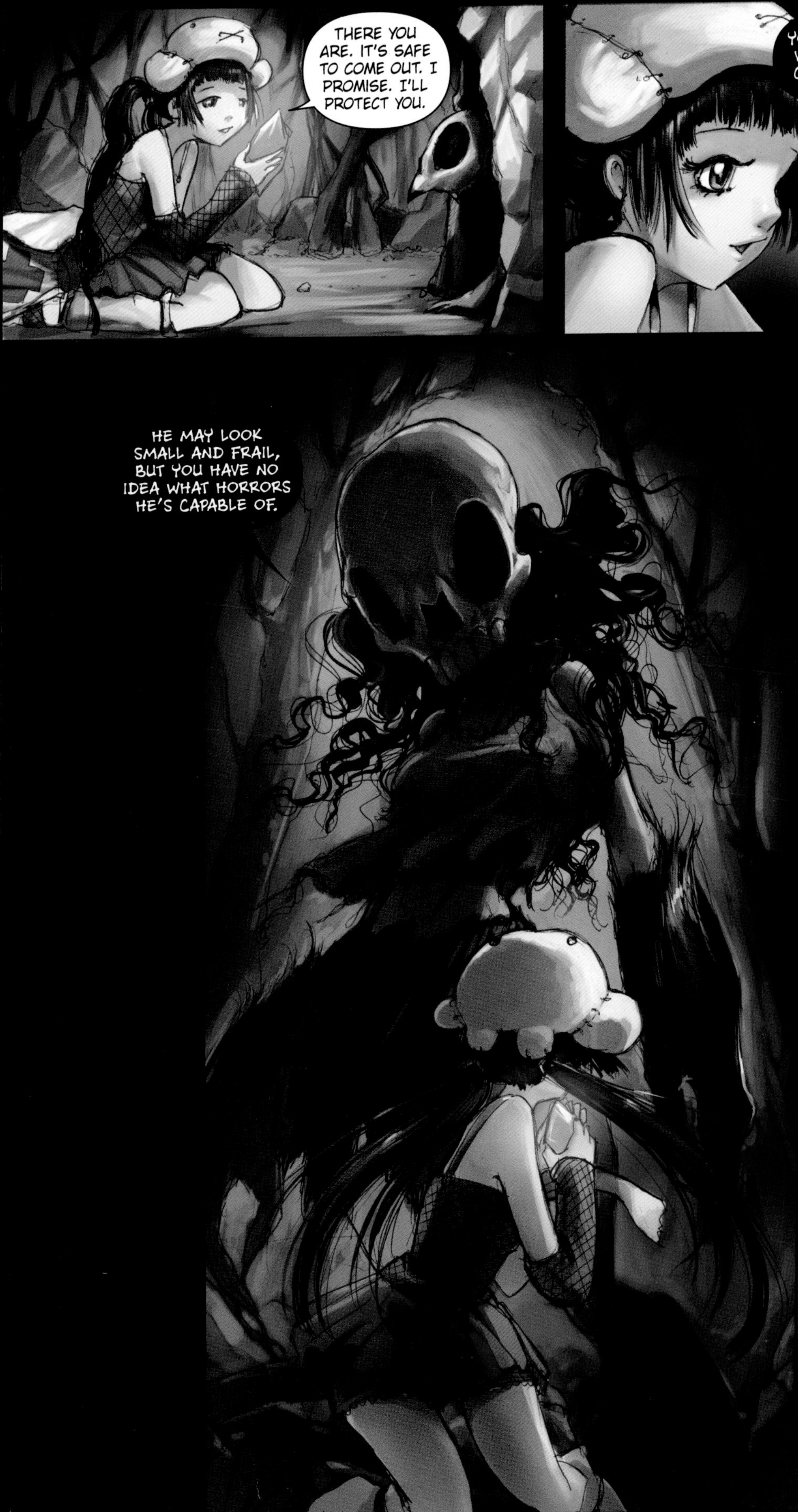
THERE YOU ARE. IT'S SAFE TO COME OUT. I PROMISE. I'LL PROTECT YOU.
YOU SHOULDN'T VENTURE TOO CLOSE TO HIS KIND.
HE MAY LOOK SMALL AND FRAIL, BUT YOU HAVE NO IDEA WHAT HORRORS HE'S CAPABLE OF.

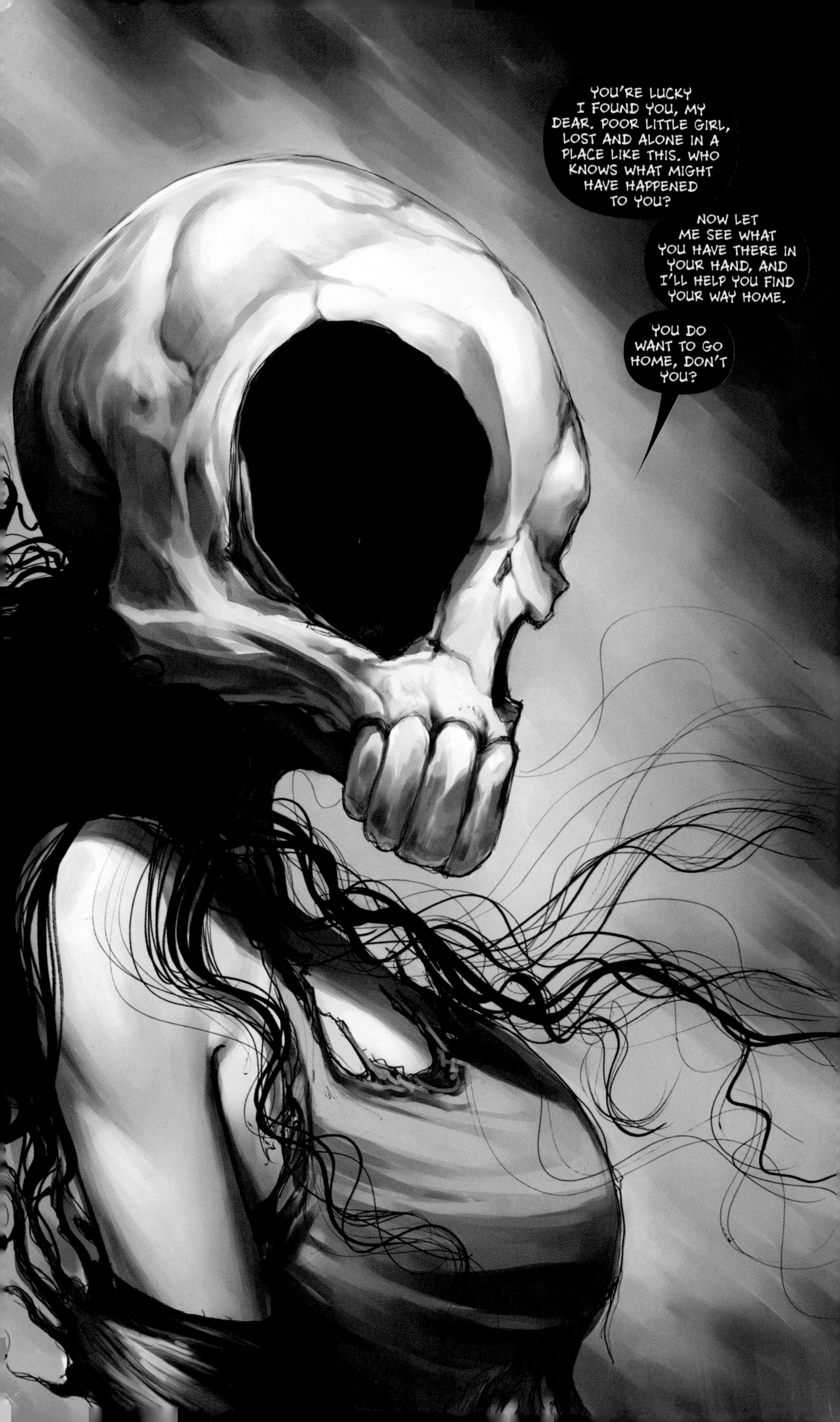
YOU'RE LUCKY I FOUND YOU, MY DEAR. POOR LITTLE GIRL, LOST AND ALONE IN A PLACE LIKE THIS. WHO KNOWS WHAT MIGHT HAVE HAPPENED TO YOU?
NOW LET ME SEE WHAT YOU HAVE THERE IN YOUR HAND, AND I'LL HELP YOU FIND YOUR WAY HOME.
YOU DO WANT TO GO HOME, DON'T YOU?

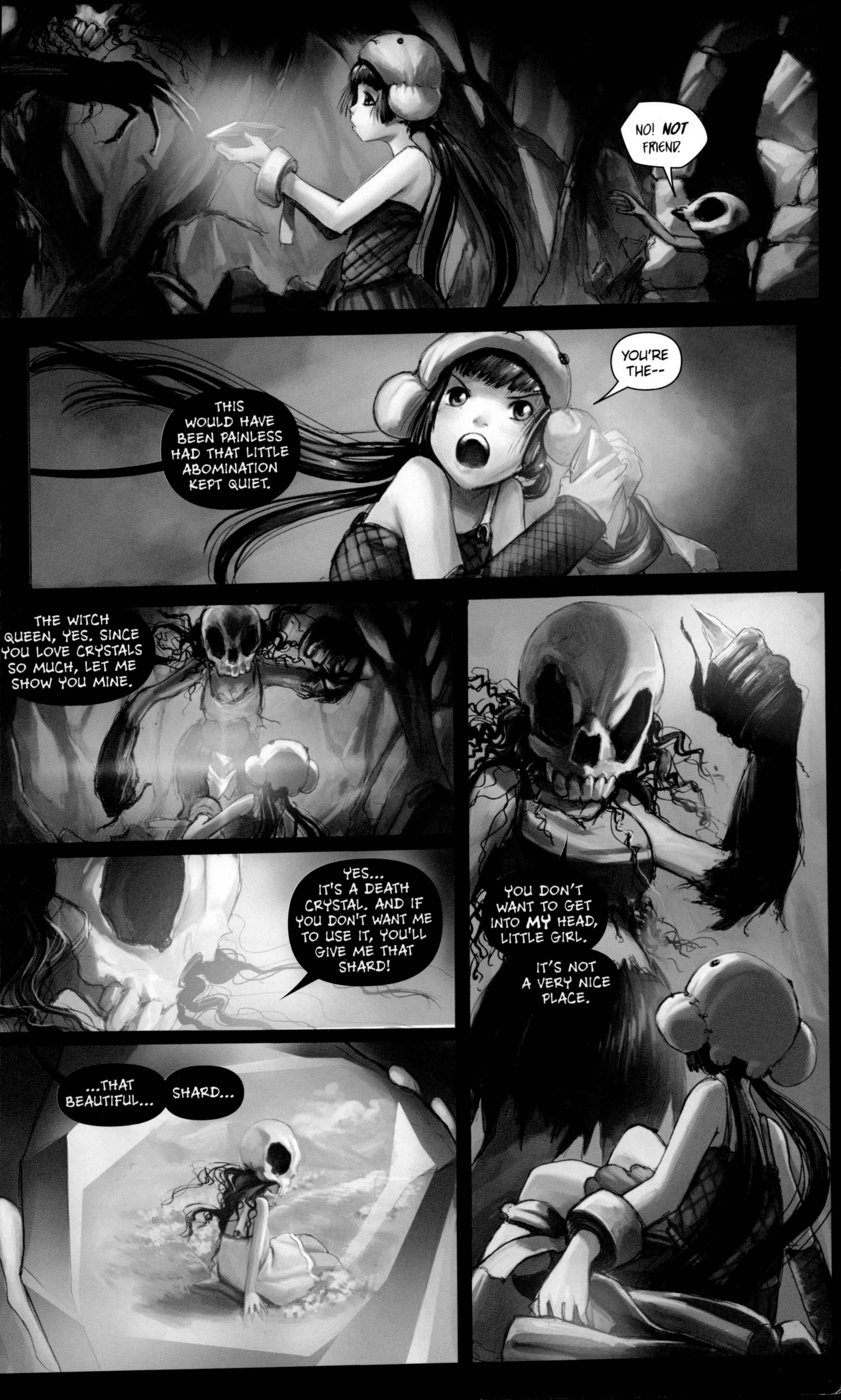
NO! NOT FRIEND.
YOU'RE THE--
THIS WOULD HAVE BEEN PAINLESS HAD THAT LITTLE ABOMINATION KEPT QUIET.
THE WITCH QUEEN, YES. SINCE YOU LOVE CRYSTALS SO MUCH, LET ME SHOW YOU MINE.
YES... IT'S A DEATH CRYSTAL. AND IF YOU DON'T WANT ME TO USE IT, YOU'LL GIVE ME THAT SHARD!
YOU DON'T WANT TO GET INTO MY HEAD, LITTLE GIRL.
IT'S NOT A VERY NICE PLACE.
...THAT BEAUTIFUL...
SHARD...

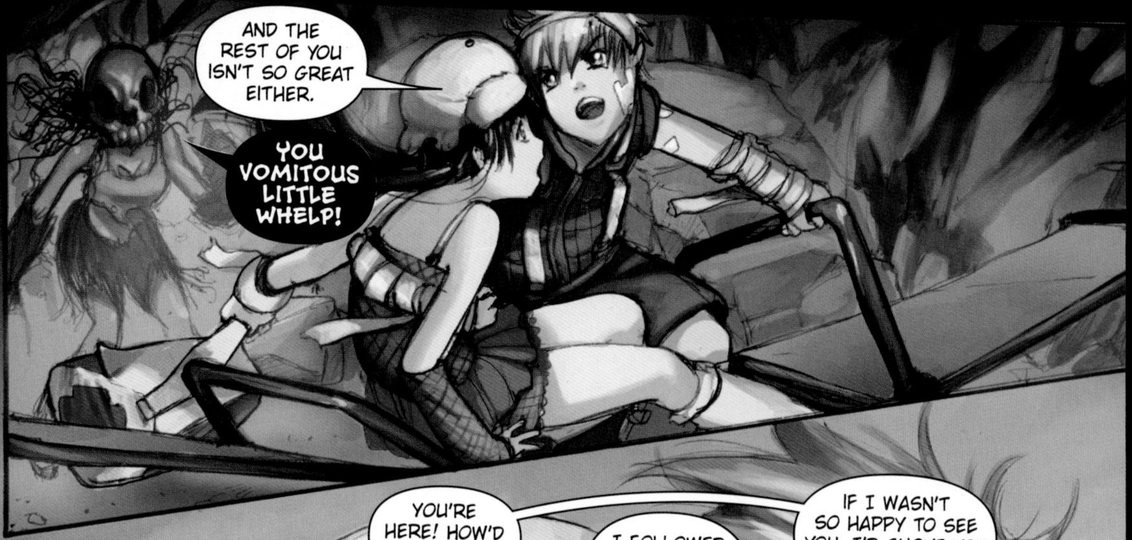
AND THE REST OF YOU ISN'T SO GREAT EITHER.
YOU VOMITOUS LITTLE WHELP!

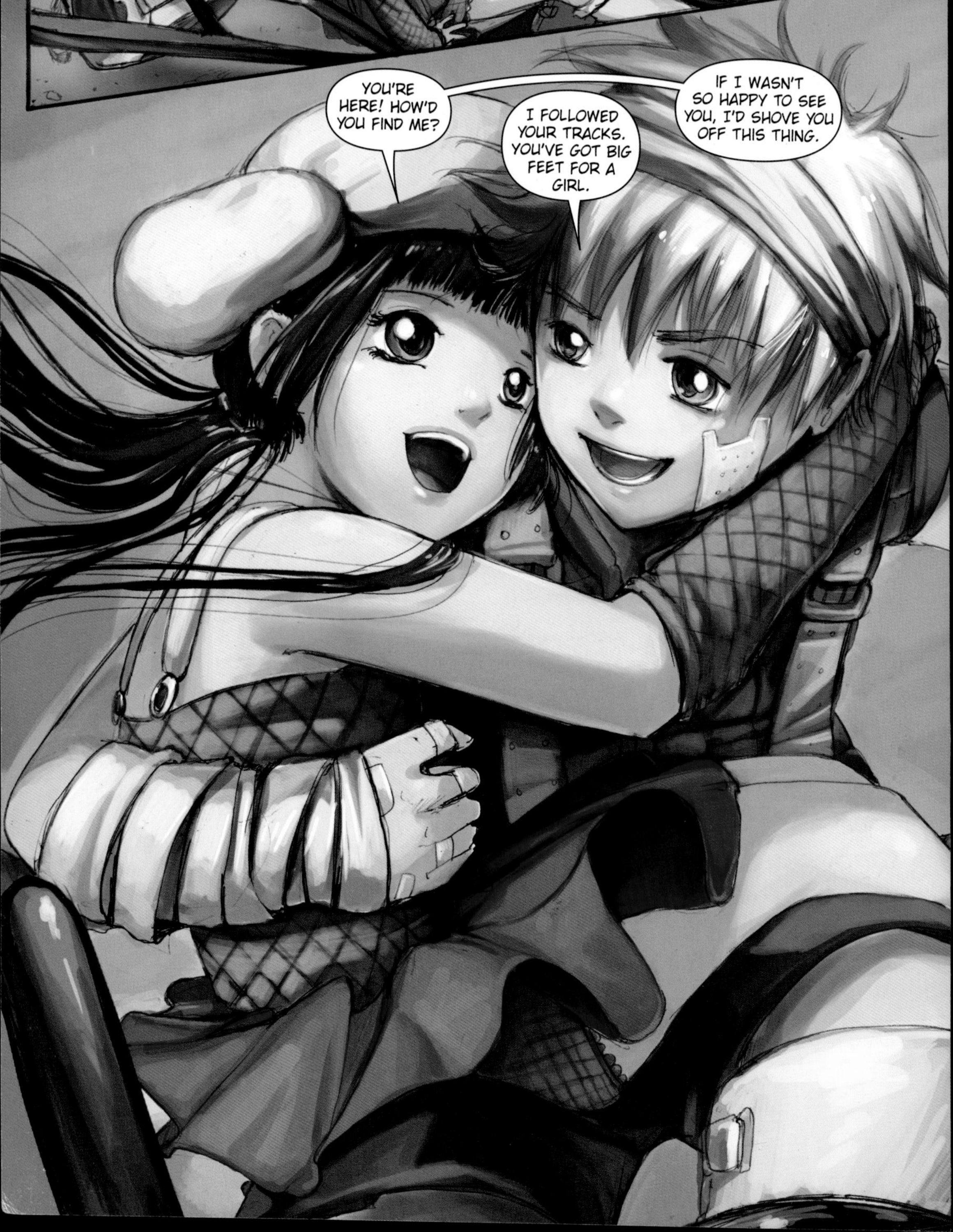
YOU'RE HERE! HOW'D YOU FIND ME?
I FOLLOWED YOUR TRACKS. YOU'VE GOT BIG FEET FOR A GIRL.
IF I WASN'T SO HAPPY TO SEE YOU, I'D SHOVE YOU OFF THIS THING.

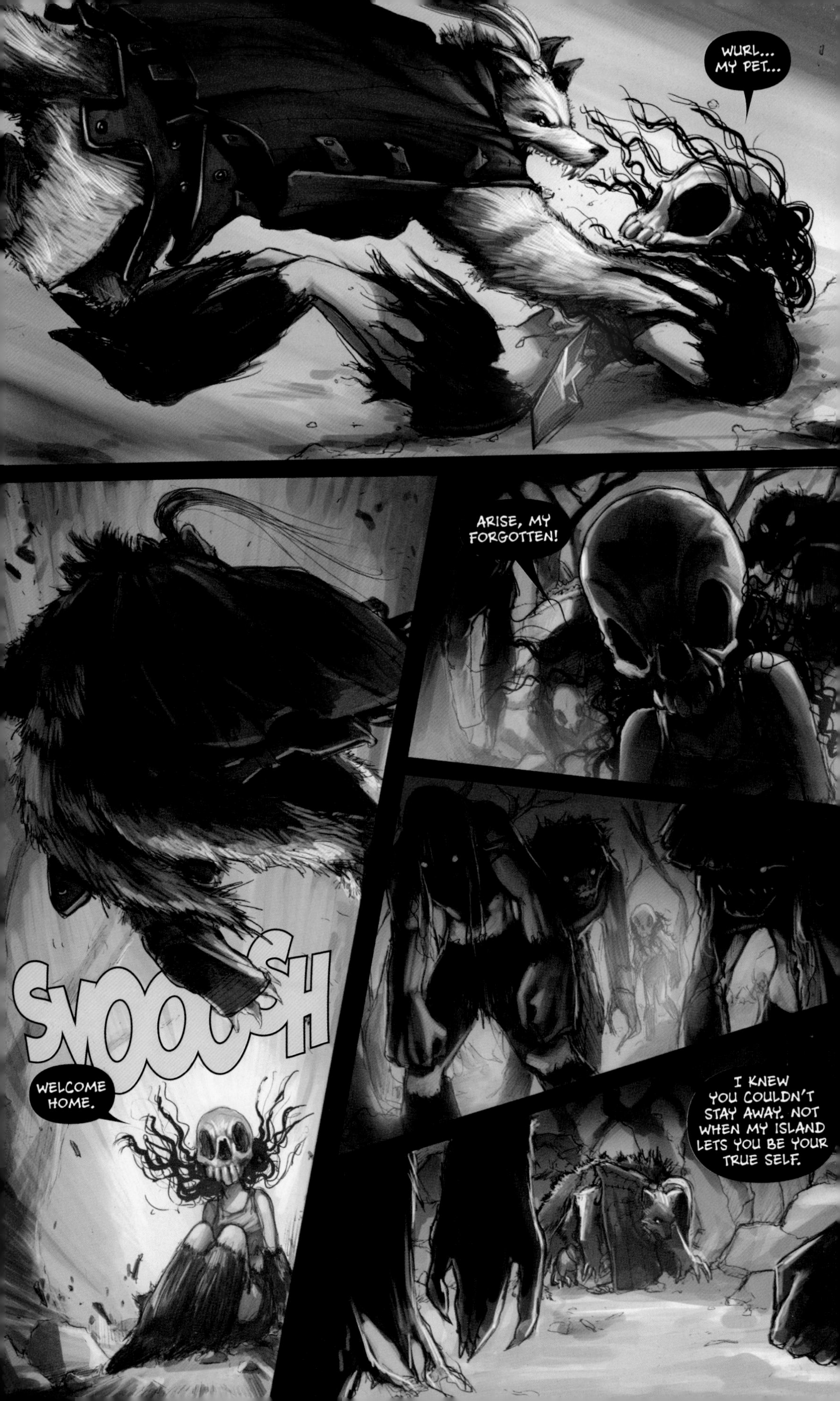
WURL... MY PET...
ARISE, MY FORGOTTEN!
SWOOOSH
WELCOME HOME.
I KNEW YOU COULDN'T STAY AWAY. NOT WHEN MY ISLAND LETS YOU BE YOUR TRUE SELF.

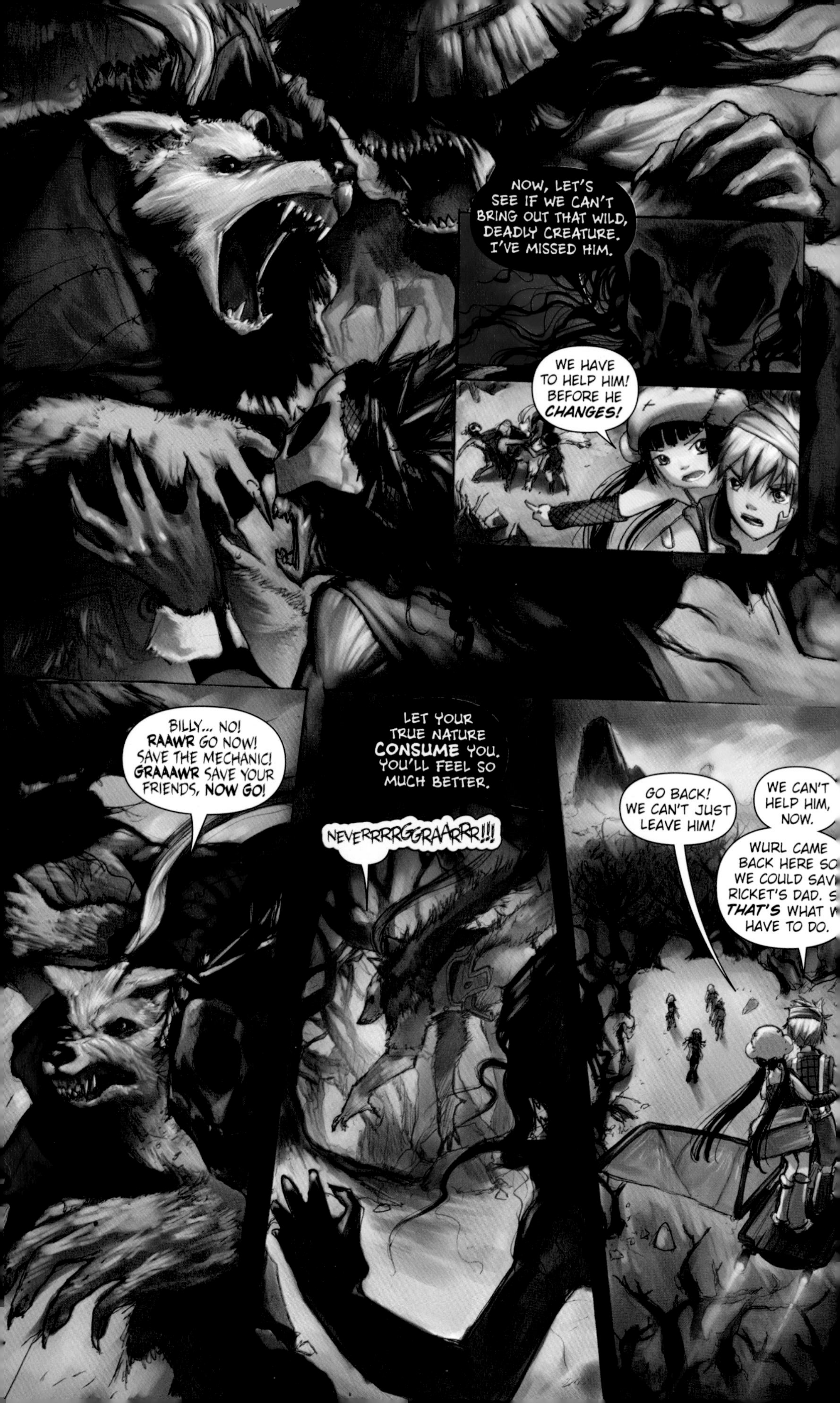
NOW, LET'S SEE IF WE CAN'T BRING OUT THAT WILD, DEADLY CREATURE. I'VE MISSED HIM.
WE HAVE TO HELP HIM! BEFORE HE CHANGES!
BILLY... NO! RAAWR GO NOW! SAVE THE MECHANIC! GRAAAWR SAVE YOUR FRIENDS, NOW GO!
LET YOUR TRUE NATURE CONSUME YOU. YOU'LL FEEL SO MUCH BETTER.
NEVERRRRGGRAARRR!!!
GO BACK! WE CAN'T JUST LEAVE HIM!
WE CAN'T HELP HIM, NOW.

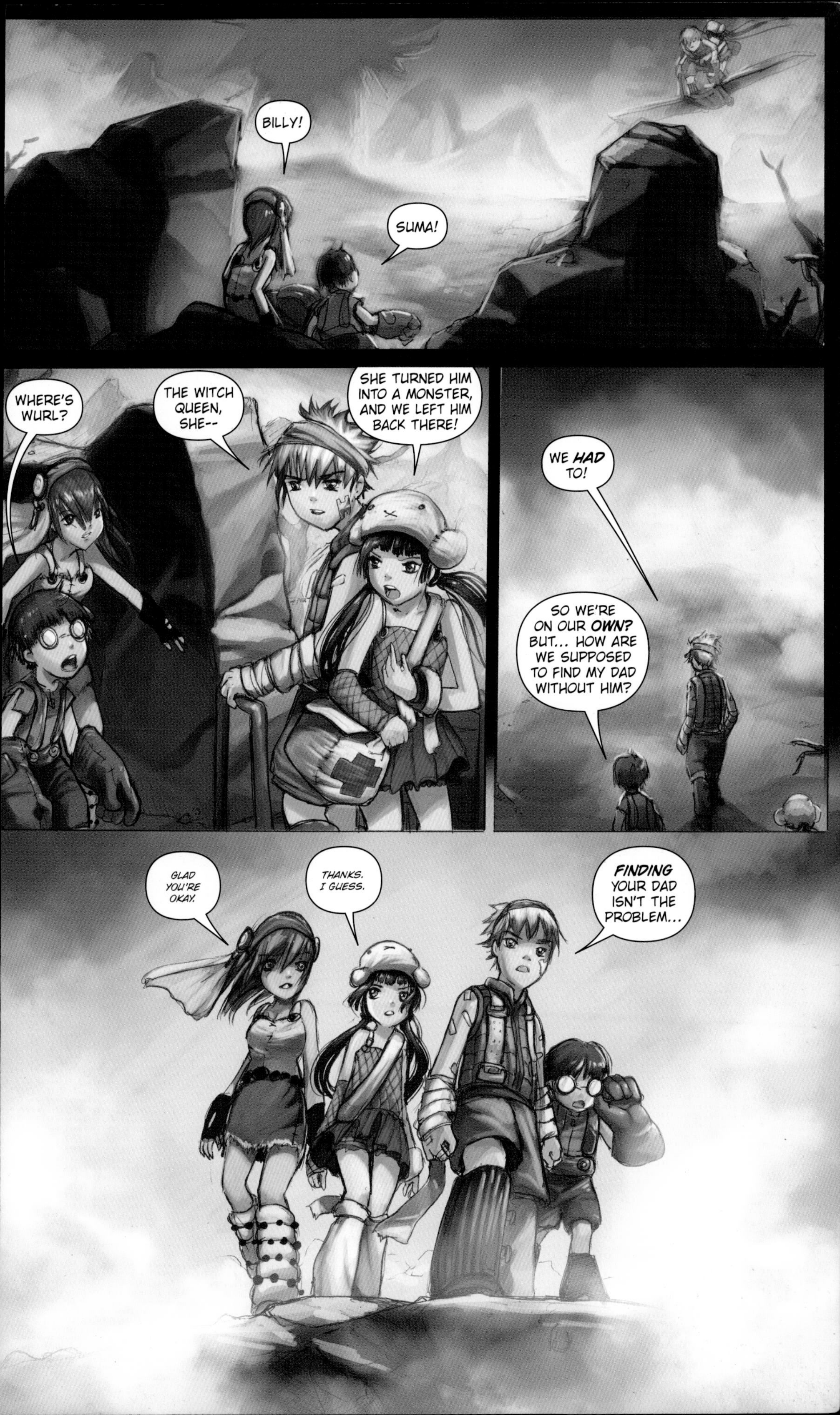
BILLY!
SUMA!
WHERE'S WURL?
THE WITCH QUEEN, SHE--
SHE TURNED HIM INTO A MONSTER, AND WE LEFT HIM BACK THERE!
WE **HAD** TO!
SO WE'RE ON OUR **OWN?** BUT... HOW ARE WE SUPPOSED TO FIND MY DAD WITHOUT HIM?
GLAD YOU'RE OKAY.
THANKS. I GUESS.
FINDING YOUR DAD ISN'T THE PROBLEM...

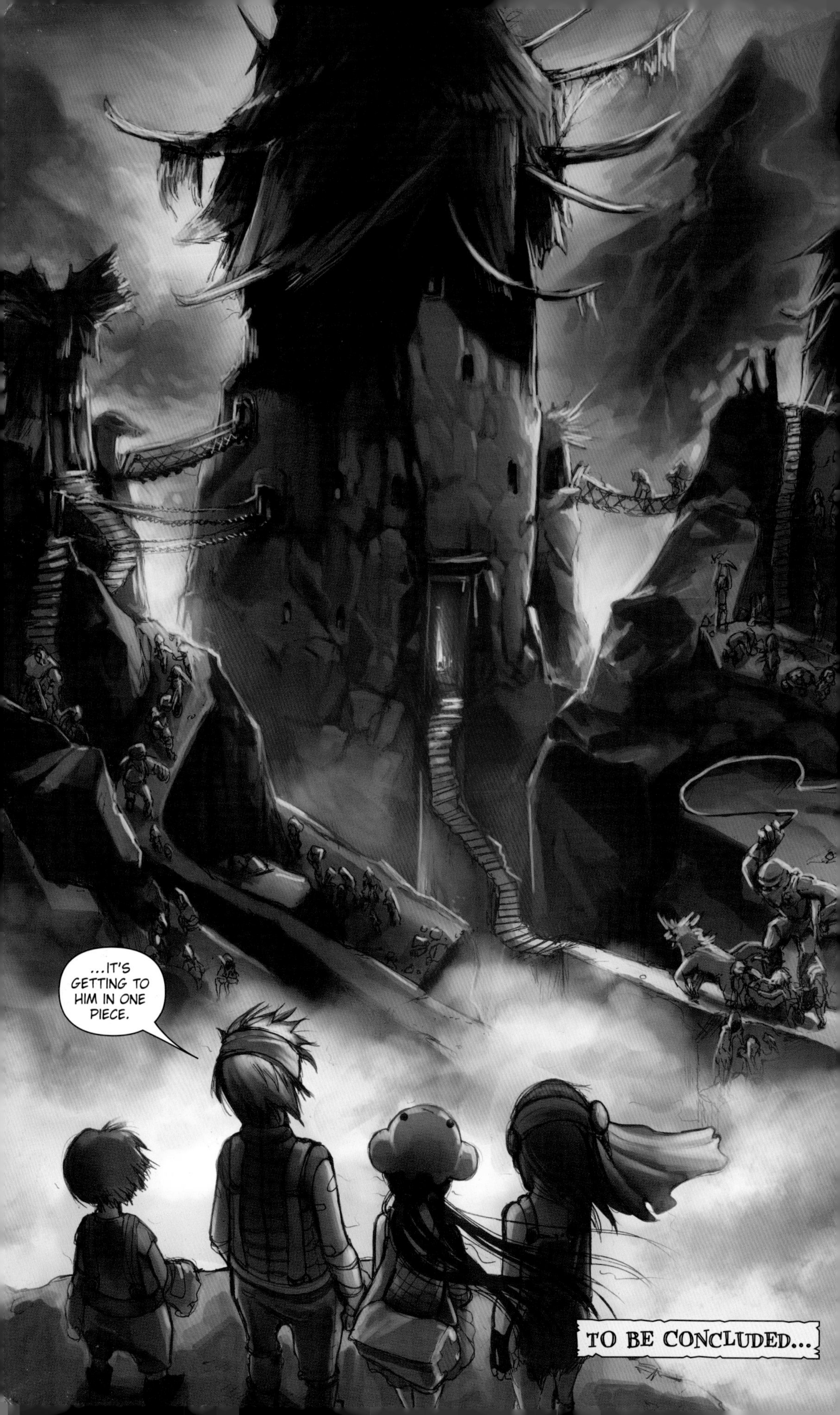
...IT'S GETTING TO HIM IN ONE PIECE.
TO BE CONCLUDED...

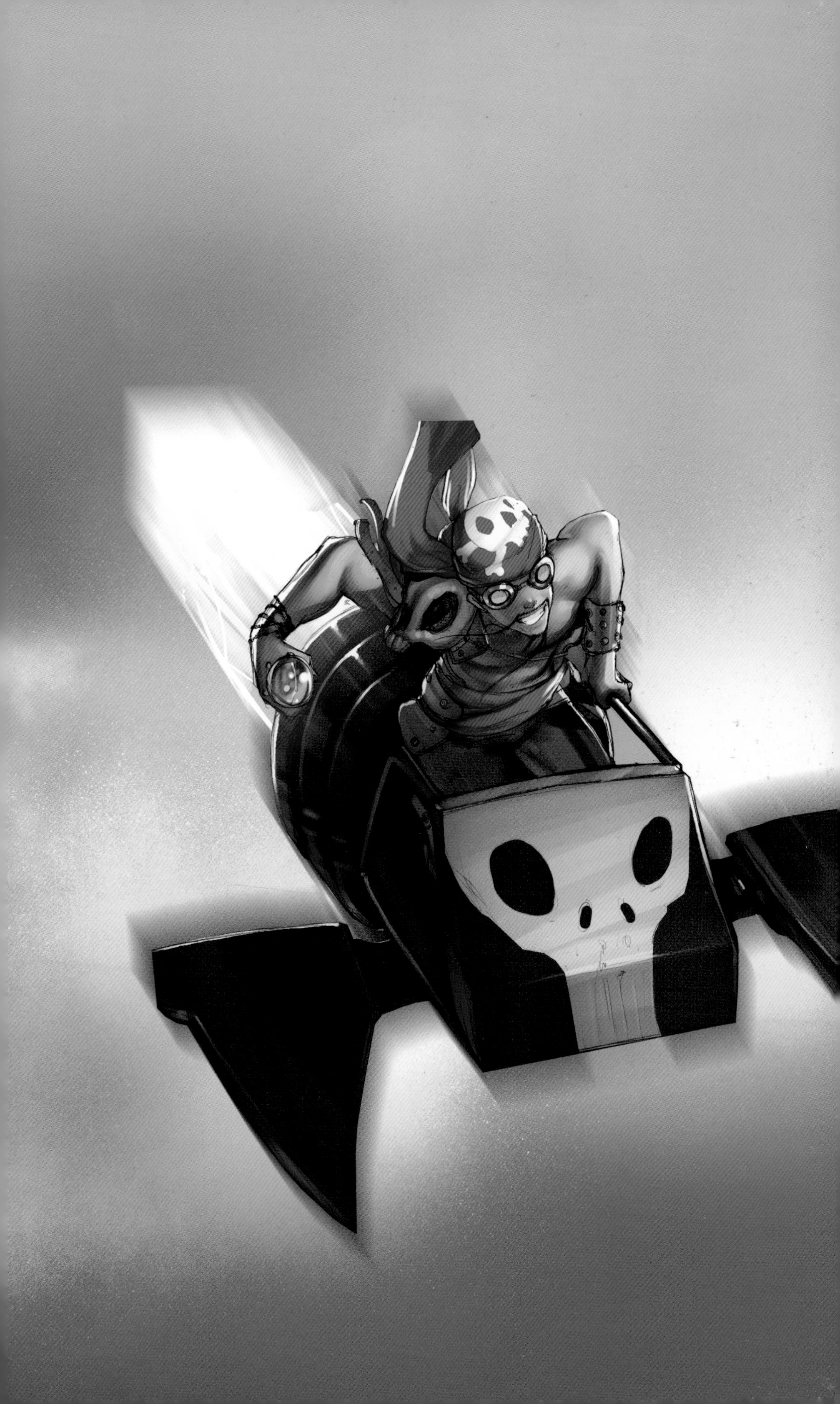

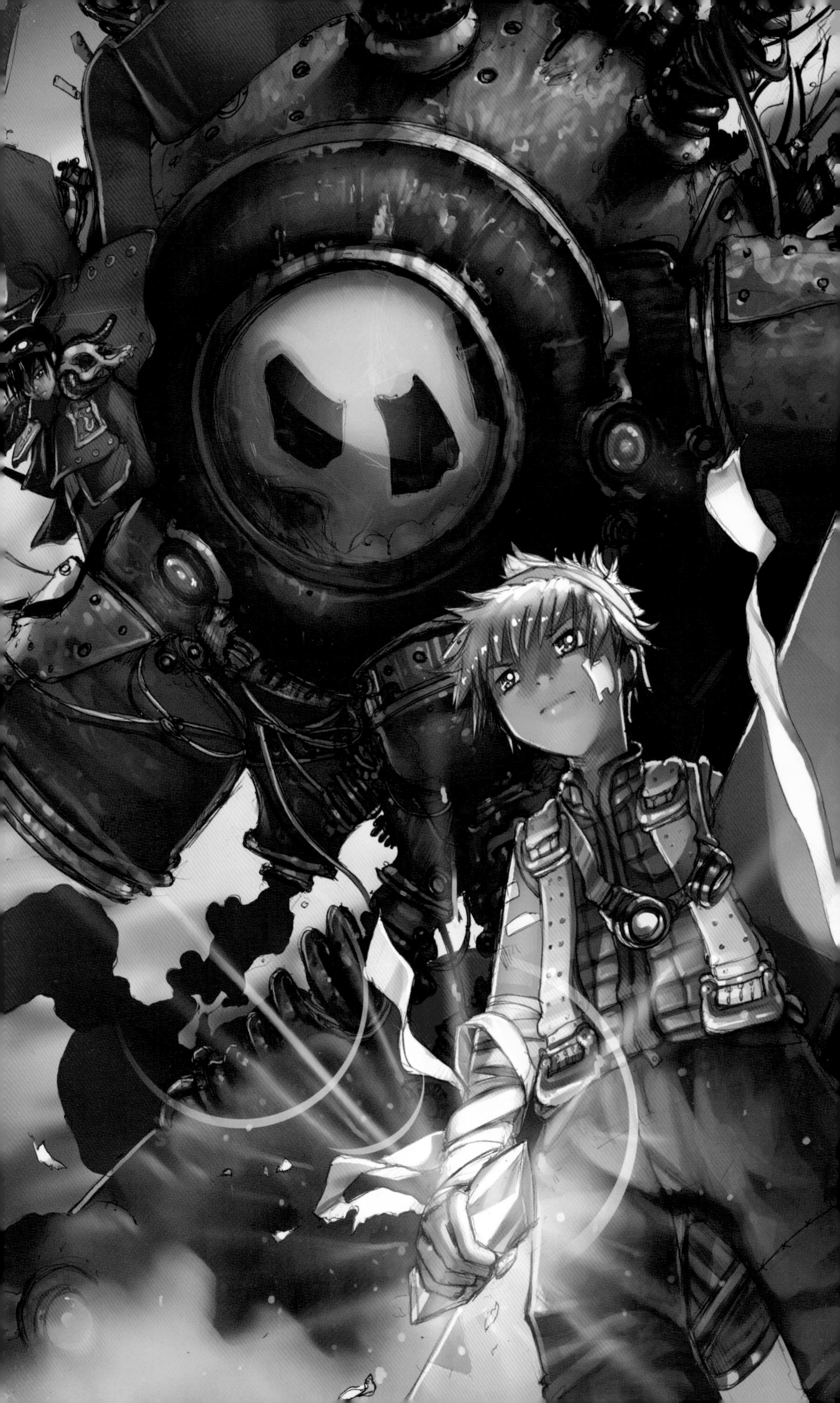

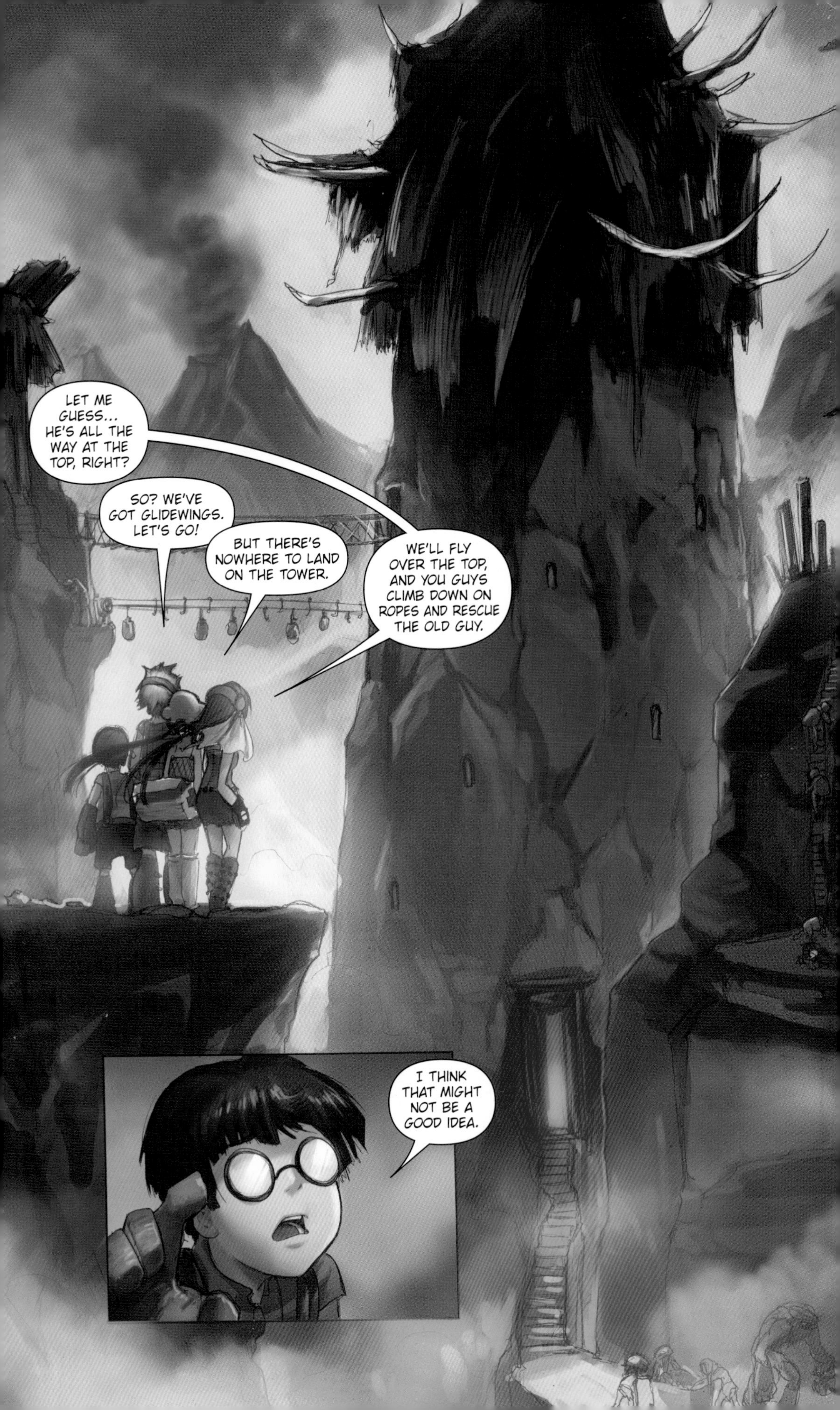

LET ME GUESS... HE'S ALL THE WAY AT THE TOP, RIGHT?
SO? WE'VE GOT GLIDEWINGS. LET'S GO!
BUT THERE'S NOWHERE TO LAND ON THE TOWER.
WE'LL FLY OVER THE TOP, AND YOU GUYS CLIMB DOWN ON ROPES AND RESCUE THE OLD GUY.
I THINK THAT MIGHT NOT BE A GOOD IDEA.

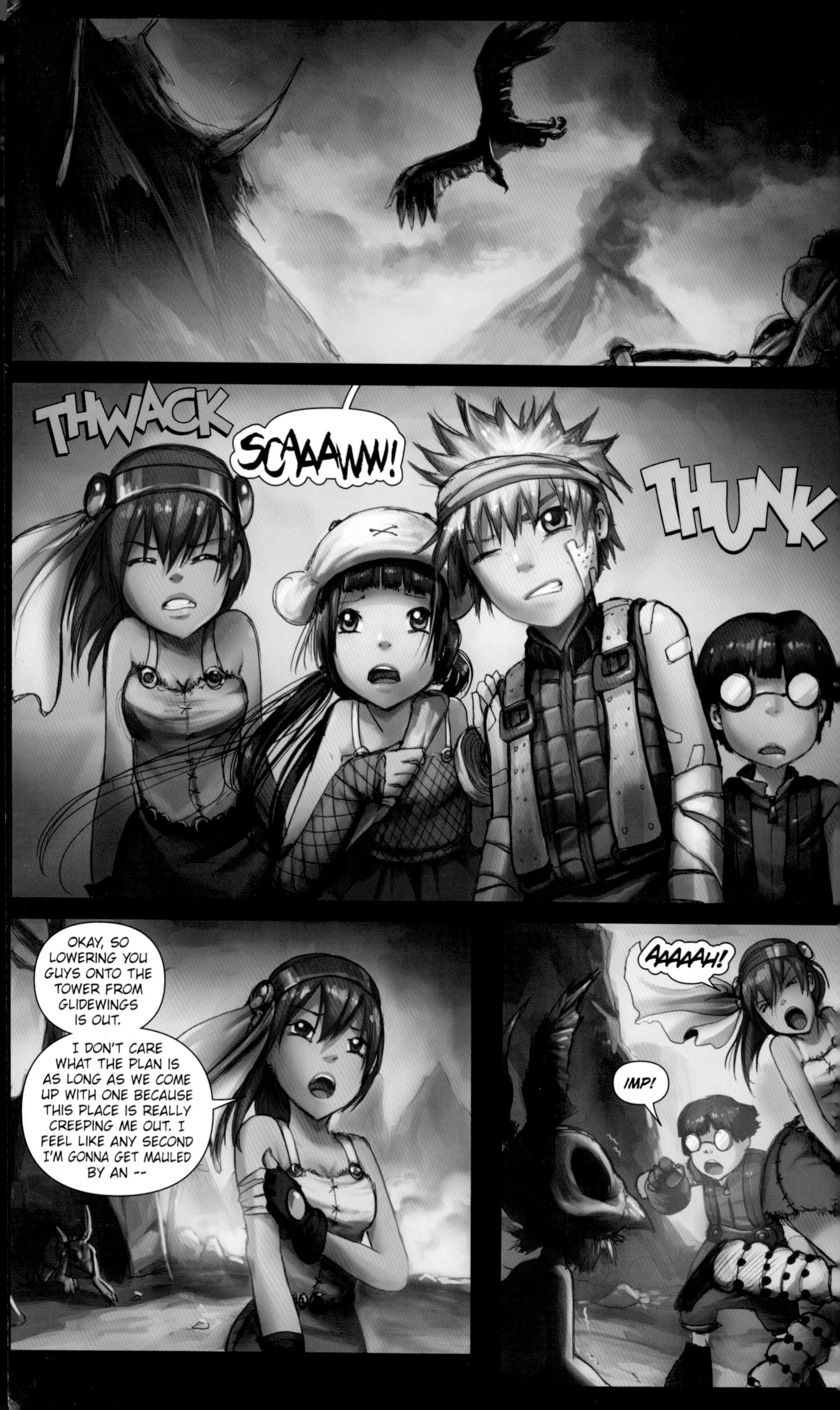
THWACK
SCAAAWW!
THUNK
OKAY, SO LOWERING YOU GUYS ONTO THE TOWER FROM GLIDEWINGS IS OUT.
I DON'T CARE WHAT THE PLAN IS AS LONG AS WE COME UP WITH ONE BECAUSE THIS PLACE IS REALLY CREEPING ME OUT. I FEEL LIKE ANY SECOND I'M GONNA GET MAULED BY AN --
AAAAAH!
IMP!

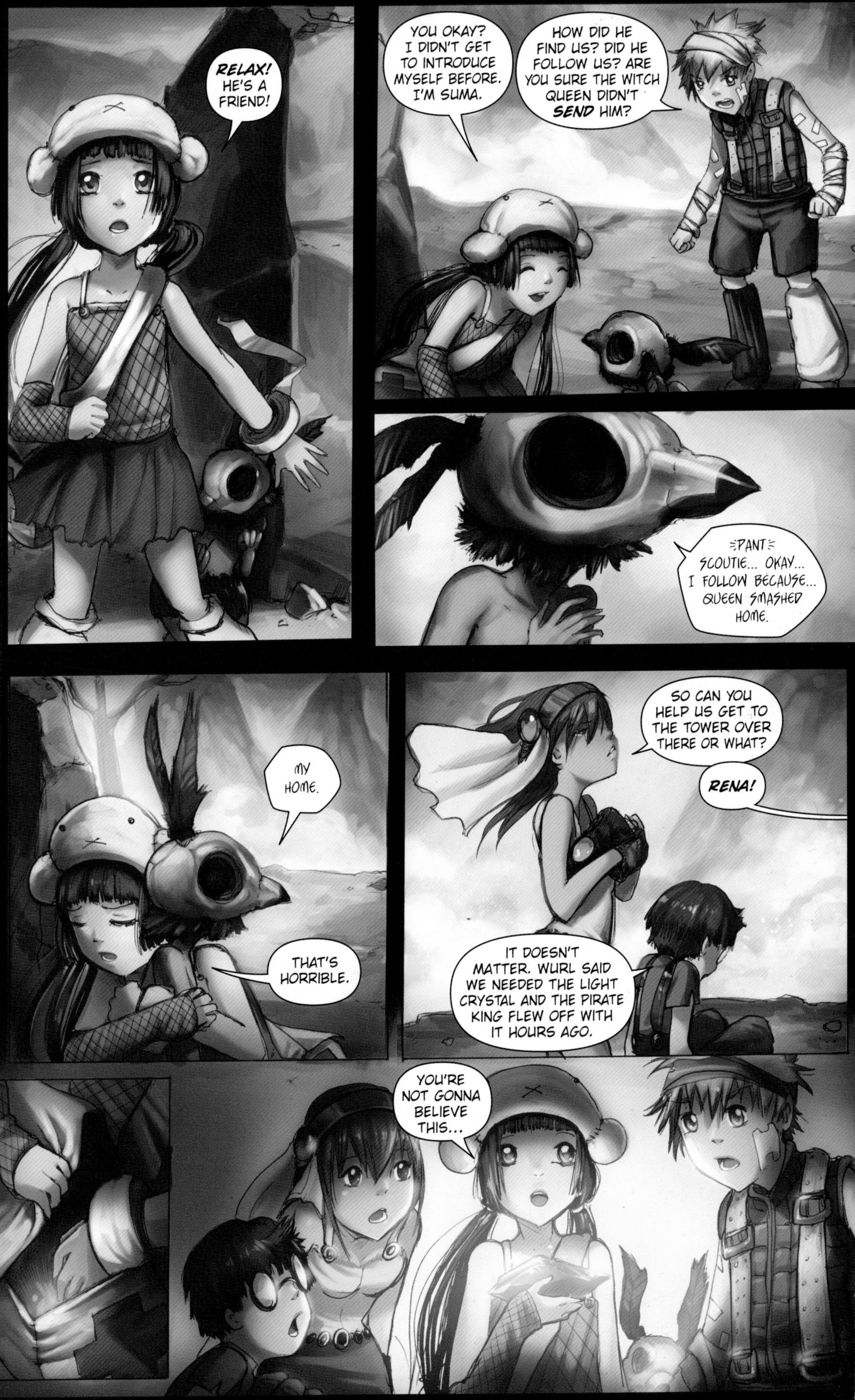
RELAX! HE'S A FRIEND!
YOU OKAY? I DIDN'T GET TO INTRODUCE MYSELF BEFORE. I'M SUMA.
HOW DID HE FIND US? DID HE FOLLOW US? ARE YOU SURE THE WITCH QUEEN DIDN'T SEND HIM?
PANT
SCOUTIE... OKAY... I FOLLOW BECAUSE... QUEEN SMASHED HOME.
MY HOME.
THAT'S HORRIBLE.
SO CAN YOU HELP US GET TO THE TOWER OVER THERE OR WHAT?
RENA!
IT DOESN'T MATTER. WURL SAID WE NEEDED THE LIGHT CRYSTAL AND THE PIRATE KING FLEW OFF WITH IT HOURS AGO.
YOU'RE NOT GONNA BELIEVE THIS...

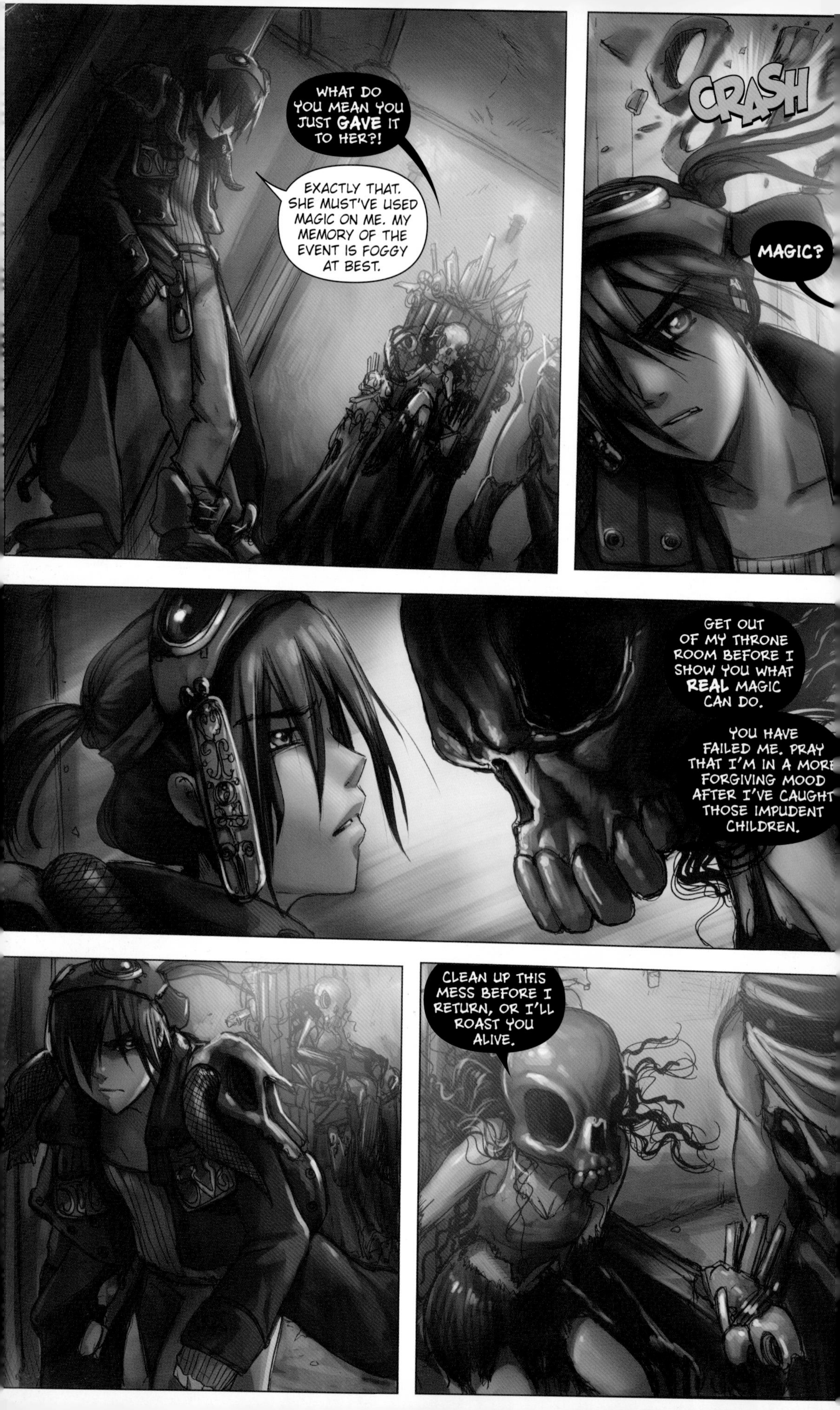
WHAT DO YOU MEAN YOU JUST GAVE IT TO HER?!
EXACTLY THAT. SHE MUST'VE USED MAGIC ON ME. MY MEMORY OF THE EVENT IS FOGGY AT BEST.
CRASH
MAGIC?
GET OUT OF MY THRONE ROOM BEFORE I SHOW YOU WHAT REAL MAGIC CAN DO.
YOU HAVE FAILED ME. PRAY THAT I'M IN A MORE FORGIVING MOOD AFTER I'VE CAUGHT THOSE IMPUDENT CHILDREN.
CLEAN UP THIS MESS BEFORE I RETURN, OR I'LL ROAST YOU ALIVE.

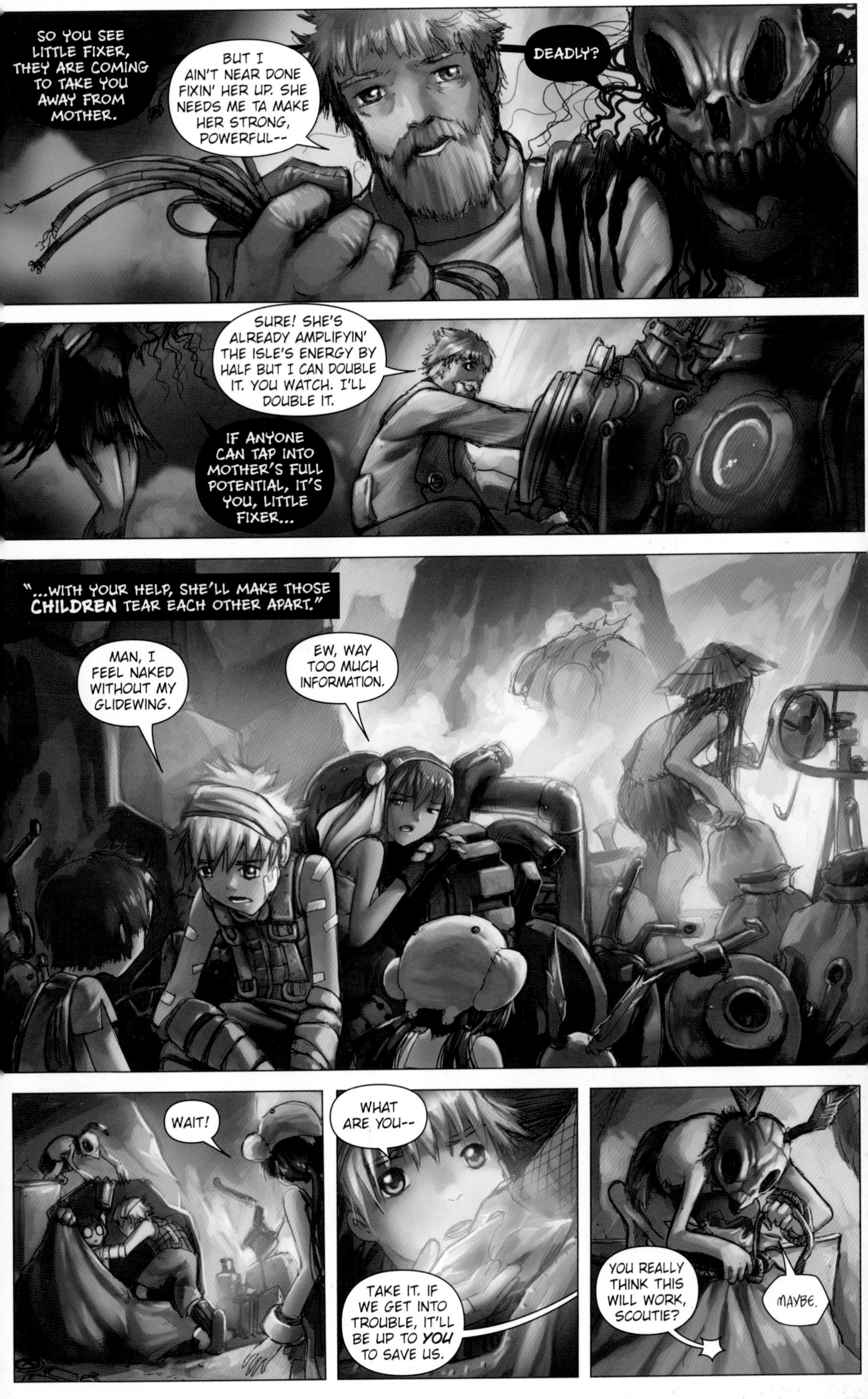
SO YOU SEE LITTLE FIXER, THEY ARE COMING TO TAKE YOU AWAY FROM MOTHER.
BUT I AIN'T NEAR DONE FIXIN' HER UP. SHE NEEDS ME TA MAKE HER STRONG, POWERFUL--
DEADLY?
SURE! SHE'S ALREADY AMPLIFYIN' THE ISLE'S ENERGY BY HALF BUT I CAN DOUBLE IT. YOU WATCH. I'LL DOUBLE IT.
IF ANYONE CAN TAP INTO MOTHER'S FULL POTENTIAL, IT'S YOU, LITTLE FIXER...
"...WITH YOUR HELP, SHE'LL MAKE THOSE CHILDREN TEAR EACH OTHER APART."
MAN, I FEEL NAKED WITHOUT MY GLIDEWING.
EW, WAY TOO MUCH INFORMATION.
WAIT!
WHAT ARE YOU--
TAKE IT. IF WE GET INTO TROUBLE, IT'LL BE UP TO YOU TO SAVE US.
YOU REALLY THINK THIS WILL WORK, SCOUTIE?
MAYBE.

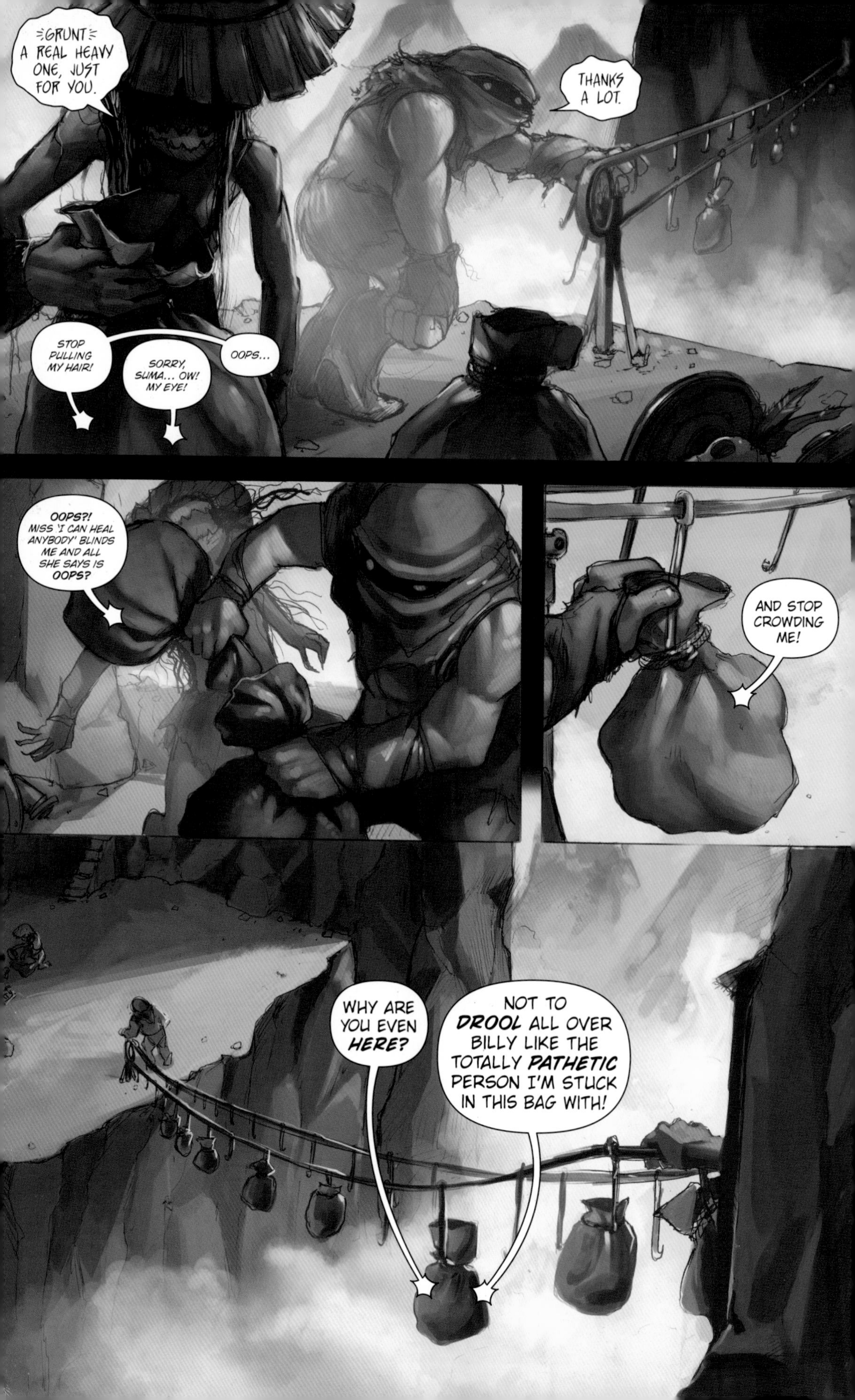
GRUNT
A REAL HEAVY ONE, JUST FOR YOU.
THANKS A LOT.
STOP PULLING MY HAIR!
OOPS...
SORRY, SUMA... OW! MY EYE!
OOPS?! MISS 'I CAN HEAL ANYBODY' BLINDS ME AND ALL SHE SAYS IS OOPS?
AND STOP CROWDING ME!
WHY ARE YOU EVEN HERE?
NOT TO DROOL ALL OVER BILLY LIKE THE TOTALLY PATHETIC PERSON I'M STUCK IN THIS BAG WITH!

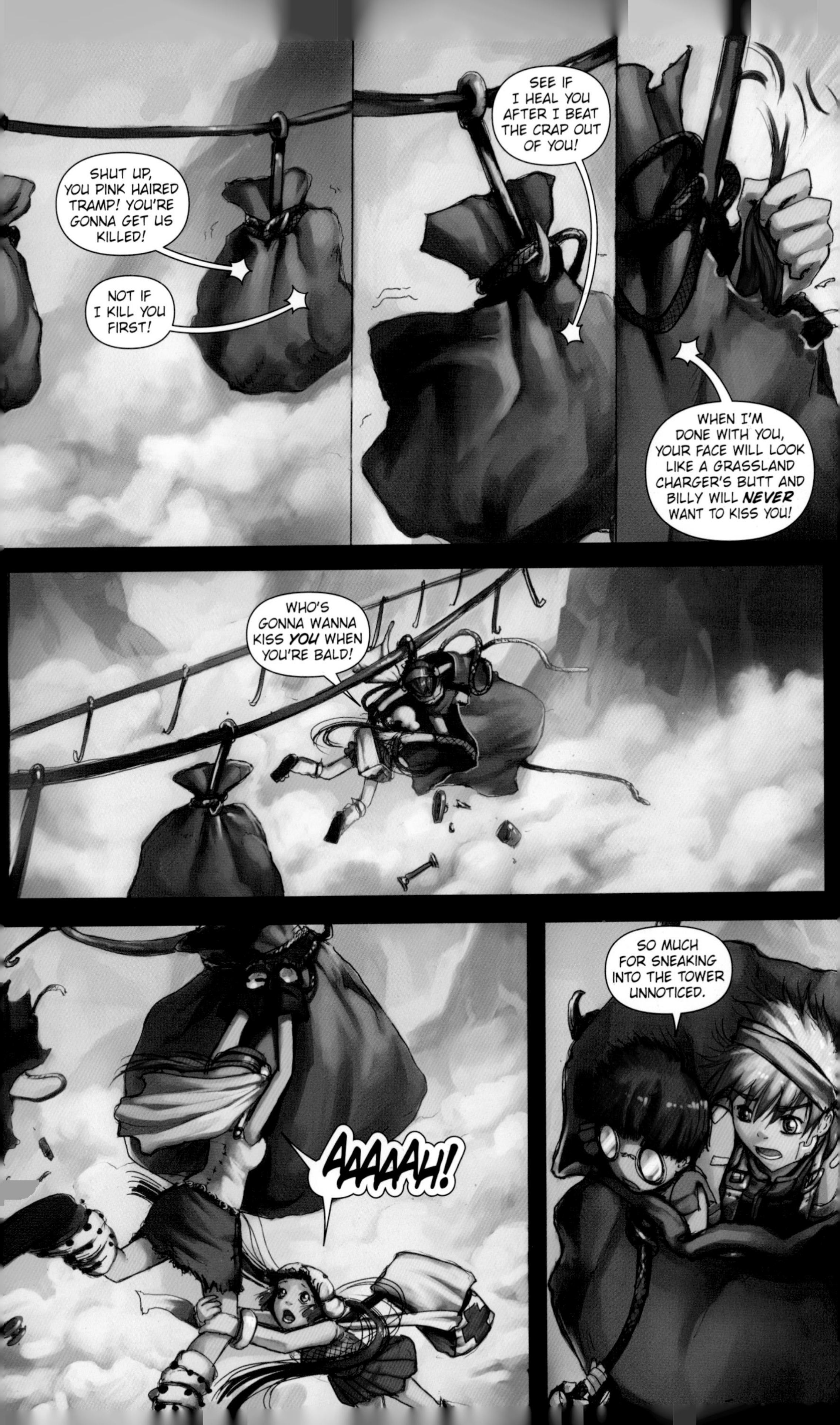
SHUT UP, YOU PINK HAIRED TRAMP! YOU'RE GONNA GET US KILLED!
NOT IF I KILL YOU FIRST!
SEE IF I HEAL YOU AFTER I BEAT THE CRAP OUT OF YOU!
WHEN I'M DONE WITH YOU, YOUR FACE WILL LOOK LIKE A GRASSLAND CHARGER'S BUTT AND BILLY WILL NEVER WANT TO KISS YOU!
WHO'S GONNA WANNA KISS YOU WHEN YOU'RE BALD!
AAAAAH!
SO MUCH FOR SNEAKING INTO THE TOWER UNNOTICED.

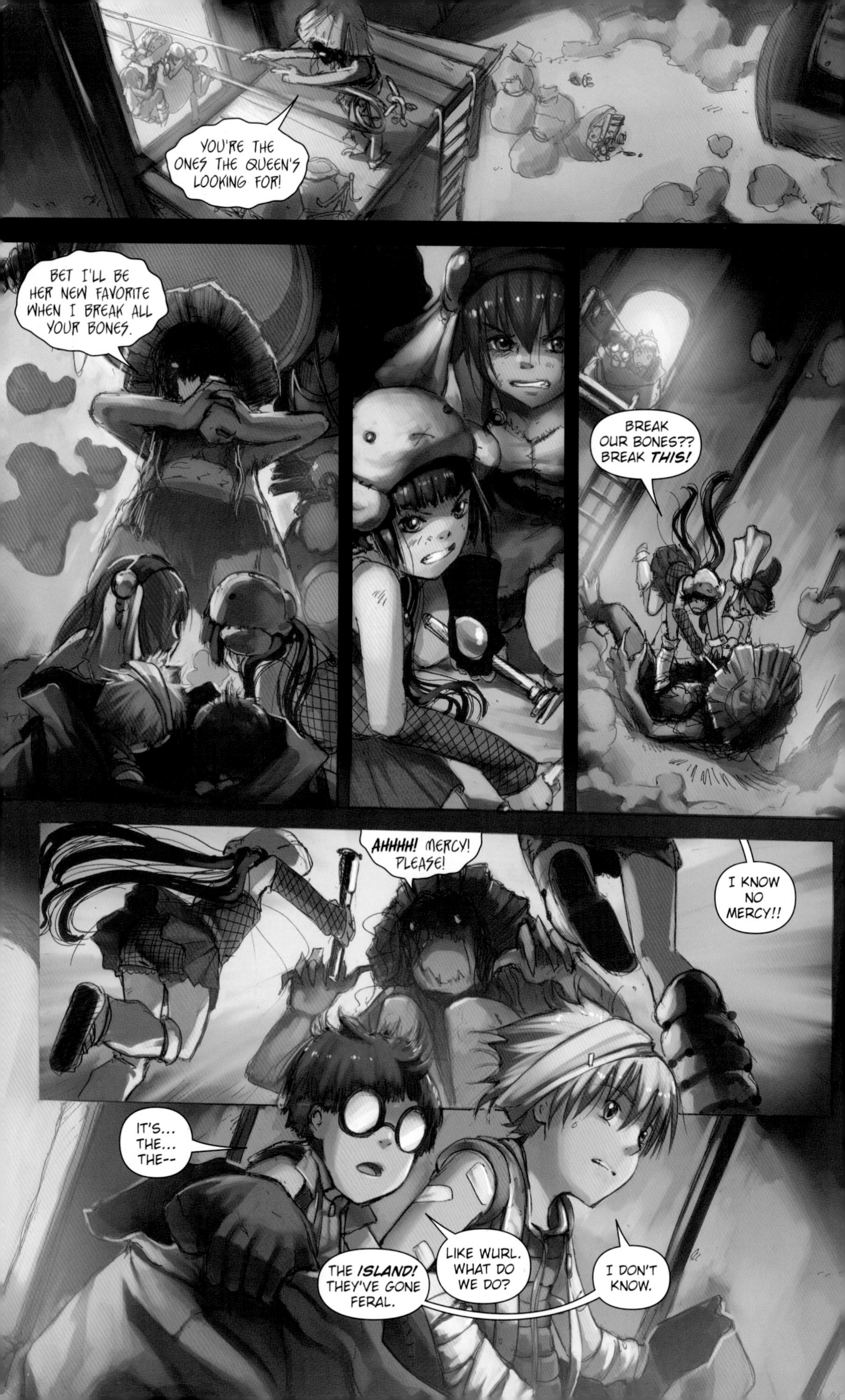
YOU'RE THE ONES THE QUEEN'S LOOKING FOR!
BET I'LL BE HER NEW FAVORITE WHEN I BREAK ALL YOUR BONES.
BREAK OUR BONES?? BREAK *THIS!*
AHHHH! MERCY! PLEASE!
I KNOW NO MERCY!!
IT'S... THE... THE--
THE *ISLAND!* THEY'VE GONE FERAL.
LIKE WURL. WHAT DO WE DO?
I DON'T KNOW.

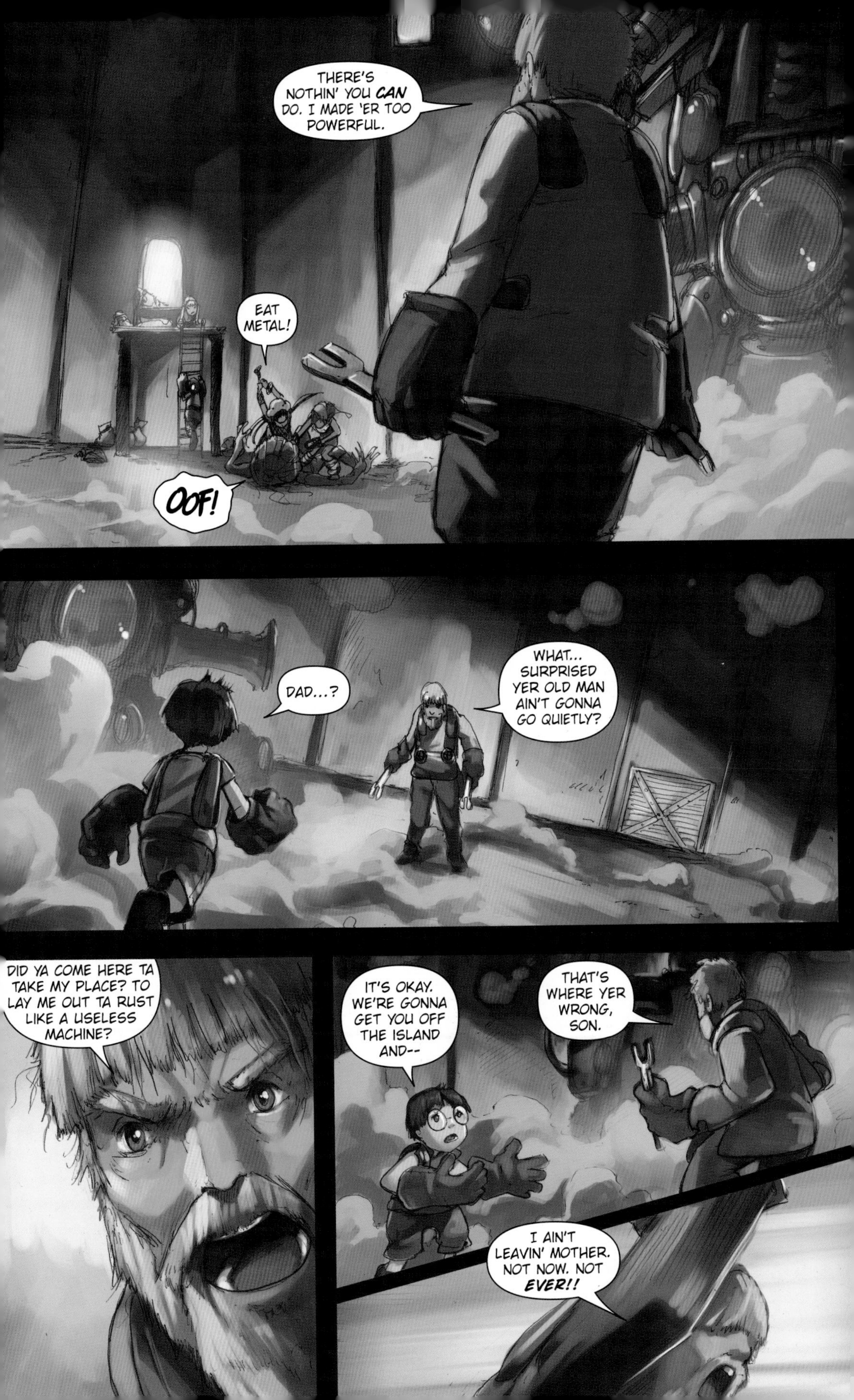
THERE'S NOTHIN' YOU CAN DO. I MADE 'ER TOO POWERFUL.
EAT METAL!
OOF!
DAD...?
WHAT... SURPRISED YER OLD MAN AIN'T GONNA GO QUIETLY?
DID YA COME HERE TA TAKE MY PLACE? TO LAY ME OUT TA RUST LIKE A USELESS MACHINE?
IT'S OKAY. WE'RE GONNA GET YOU OFF THE ISLAND AND--
THAT'S WHERE YER WRONG, SON.
I AIN'T LEAVIN' MOTHER. NOT NOW. NOT EVER!!

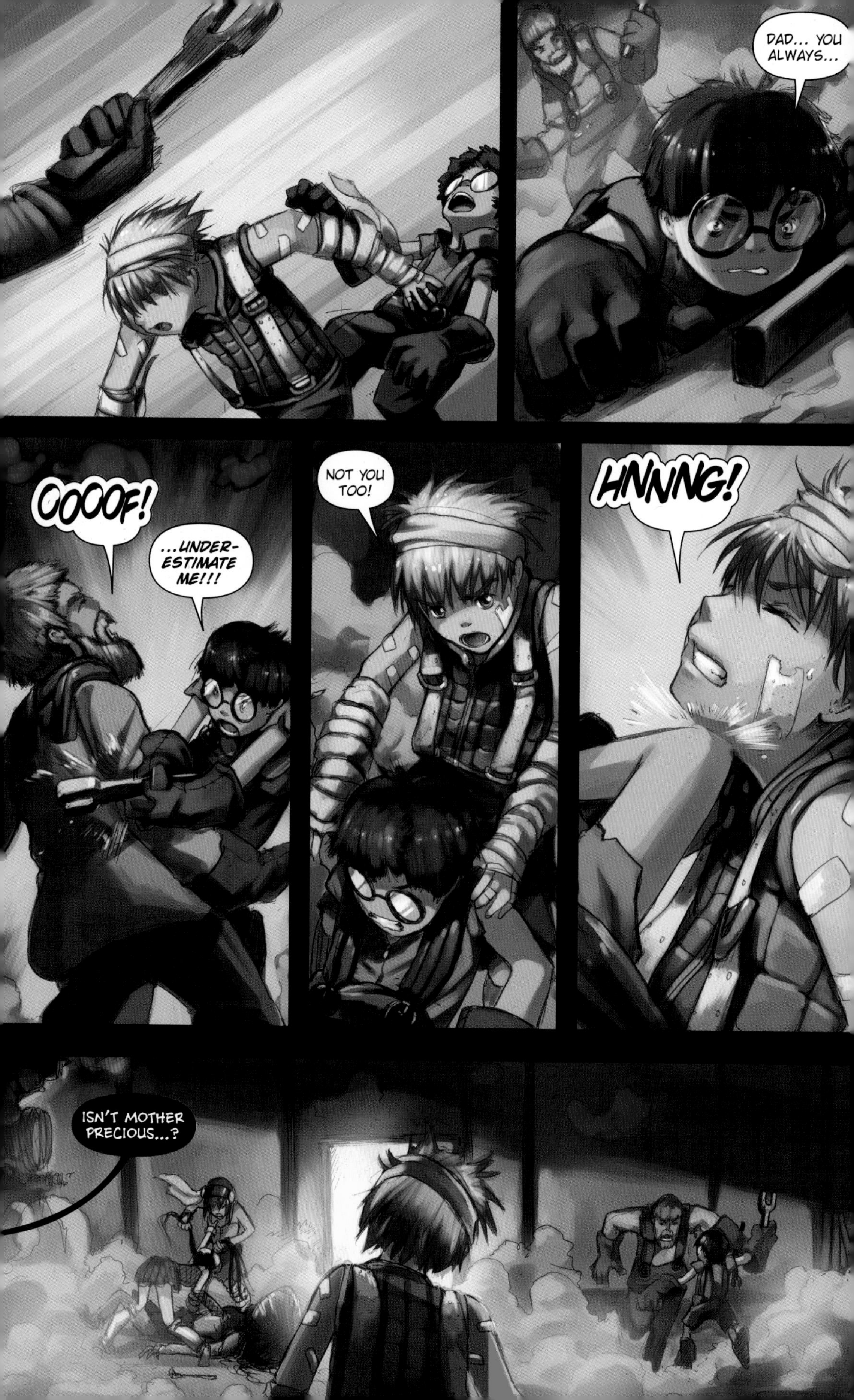
DAD... YOU ALWAYS...
OOOOF!
...UNDER-ESTIMATE ME!!!
NOT YOU TOO!
HNNNG!
ISN'T MOTHER PRECIOUS...?

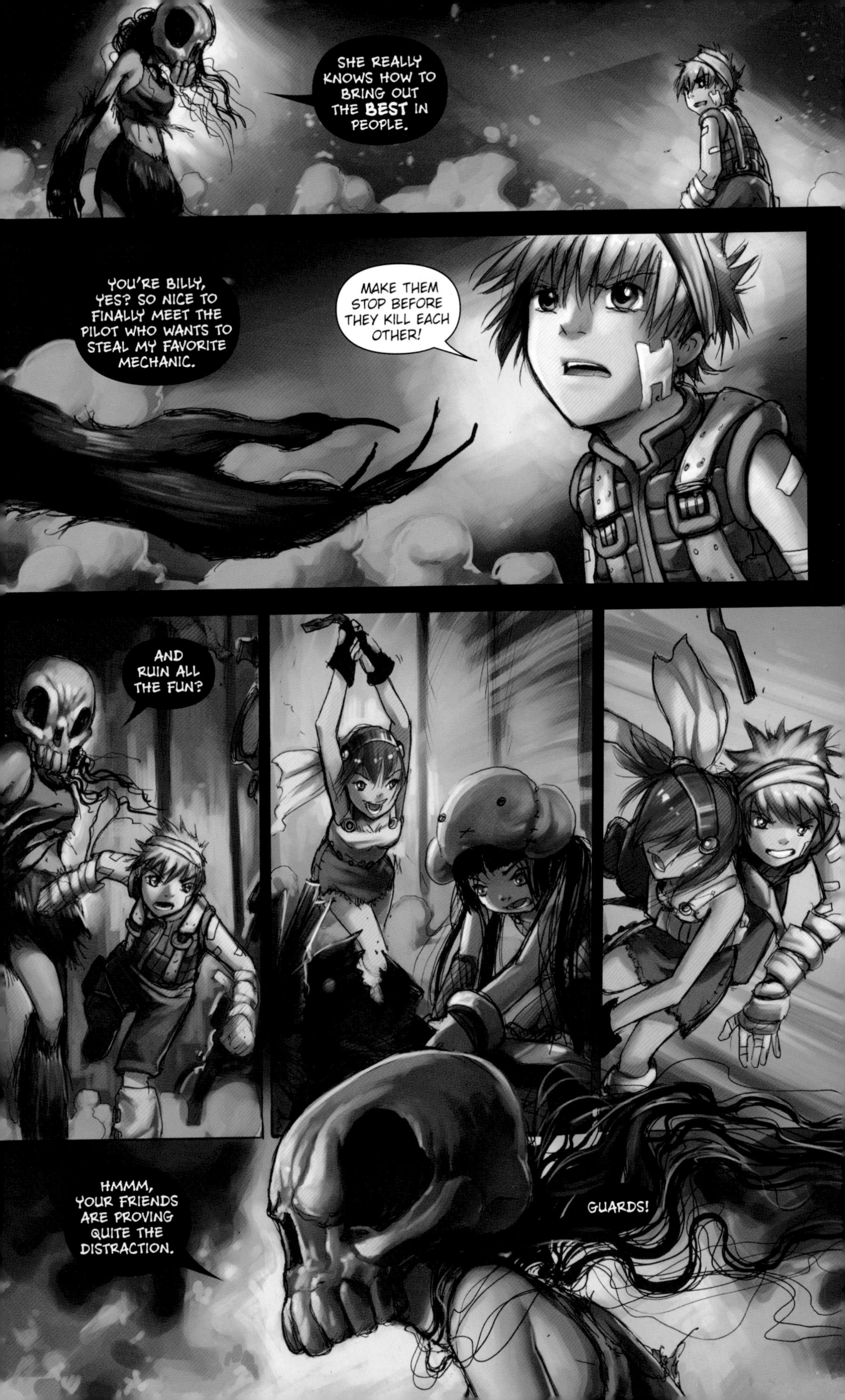
SHE REALLY KNOWS HOW TO BRING OUT THE **BEST** IN PEOPLE.
YOU'RE BILLY, YES? SO NICE TO FINALLY MEET THE PILOT WHO WANTS TO STEAL MY FAVORITE MECHANIC.
MAKE THEM STOP BEFORE THEY KILL EACH OTHER!
AND RUIN ALL THE FUN?
HMMM, YOUR FRIENDS ARE PROVING QUITE THE DISTRACTION.
GUARDS!

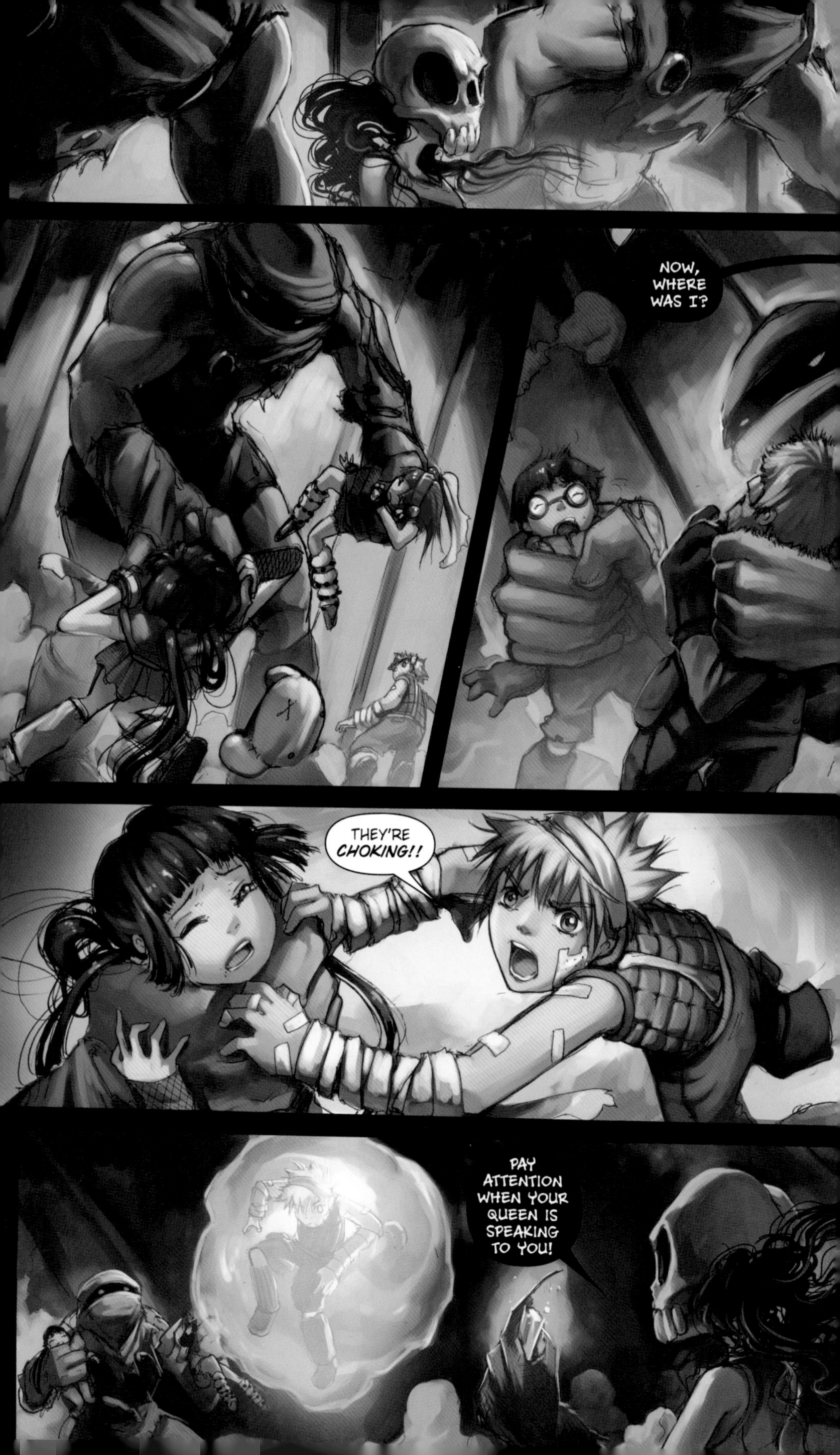
NOW, WHERE WAS I?
THEY'RE *CHOKING!!*
PAY ATTENTION WHEN YOUR QUEEN IS SPEAKING TO YOU!

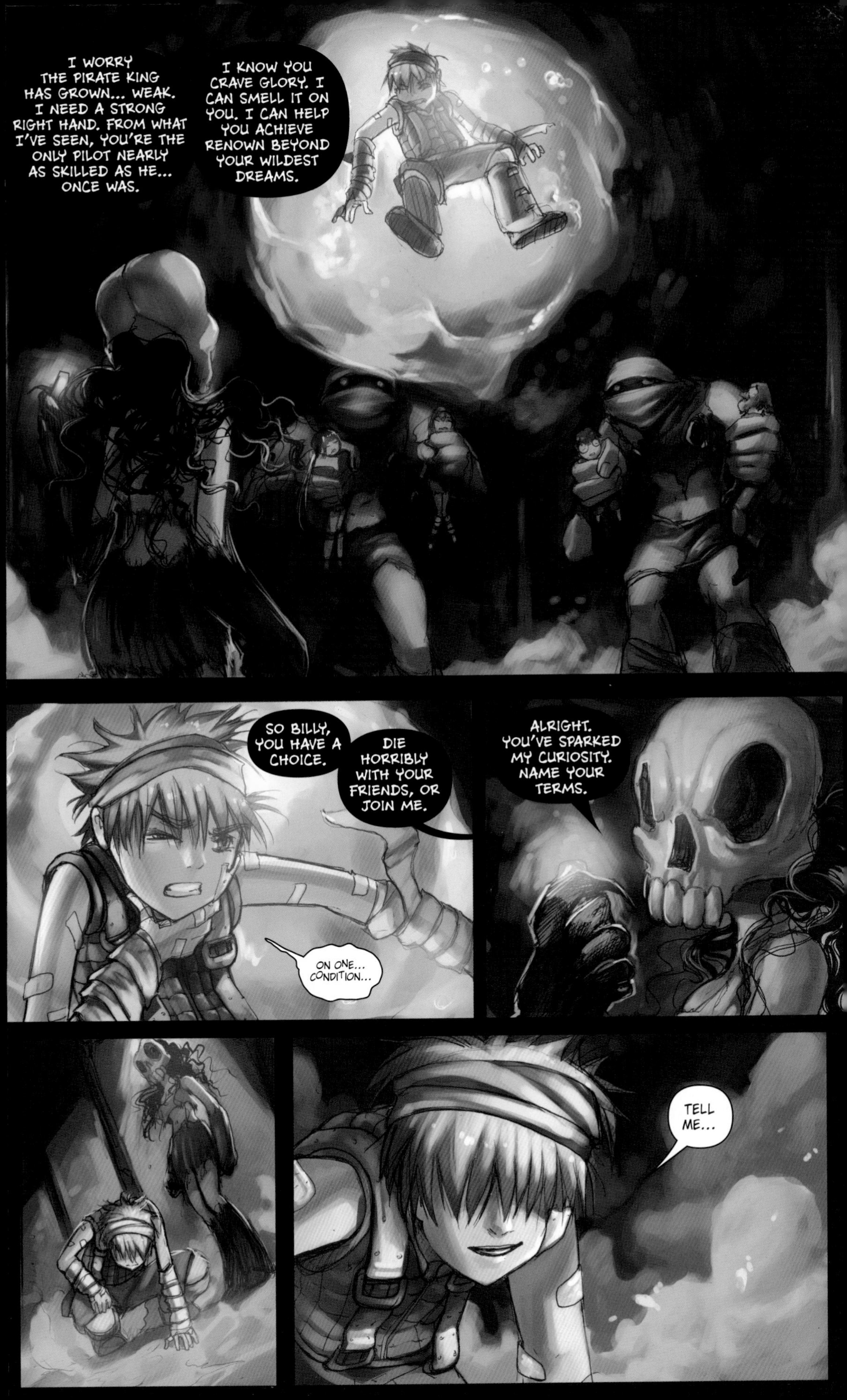
I WORRY THE PIRATE KING HAS GROWN... WEAK. I NEED A STRONG RIGHT HAND. FROM WHAT I'VE SEEN, YOU'RE THE ONLY PILOT NEARLY AS SKILLED AS HE... ONCE WAS.
I KNOW YOU CRAVE GLORY. I CAN SMELL IT ON YOU. I CAN HELP YOU ACHIEVE RENOWN BEYOND YOUR WILDEST DREAMS.
SO BILLY, YOU HAVE A CHOICE.
DIE HORRIBLY WITH YOUR FRIENDS, OR JOIN ME.
ON ONE... CONDITION...
ALRIGHT. YOU'VE SPARKED MY CURIOSITY. NAME YOUR TERMS.
TELL ME...

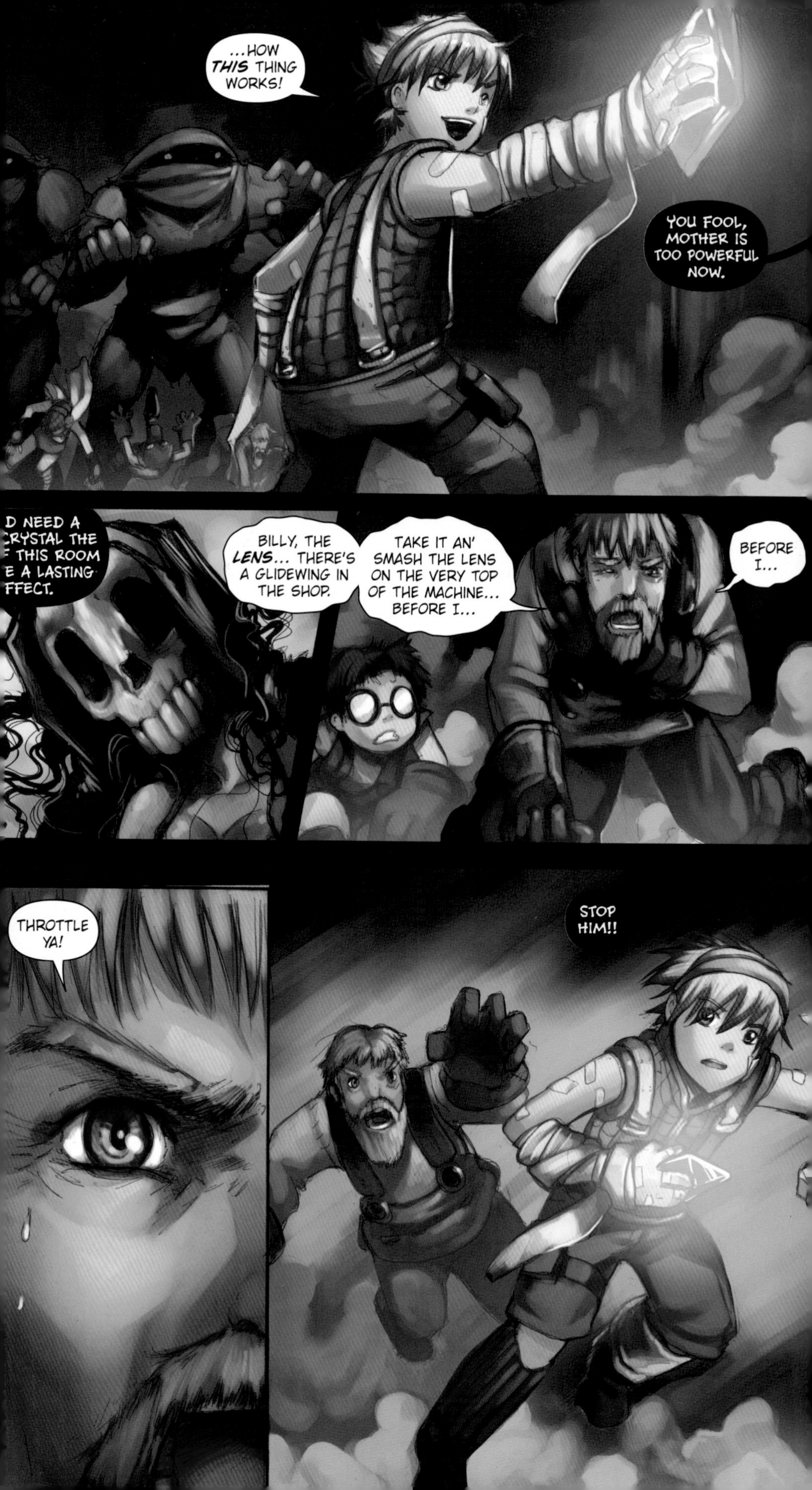
...HOW THIS THING WORKS!
YOU FOOL, MOTHER IS TOO POWERFUL NOW.
D NEED A CRYSTAL THE F THIS ROOM E A LASTING FFECT.
BILLY, THE LENS... THERE'S A GLIDEWING IN THE SHOP.
TAKE IT AN' SMASH THE LENS ON THE VERY TOP OF THE MACHINE... BEFORE I...
BEFORE I...
THROTTLE YA!
STOP HIM!!

I'VE BEEN LOOKING FOR THAT CRYSTAL ALL DAY, KID.

THOUGHT IF I PUT A LITTLE B ON IT AND GAVE TO THE WITCH QUEEN, SHE'D FORGIVE ME.

RACE YA TO THE TOP!

WILL YOU *STOP* GETTING IN MY WAY!

RELAX, I JUST WANT TO THANK YOU...

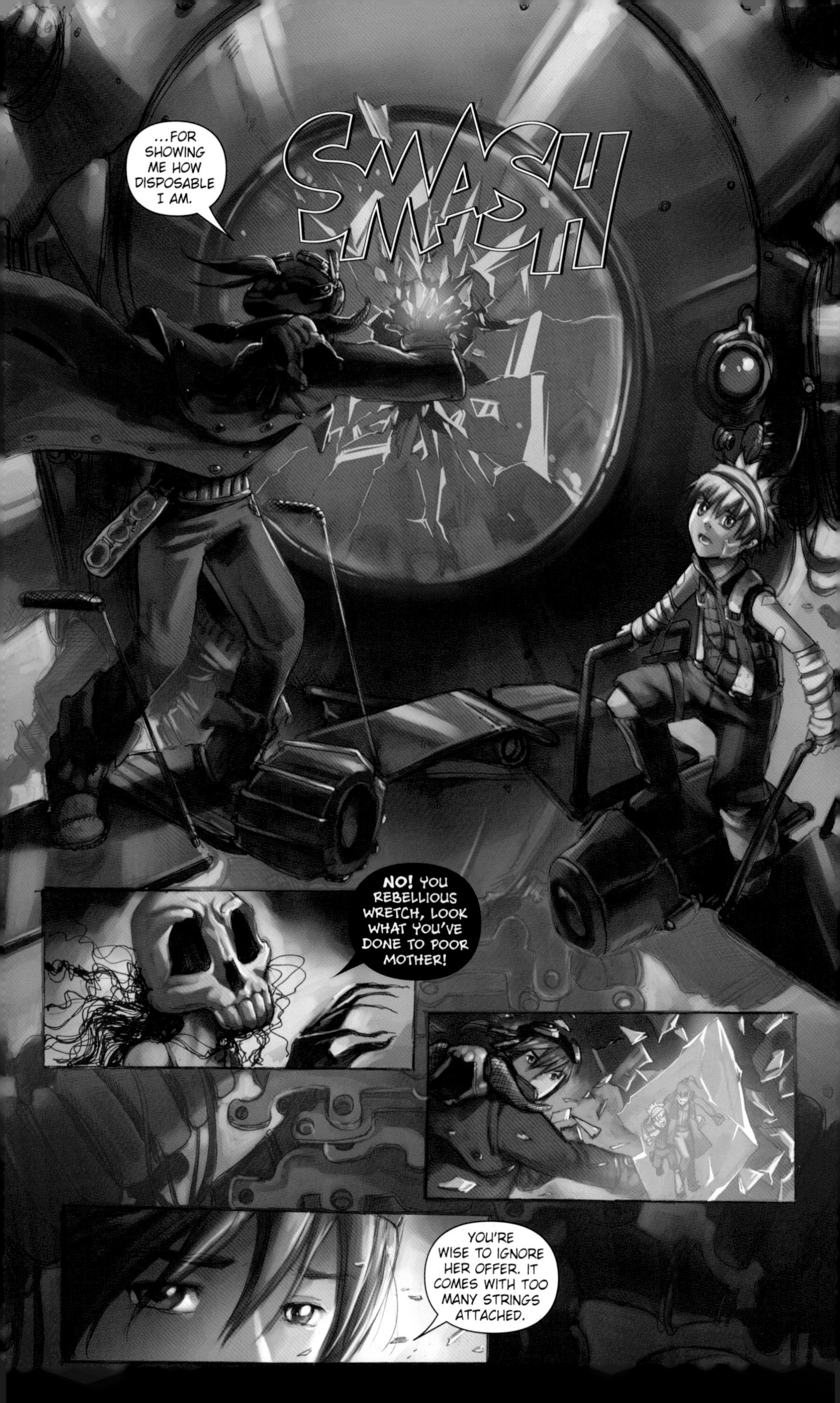
...FOR SHOWING ME HOW DISPOSABLE I AM.
SMASH
NO! YOU REBELLIOUS WRETCH, LOOK WHAT YOU'VE DONE TO POOR MOTHER!
YOU'RE WISE TO IGNORE HER OFFER. IT COMES WITH TOO MANY STRINGS ATTACHED.

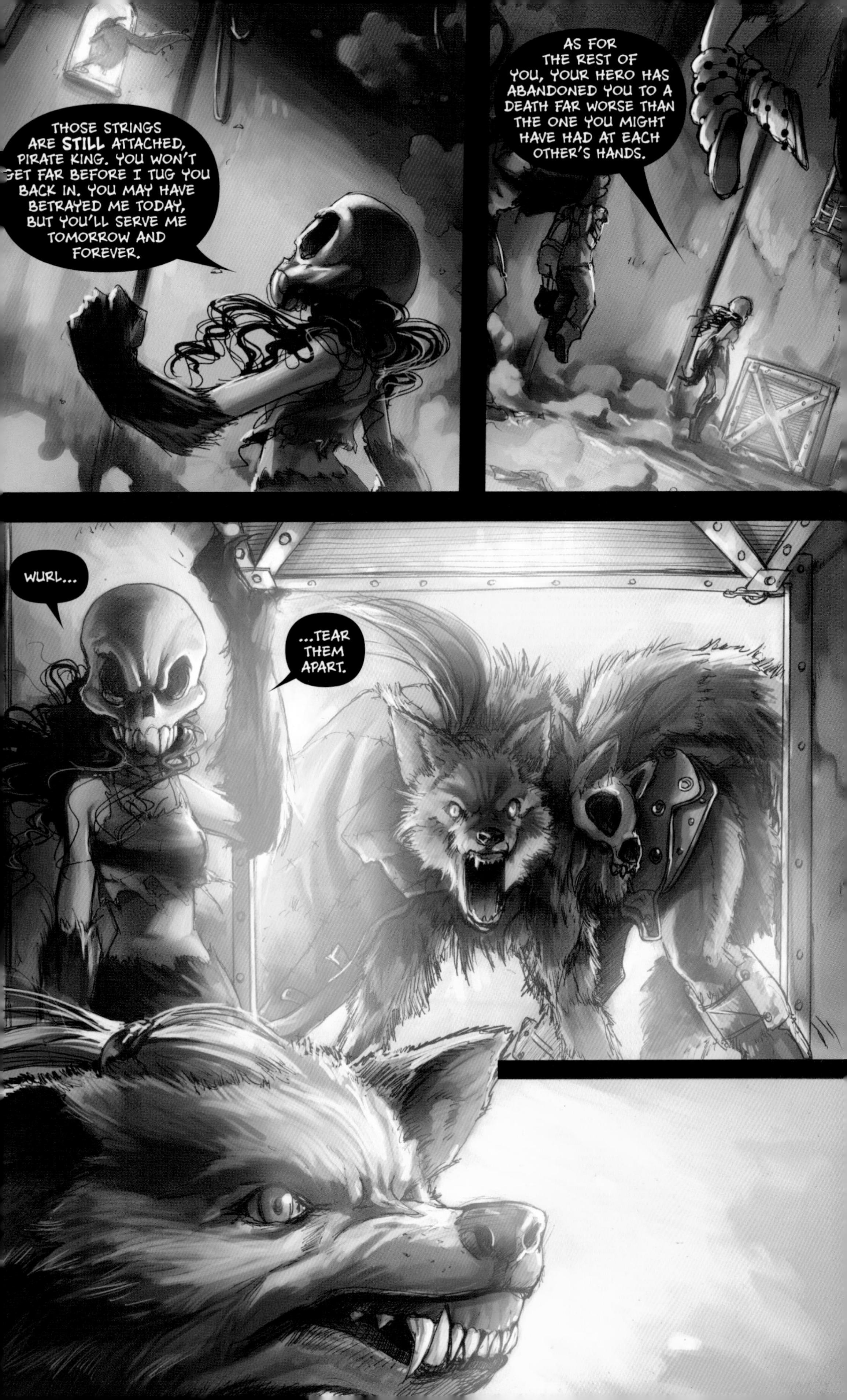
THOSE STRINGS ARE STILL ATTACHED, PIRATE KING. YOU WON'T GET FAR BEFORE I TUG YOU BACK IN. YOU MAY HAVE BETRAYED ME TODAY, BUT YOU'LL SERVE ME TOMORROW AND FOREVER.
AS FOR THE REST OF YOU, YOUR HERO HAS ABANDONED YOU TO A DEATH FAR WORSE THAN THE ONE YOU MIGHT HAVE HAD AT EACH OTHER'S HANDS.
WURL...
...TEAR THEM APART.

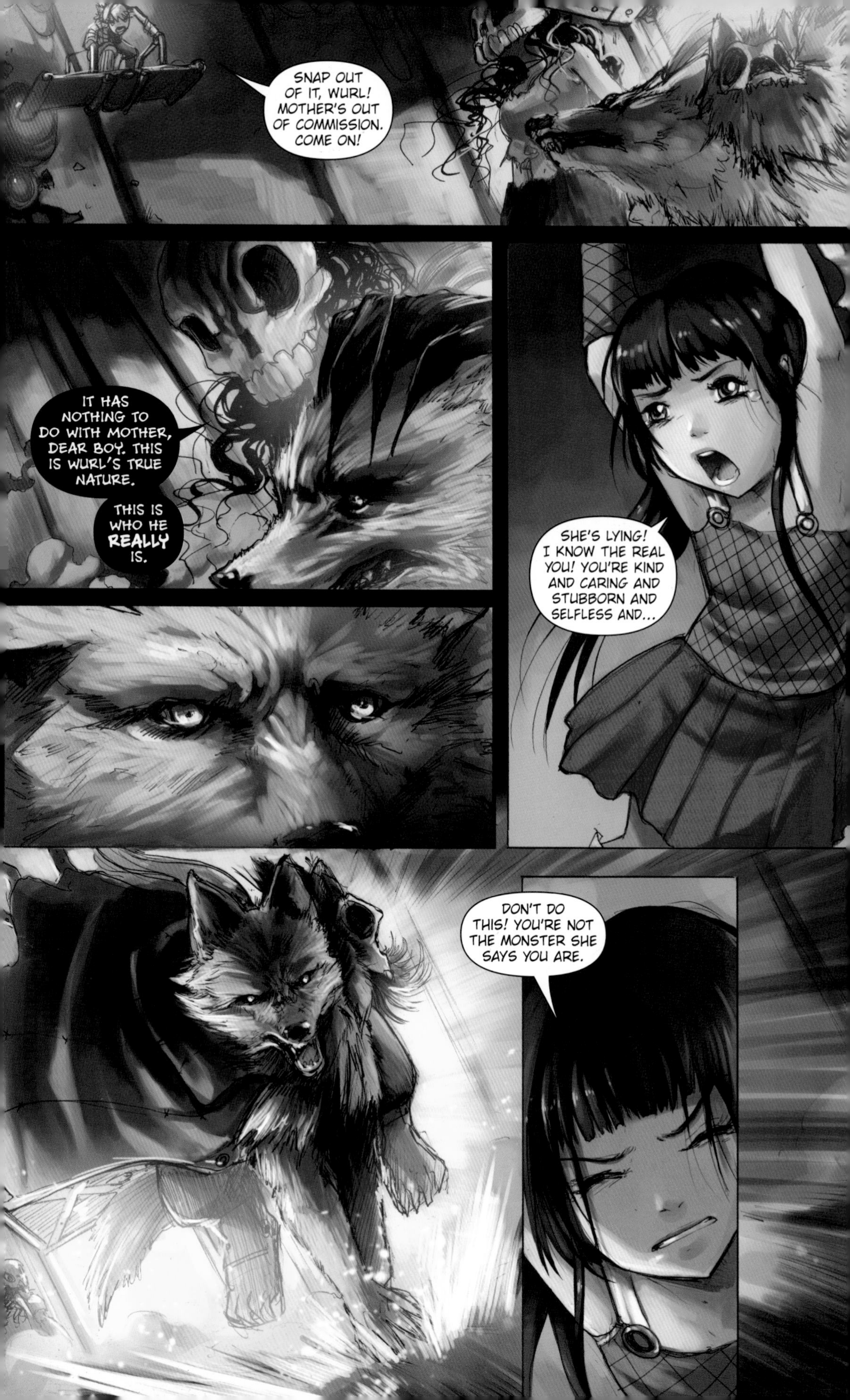
SNAP OUT OF IT, WURL! MOTHER'S OUT OF COMMISSION. COME ON!
IT HAS NOTHING TO DO WITH MOTHER, DEAR BOY. THIS IS WURL'S TRUE NATURE.
THIS IS WHO HE REALLY IS.
SHE'S LYING! I KNOW THE REAL YOU! YOU'RE KIND AND CARING AND STUBBORN AND SELFLESS AND...
DON'T DO THIS! YOU'RE NOT THE MONSTER SHE SAYS YOU ARE.

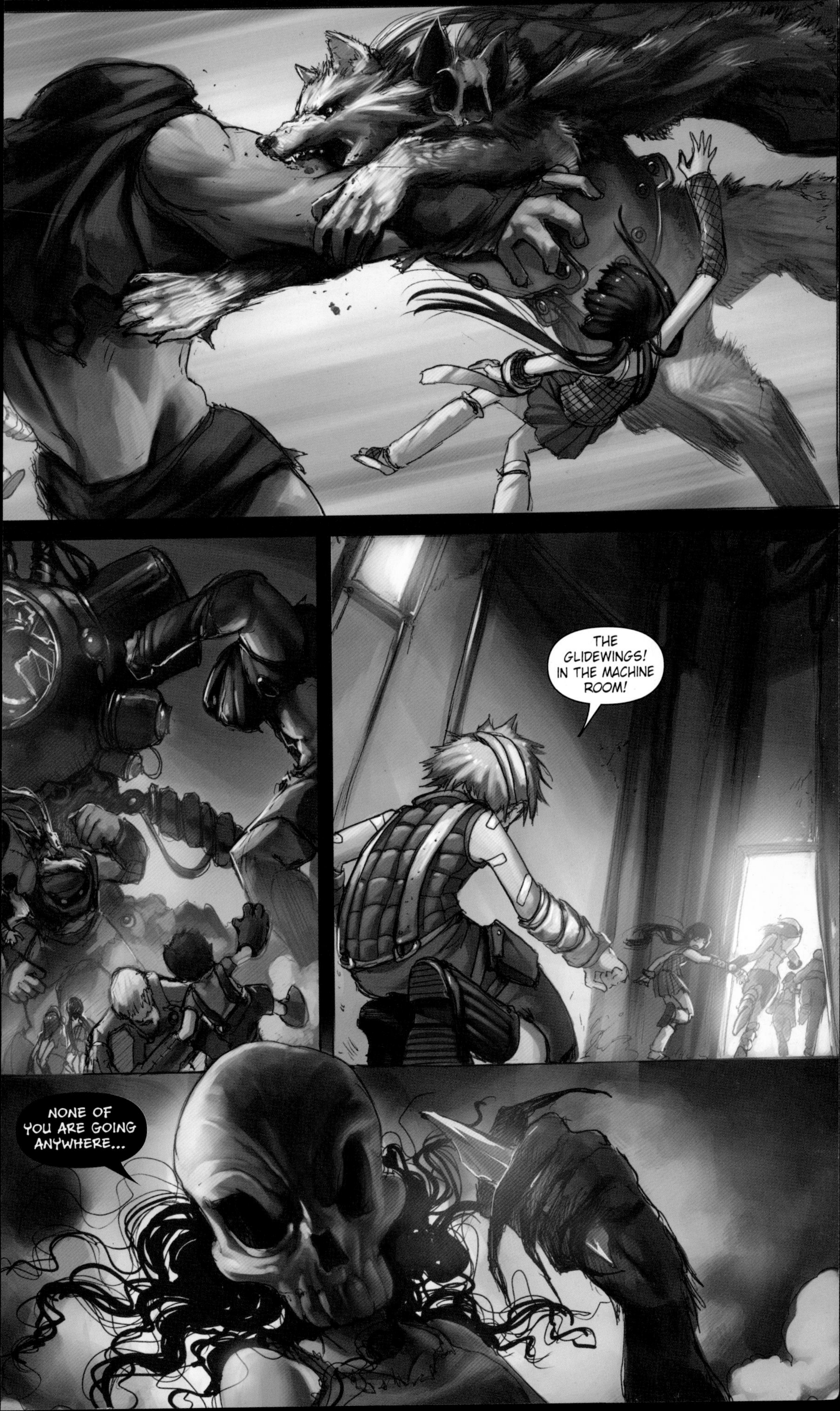
THE GLIDEWINGS! IN THE MACHINE ROOM!
NONE OF YOU ARE GOING ANYWHERE...

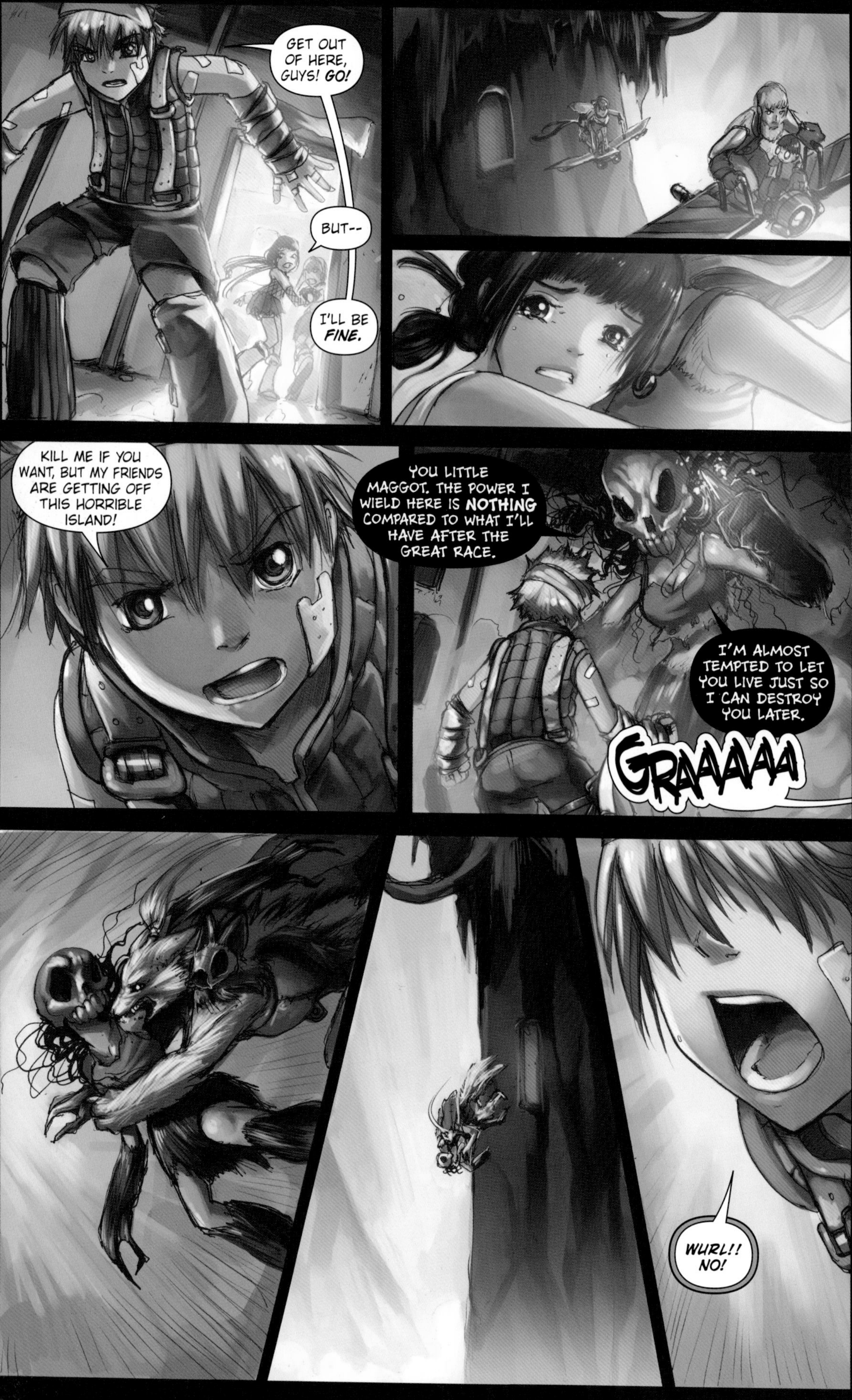
GET OUT OF HERE, GUYS! GO!
BUT--
I'LL BE FINE.
KILL ME IF YOU WANT, BUT MY FRIENDS ARE GETTING OFF THIS HORRIBLE ISLAND!
YOU LITTLE MAGGOT. THE POWER I WIELD HERE IS NOTHING COMPARED TO WHAT I'LL HAVE AFTER THE GREAT RACE.
I'M ALMOST TEMPTED TO LET YOU LIVE JUST SO I CAN DESTROY YOU LATER.
GRAAAAAA
WURL!! NO!

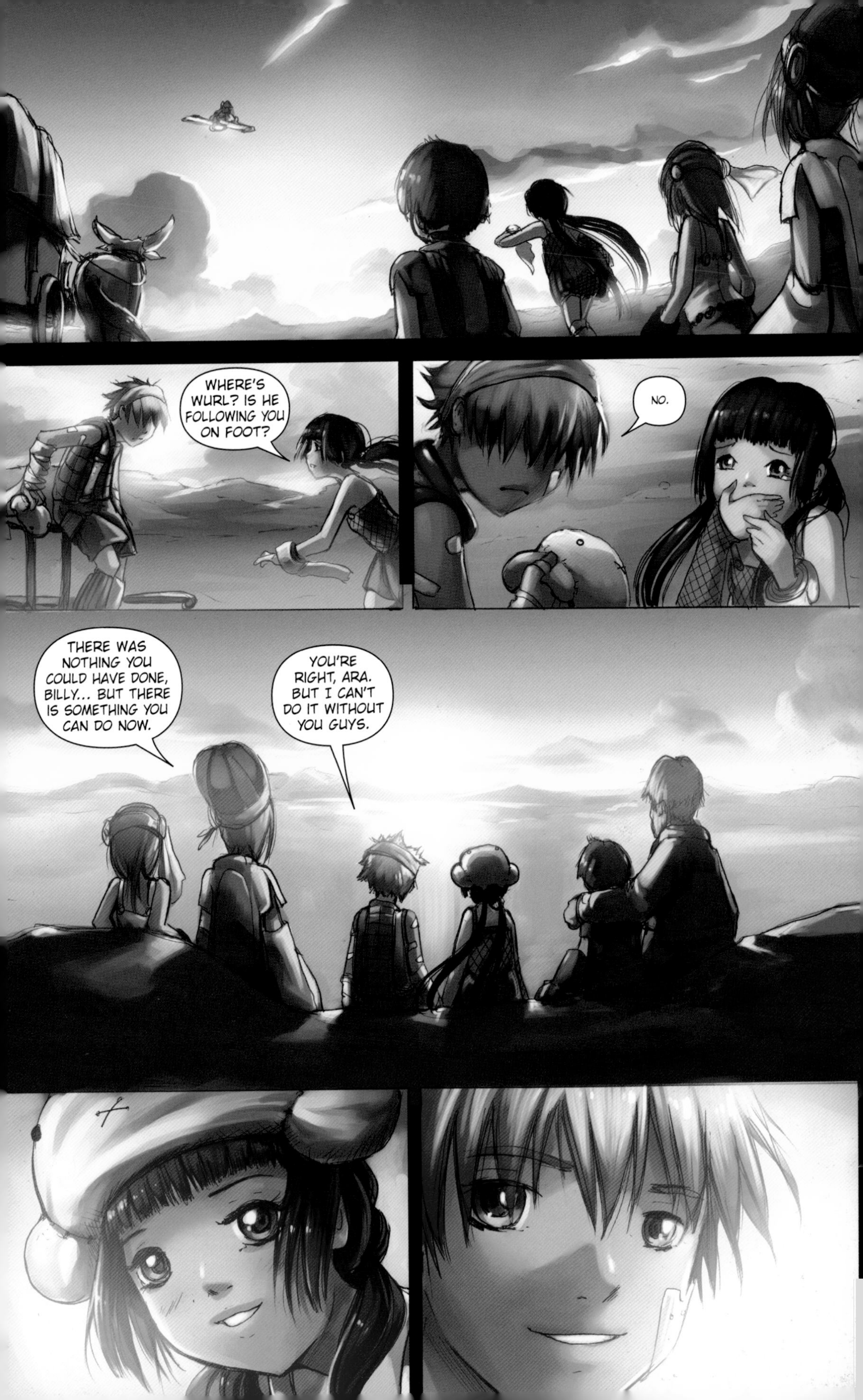
WHERE'S WURL? IS HE FOLLOWING YOU ON FOOT?
NO.
THERE WAS NOTHING YOU COULD HAVE DONE, BILLY... BUT THERE IS SOMETHING YOU CAN DO NOW.
YOU'RE RIGHT, ARA. BUT I CAN'T DO IT WITHOUT YOU GUYS.

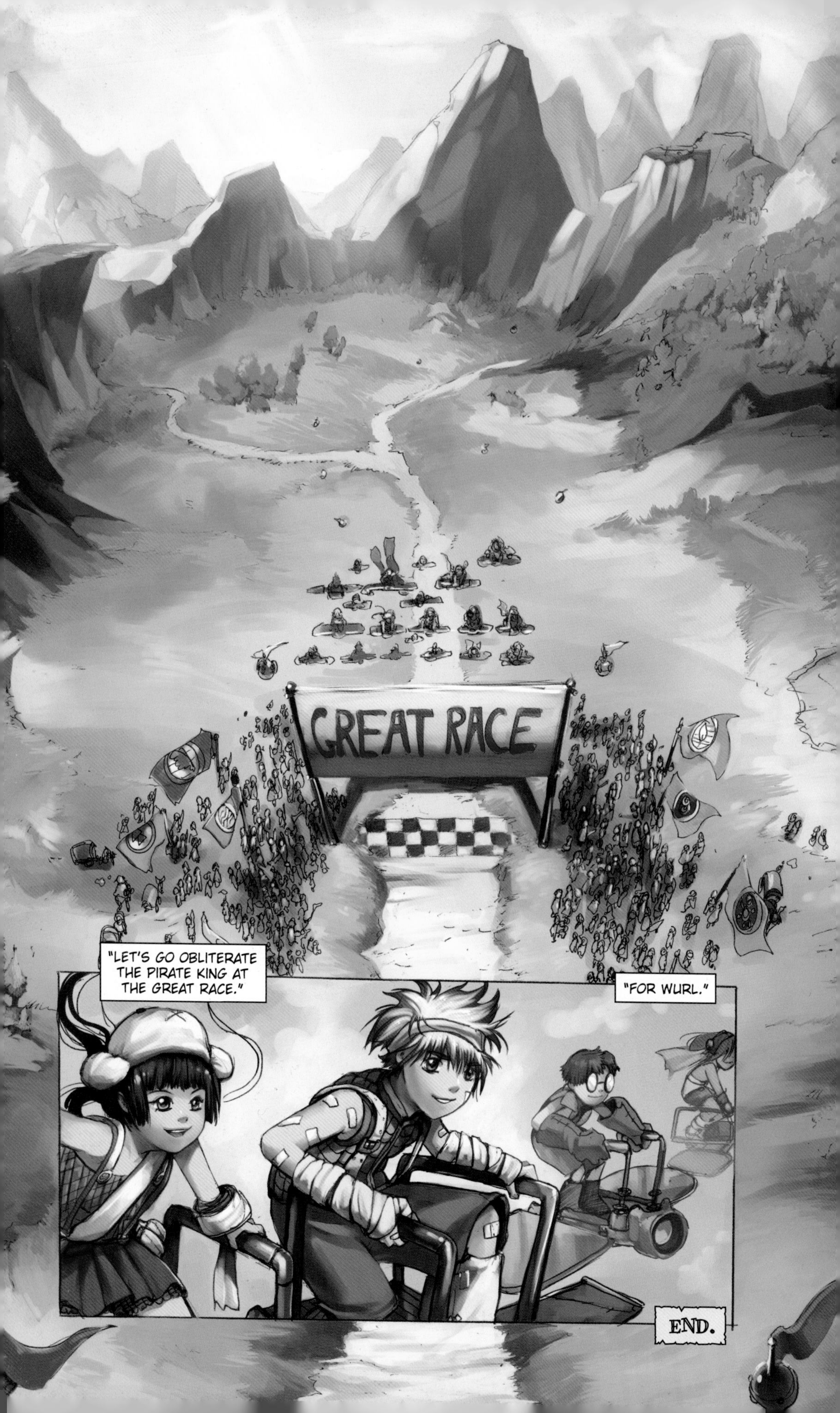
GREAT RACE
"LET'S GO OBLITERATE THE PIRATE KING AT THE GREAT RACE."
"FOR WURL."
END.

Hi Everyone!

Thanks for picking up our graphic novel! One Day in 2005 I saw Camilla's artwork at a local Vancouver Comic Con and fell in love with it. I had the name kicking around in my head "Billy Boom Boom" and asked her to draw a few things for me. Little did I know this chance meeting would change the last five years of my life so dramatically.

What you are looking at here is the first version of the comic that we did- issue 0. It was made to set up the world and introduces the Glidewings and the Great Race; I think it does a great job. The Pirate King comes across as cocky and evil and Billy, Suma and Ricket are kids who are just about to begin the adventure of their lives. I'm happy it's finally in print for the world to see... Enjoy!

I have to thank Tyler Sigman for helping me come up with these interesting characters and world, without him there would be no Sky Pirates of Neo Terra. I'd also like to thank Jeff Simpson who's colors on the early Sky Pirates stuff and the game is incredible work.

Extra special thanks to Day 21 Studios - Torval and Greg Mork and everyone at Image Comics for helping us get this book onto the shelves.

Double extra special thanks to the team - Tim, Josh, Camilla, Simon, Ed, Adapia, Pitipat, Sarah for making this book a reality.

Keep checking www.billyboomboom.com for new updates, information on the game, flash games and new books we are working on.

As we say- Time Flies!
Sean Megaw - Creator - Sky Pirates of Neo Terra

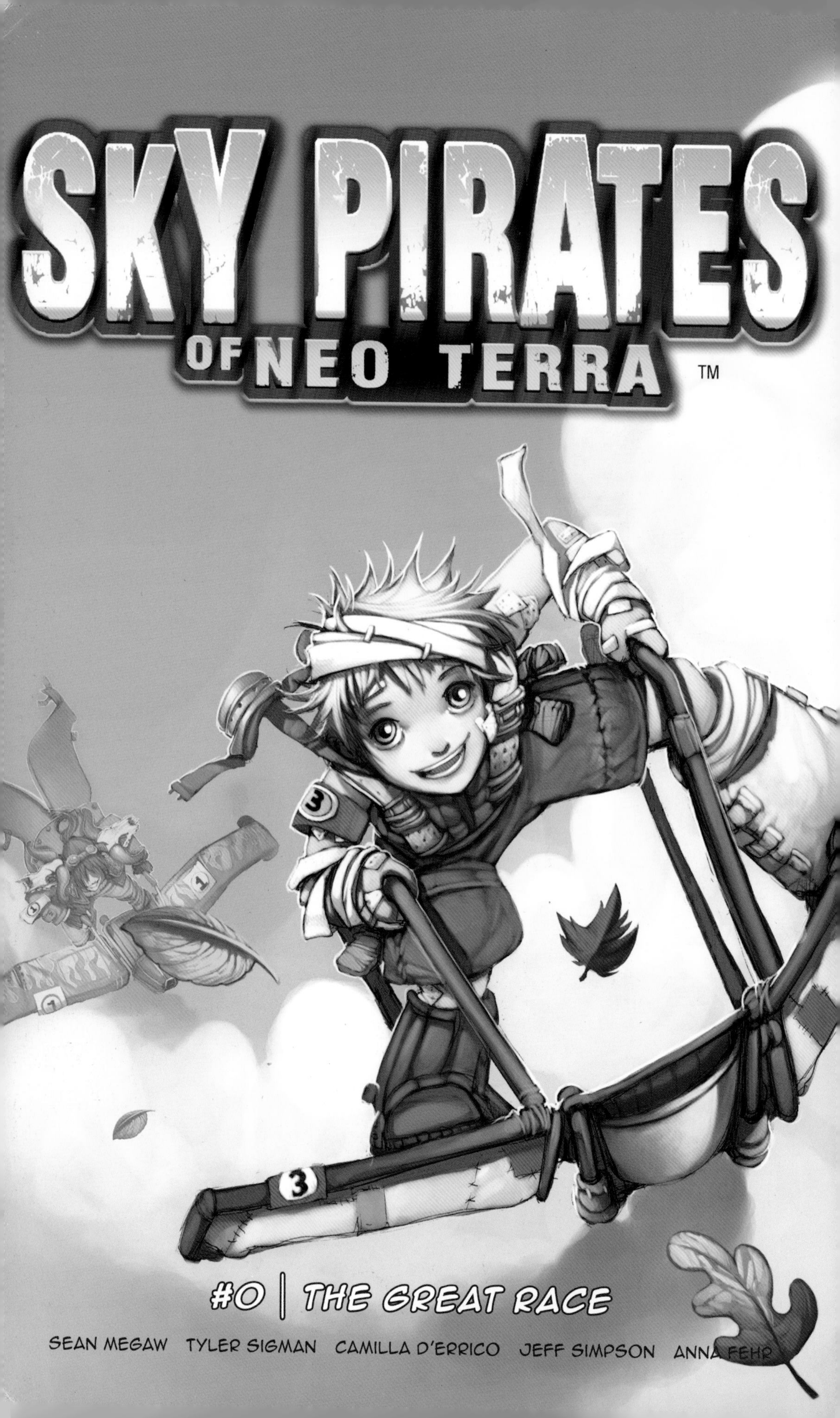
SKY PIRATES
OF NEO TERRA
TM
3
1
1
1
3
#0 | THE GREAT RACE
SEAN MEGAW TYLER SIGMAN CAMILLA D'ERRICO JEFF SIMPSON ANNA FEHR

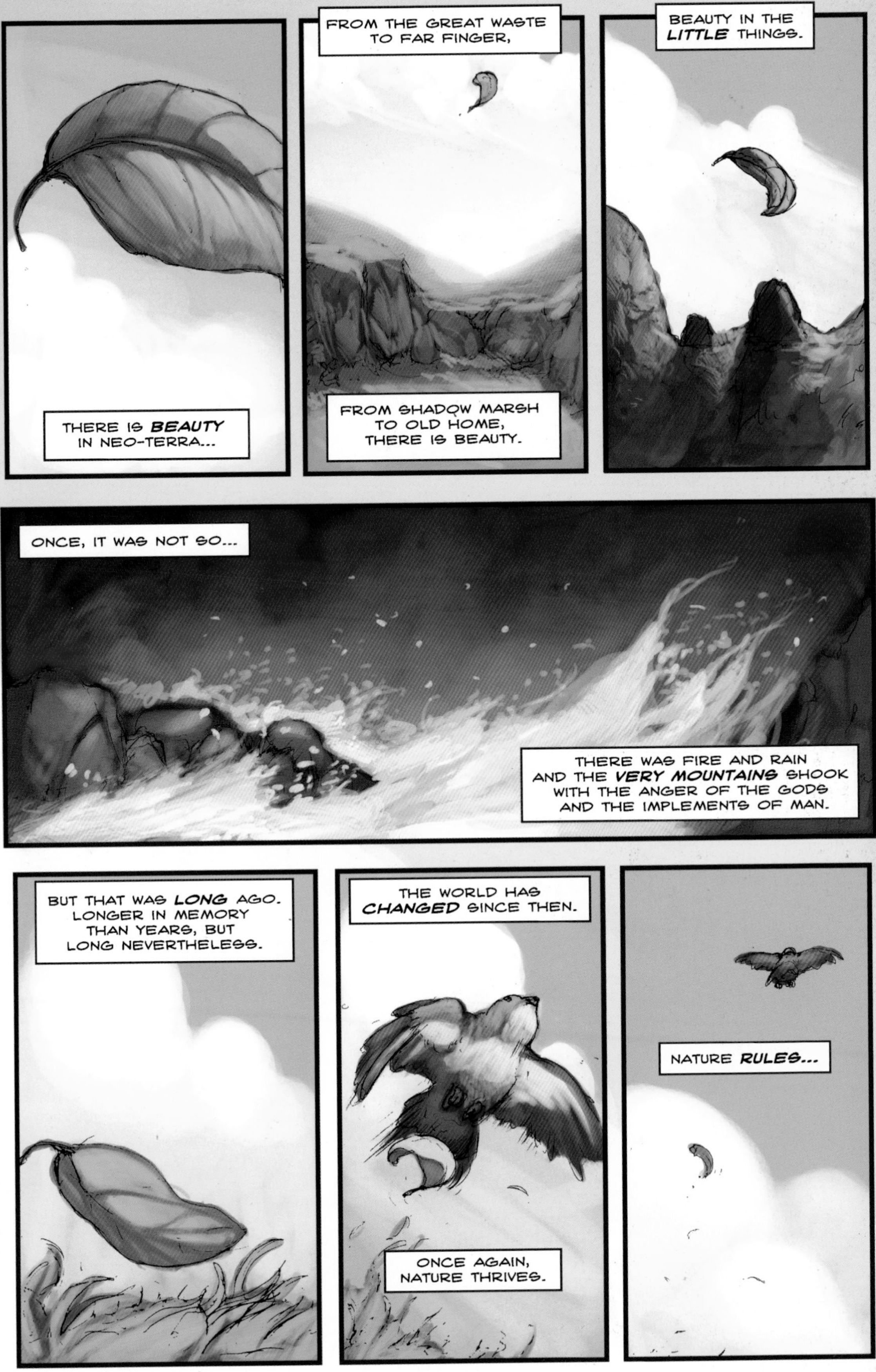
THERE IS BEAUTY IN NEO-TERRA...
FROM THE GREAT WASTE TO FAR FINGER,
FROM SHADOW MARSH TO OLD HOME, THERE IS BEAUTY.
BEAUTY IN THE LITTLE THINGS.
ONCE, IT WAS NOT SO...
THERE WAS FIRE AND RAIN AND THE VERY MOUNTAINS SHOOK WITH THE ANGER OF THE GODS AND THE IMPLEMENTS OF MAN.
BUT THAT WAS LONG AGO. LONGER IN MEMORY THAN YEARS, BUT LONG NEVERTHELESS.
THE WORLD HAS CHANGED SINCE THEN.
ONCE AGAIN, NATURE THRIVES.
NATURE RULES...

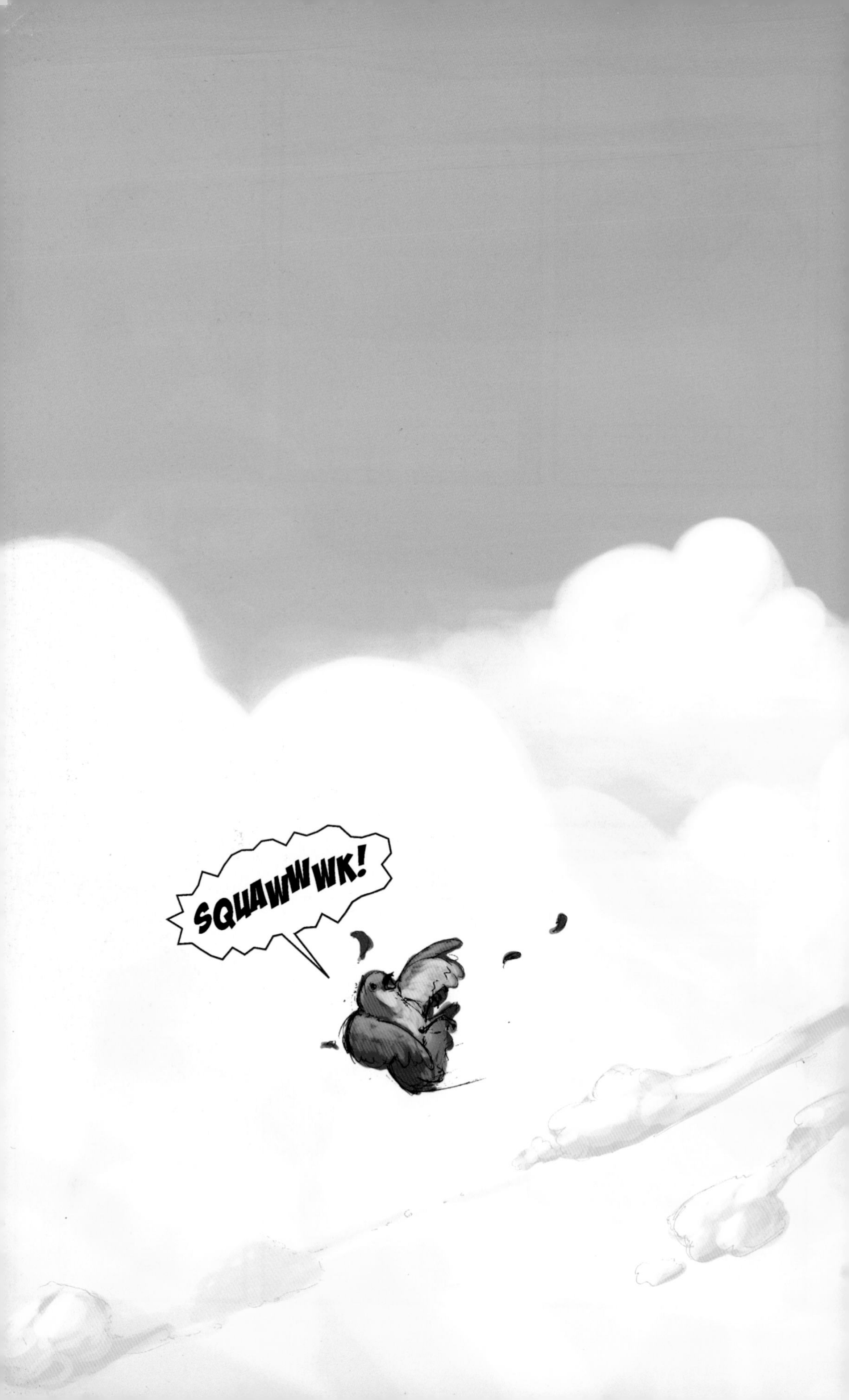
SQUAWWWK!

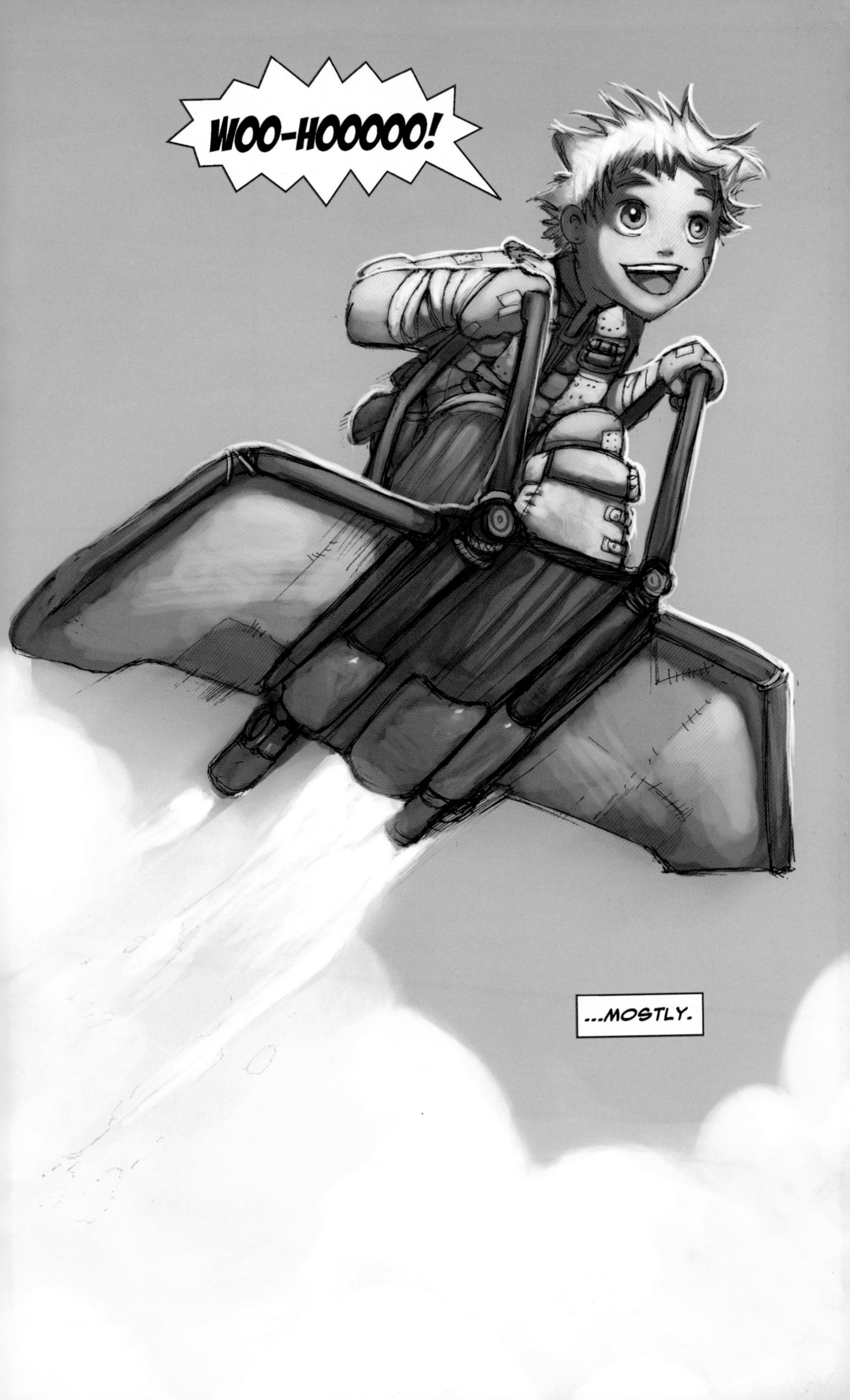
WOO-HOOOOO!
...MOSTLY.

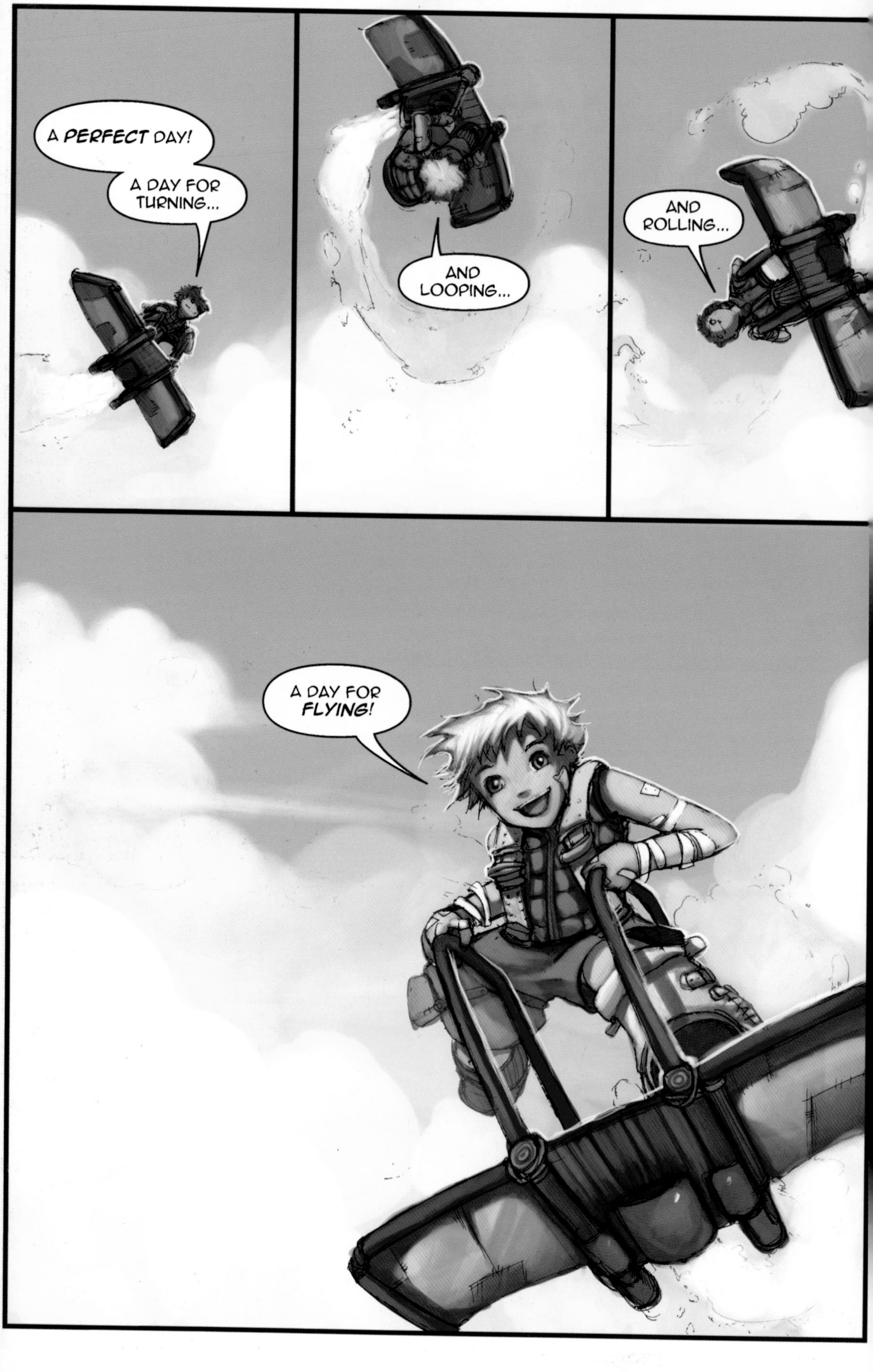
A PERFECT DAY!
A DAY FOR TURNING...
AND LOOPING...
AND ROLLING...
A DAY FOR FLYING!

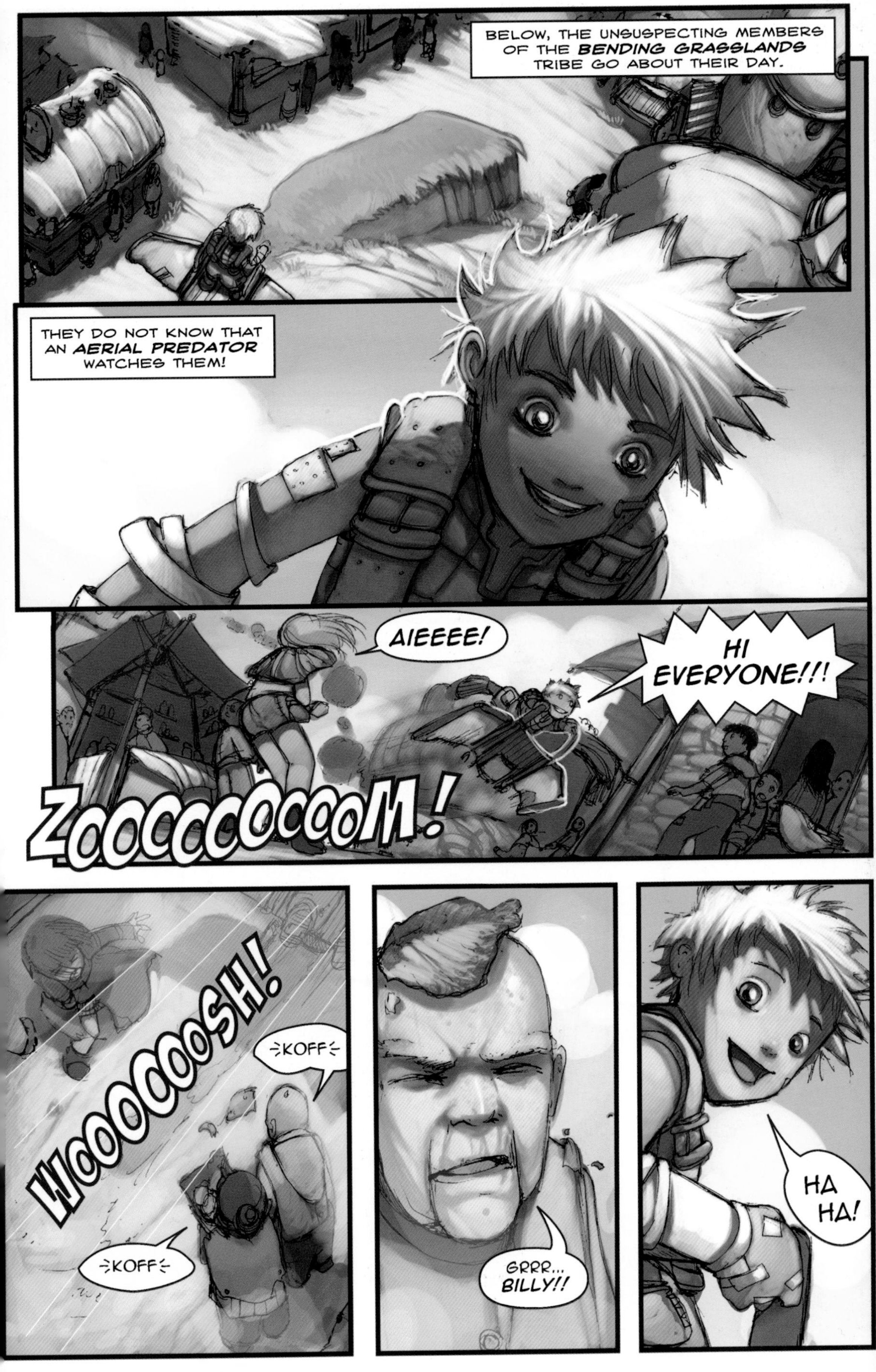
BELOW, THE UNSUSPECTING MEMBERS OF THE BENDING GRASSLANDS TRIBE GO ABOUT THEIR DAY.
THEY DO NOT KNOW THAT AN AERIAL PREDATOR WATCHES THEM!
AIEEEE!
HI EVERYONE!!!
ZOOCCCOOOOM!
WOOOOOSH!
KOFF
KOFF
GRRR... BILLY!!
HA HA!

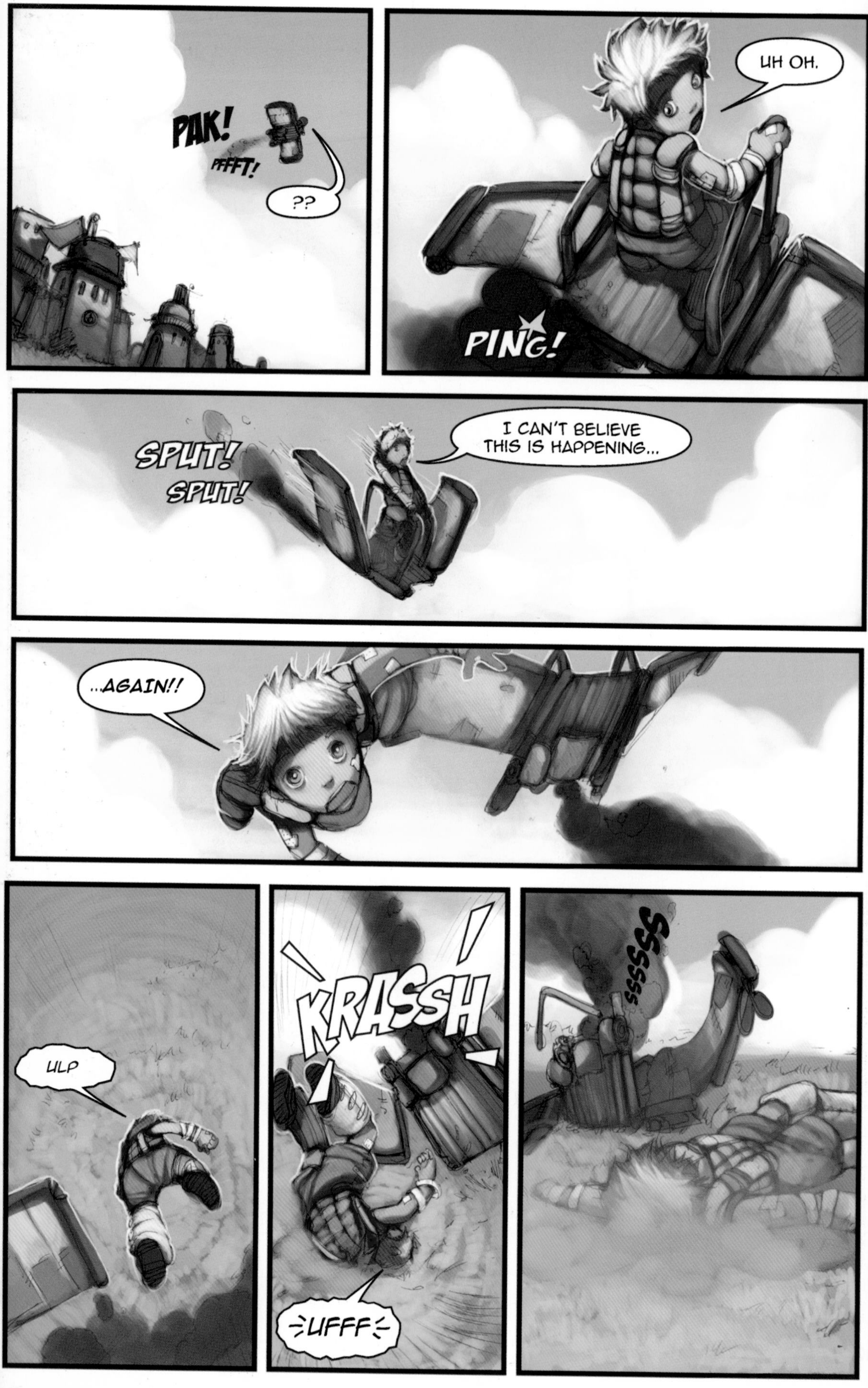
PAK!
PFFFT!
??
UH OH.
PING!
SPUT!
SPUT!
I CAN'T BELIEVE THIS IS HAPPENING...
...AGAIN!!
ULP
KRASSH
UFFF
SSSSSS

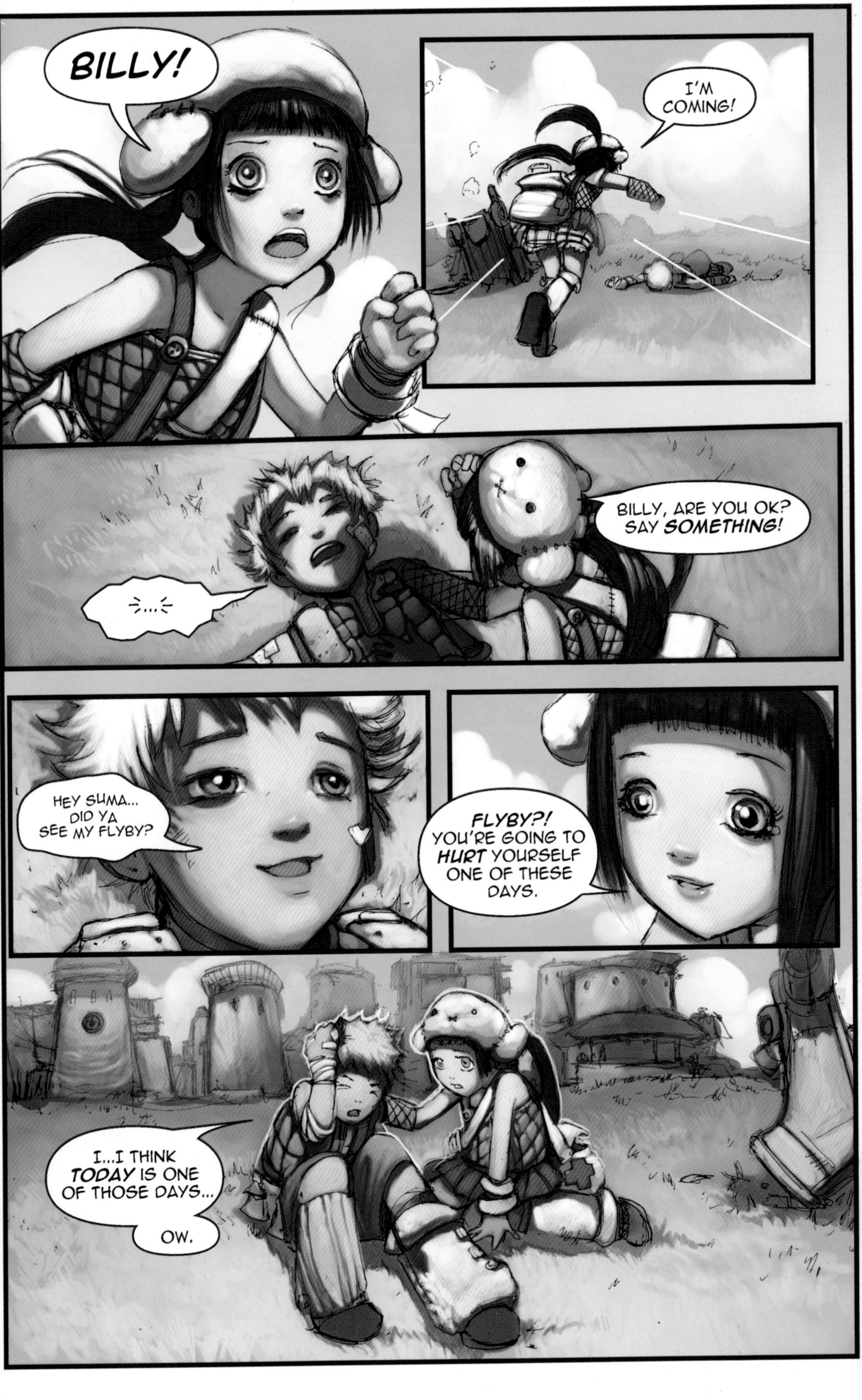
BILLY!
I'M COMING!
BILLY, ARE YOU OK? SAY *SOMETHING*!
...
HEY SUMA... DID YA SEE MY FLYBY?
FLYBY?! YOU'RE GOING TO *HURT* YOURSELF ONE OF THESE DAYS.
I...I THINK *TODAY* IS ONE OF THOSE DAYS...
OW.

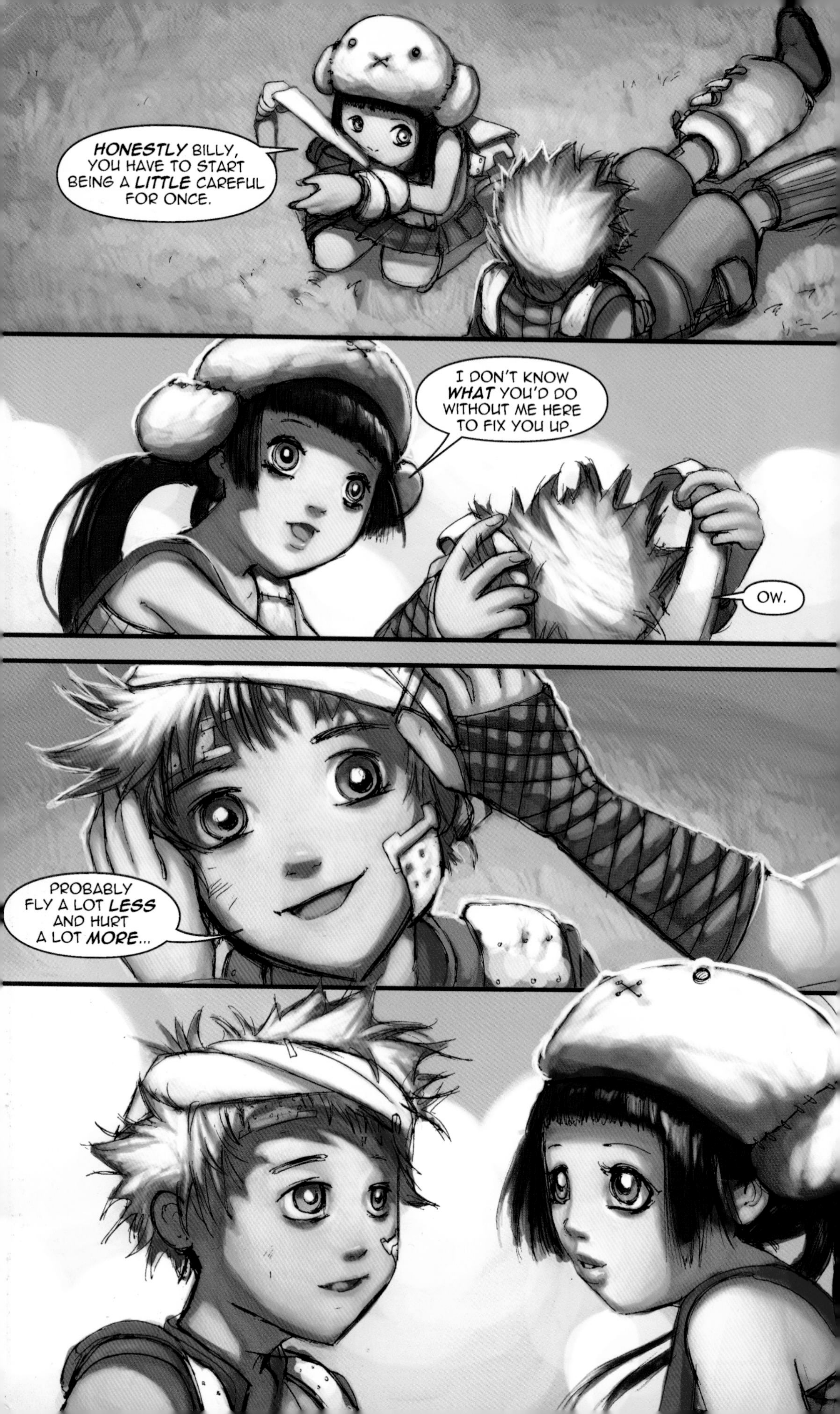
HONESTLY BILLY, YOU HAVE TO START BEING A LITTLE CAREFUL FOR ONCE.
I DON'T KNOW WHAT YOU'D DO WITHOUT ME HERE TO FIX YOU UP.
OW.
PROBABLY FLY A LOT LESS AND HURT A LOT MORE...

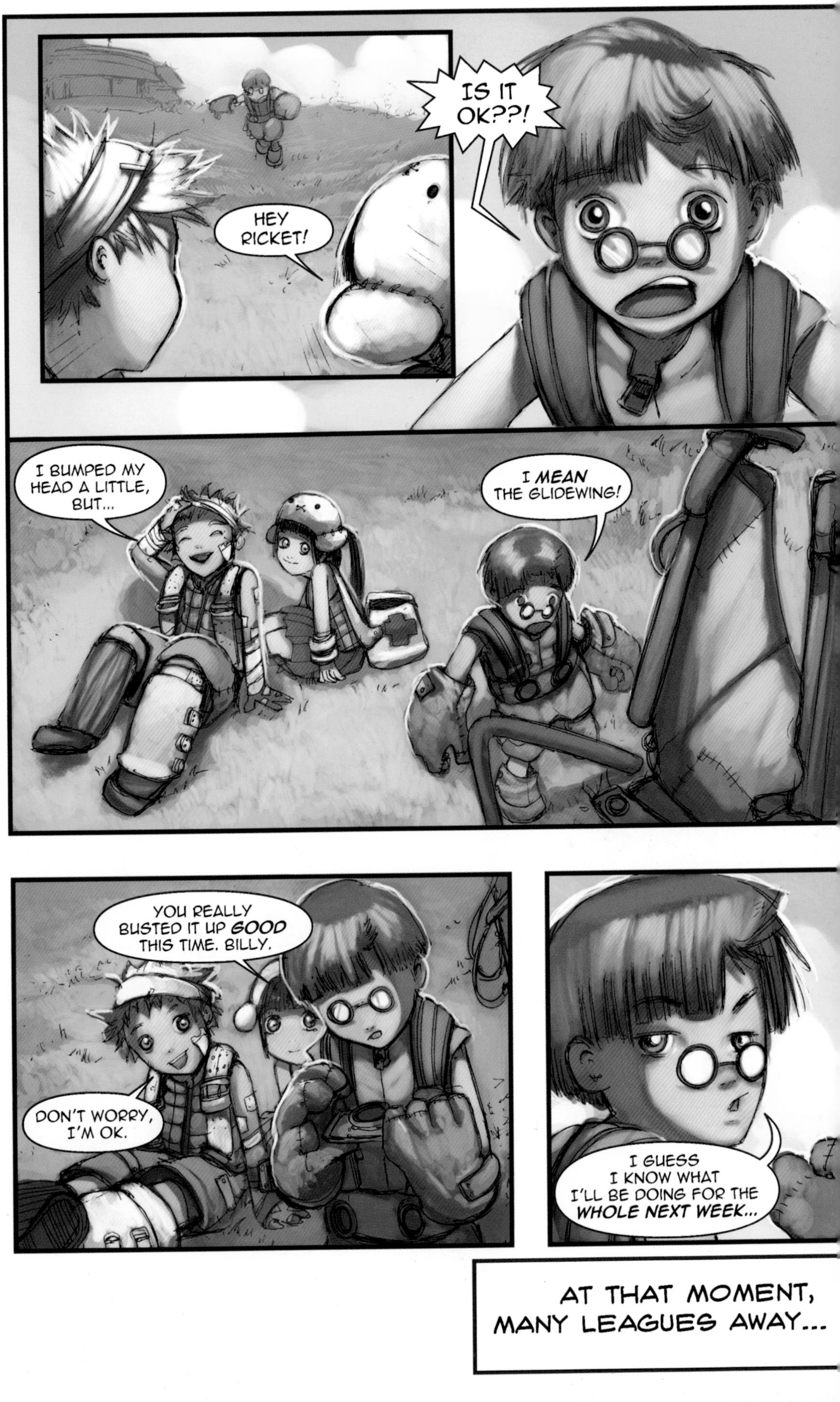
HEY RICKET!
IS IT OK??!
I BUMPED MY HEAD A LITTLE, BUT...
I MEAN THE GLIDEWING!
YOU REALLY BUSTED IT UP GOOD THIS TIME, BILLY.
DON'T WORRY, I'M OK.
I GUESS I KNOW WHAT I'LL BE DOING FOR THE WHOLE NEXT WEEK...
AT THAT MOMENT, MANY LEAGUES AWAY...

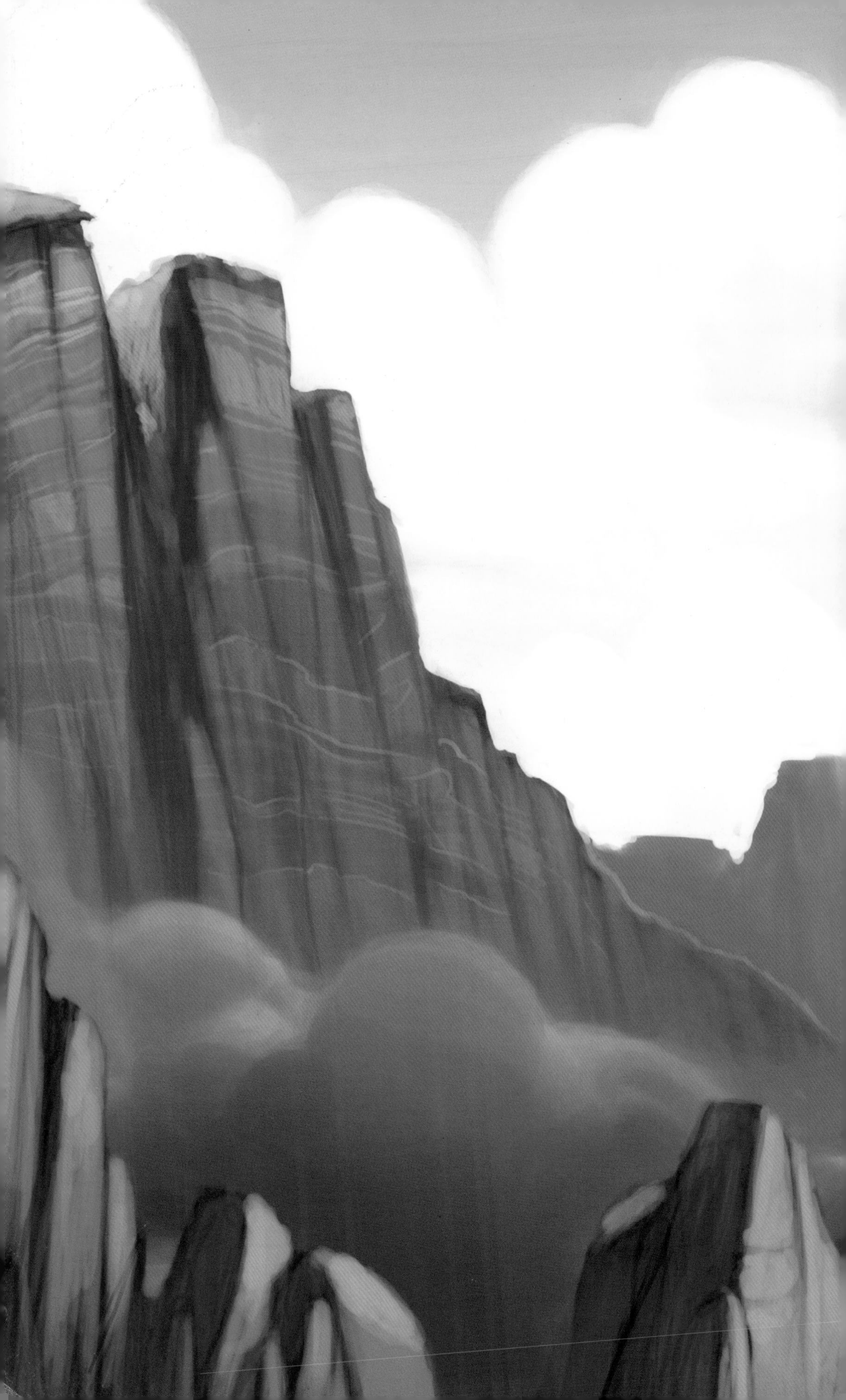

NEO EDEN.
WHERE THE REBIRTH BEGAN.

TWO CENTURIES AGO, THE TRIBES SPREAD FROM HERE TO FIND THEIR NEW HOMES IN THE *DISTANT REACHES* OF NEO TERRA.

NOW, THE VALLEY IS A SITE OF *CEREMONIAL IMPORTANCE.*

IT'S A PLACE FOR THE ANNUAL COUNCIL AND THE GREAT RACE WHICH ALWAYS FOLLOWS IT.

THIS YEAR'S COUNCIL HAS JUST ENDED, AND THE GREAT RACE IS ON.

THERE'S MORE THAN JUST *PRIDE* AT STAKE THIS YEAR, THOUGH MANY DON'T KNOW IT.

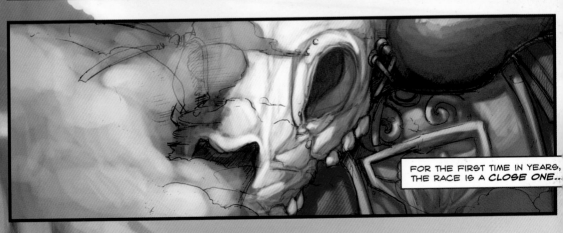

FOR THE FIRST TIME IN YEARS, THE RACE IS A *CLOSE ONE...*

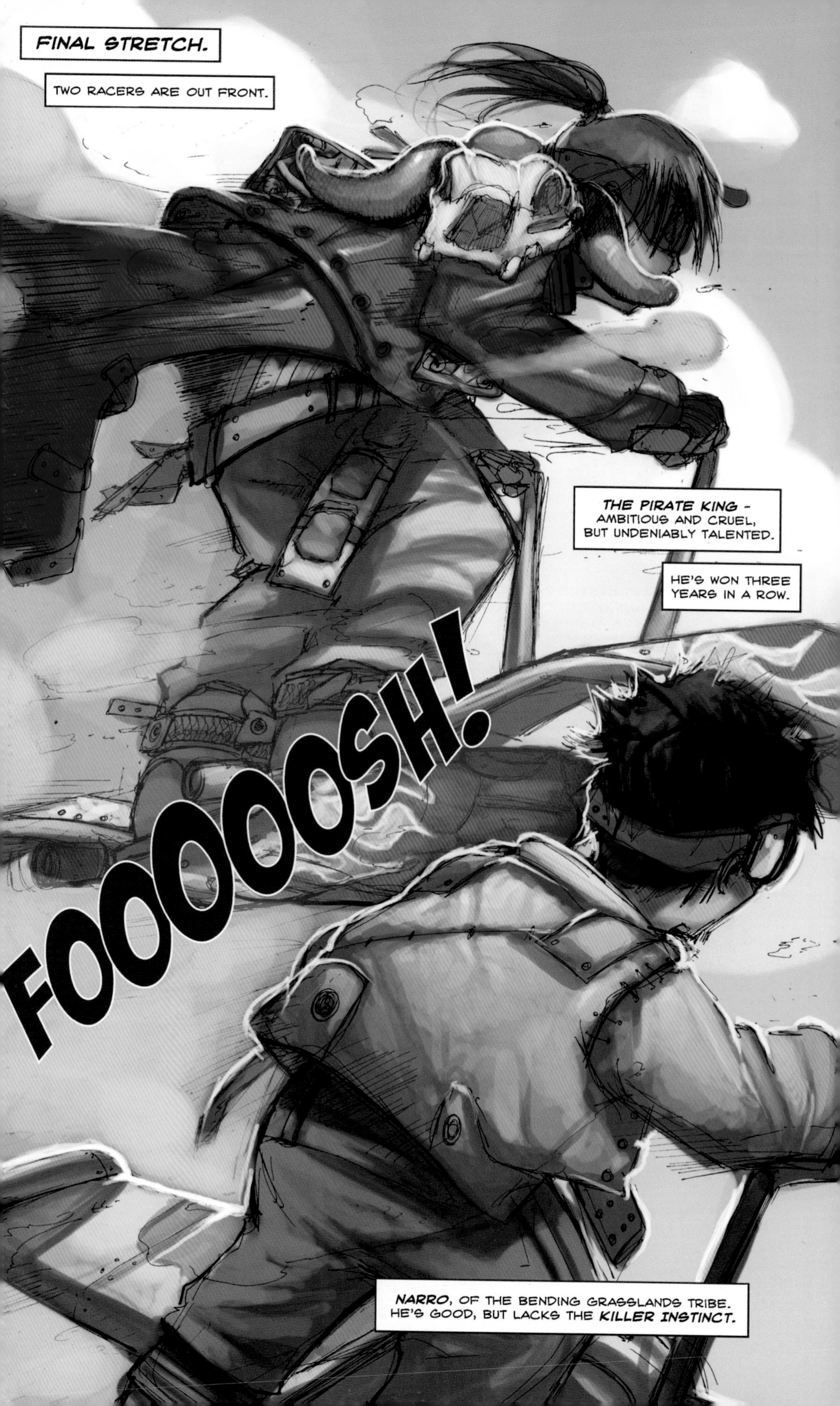
FINAL STRETCH.
TWO RACERS ARE OUT FRONT.
THE PIRATE KING - AMBITIOUS AND CRUEL, BUT UNDENIABLY TALENTED.
HE'S WON THREE YEARS IN A ROW.
FOOOOOSH!
NARRO, OF THE BENDING GRASSLANDS TRIBE. HE'S GOOD, BUT LACKS THE KILLER INSTINCT.

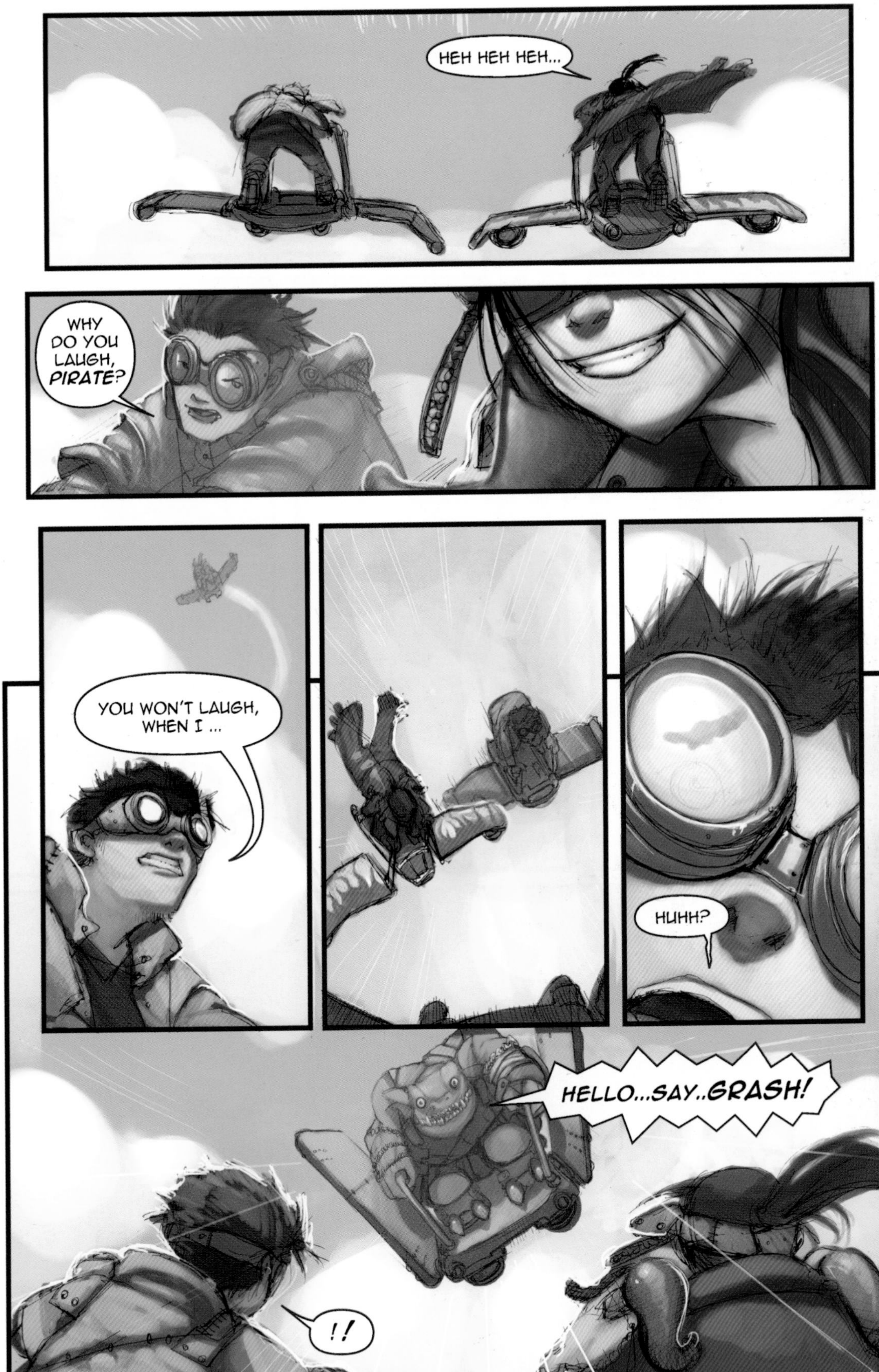
HEH HEH HEH...
WHY DO YOU LAUGH, *PIRATE*?
YOU WON'T LAUGH, WHEN I ...
HUHH?
HELLO...SAY..GRASH!
!!

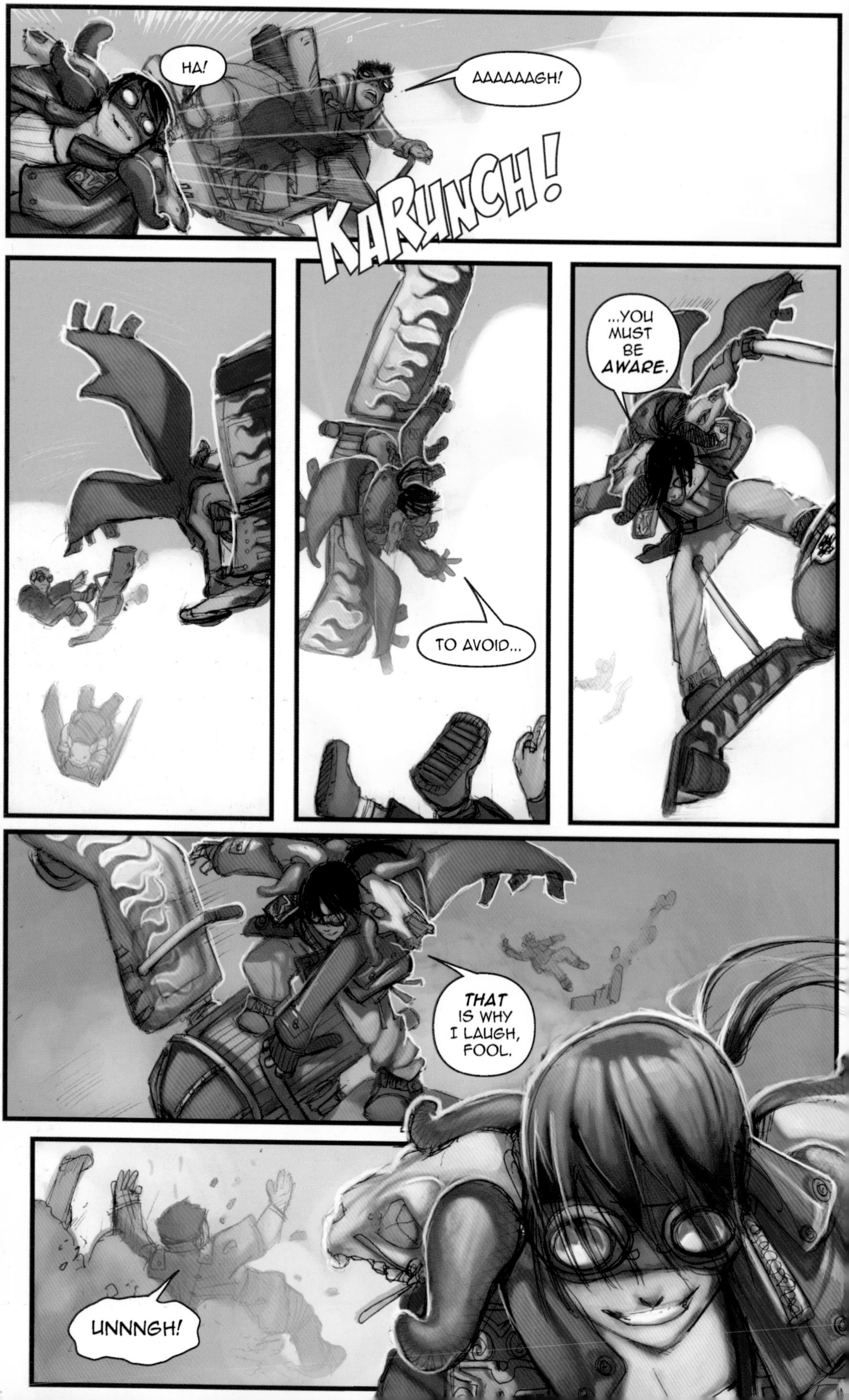
HA!
AAAAAAGH!
KARUNCH!
TO AVOID...
...YOU MUST BE AWARE.
THAT IS WHY I LAUGH, FOOL.
UNNNGH!

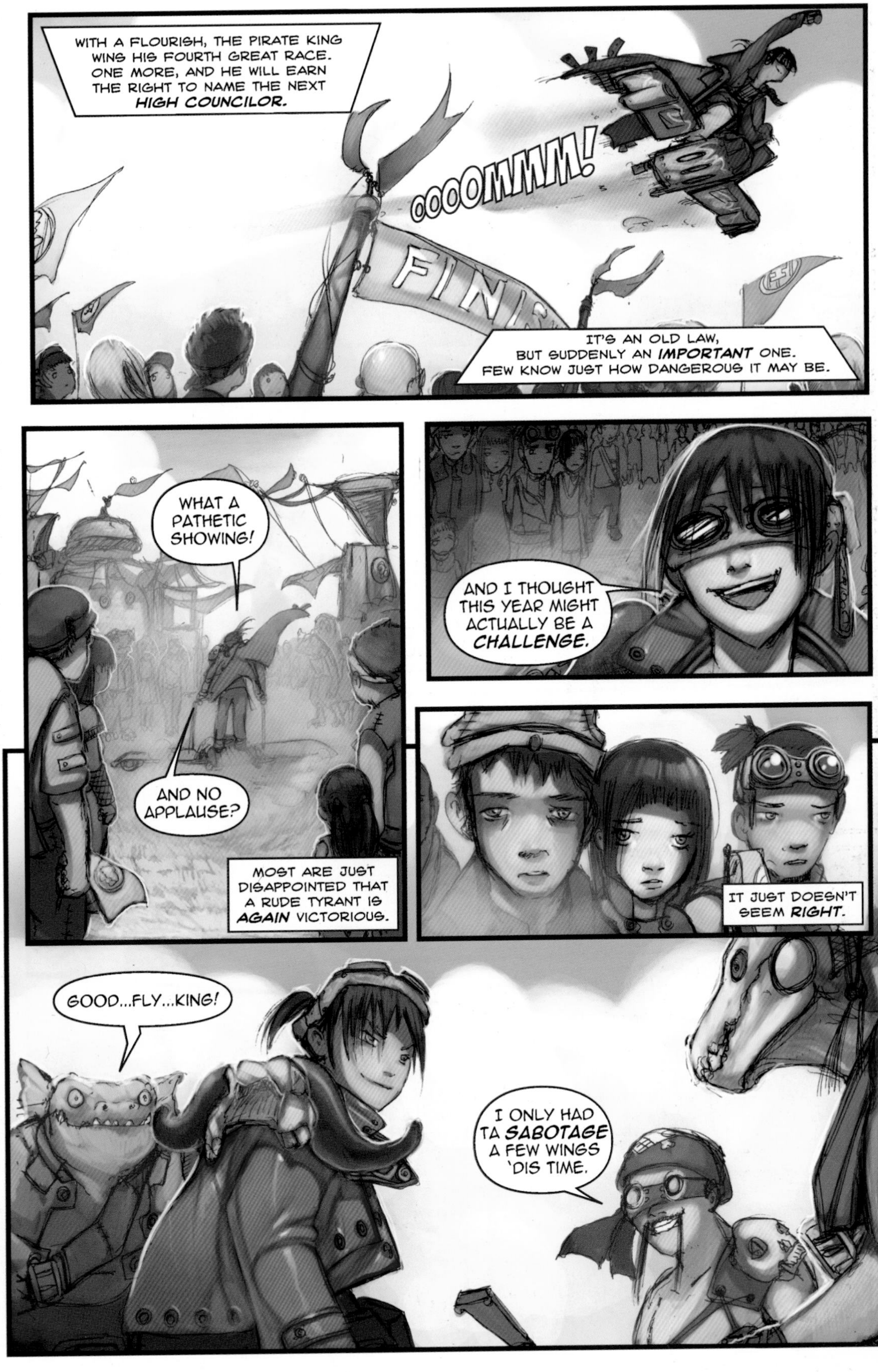
WITH A FLOURISH, THE PIRATE KING WINS HIS FOURTH GREAT RACE. ONE MORE, AND HE WILL EARN THE RIGHT TO NAME THE NEXT HIGH COUNCILOR.
OOOOMMM!
FINI
IT'S AN OLD LAW, BUT SUDDENLY AN IMPORTANT ONE. FEW KNOW JUST HOW DANGEROUS IT MAY BE.
WHAT A PATHETIC SHOWING!
AND NO APPLAUSE?
MOST ARE JUST DISAPPOINTED THAT A RUDE TYRANT IS AGAIN VICTORIOUS.
AND I THOUGHT THIS YEAR MIGHT ACTUALLY BE A CHALLENGE.
IT JUST DOESN'T SEEM RIGHT.
GOOD...FLY...KING!
I ONLY HAD TA SABOTAGE A FEW WINGS 'DIS TIME.

SSSUPERB, MAJESSSTY.

WHAT DID YOU EXPECT?

FOR SOME, THE PIRATE KING VICTORY IS *TOO MUCH* TO BEAR.

I AM SORRY, COUNCILOR.

DON'T. THERE IS NO SHAME IN DEFEAT. YOU CAN STILL—

NO. I AM NOT A YOUNG RACER ANYMORE.

NEXT YEAR I WILL BE NO *YOUNGER.*

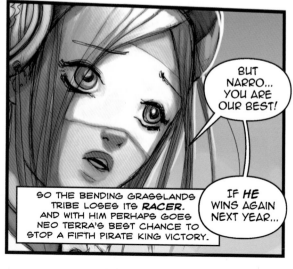

BUT NARRO... YOU ARE OUR BEST!

IF *HE* WINS AGAIN NEXT YEAR...

SO THE BENDING GRASSLANDS TRIBE LOSES ITS *RACER.* AND WITH HIM PERHAPS GOES NEO TERRA'S BEST CHANCE TO STOP A FIFTH PIRATE KING VICTORY.

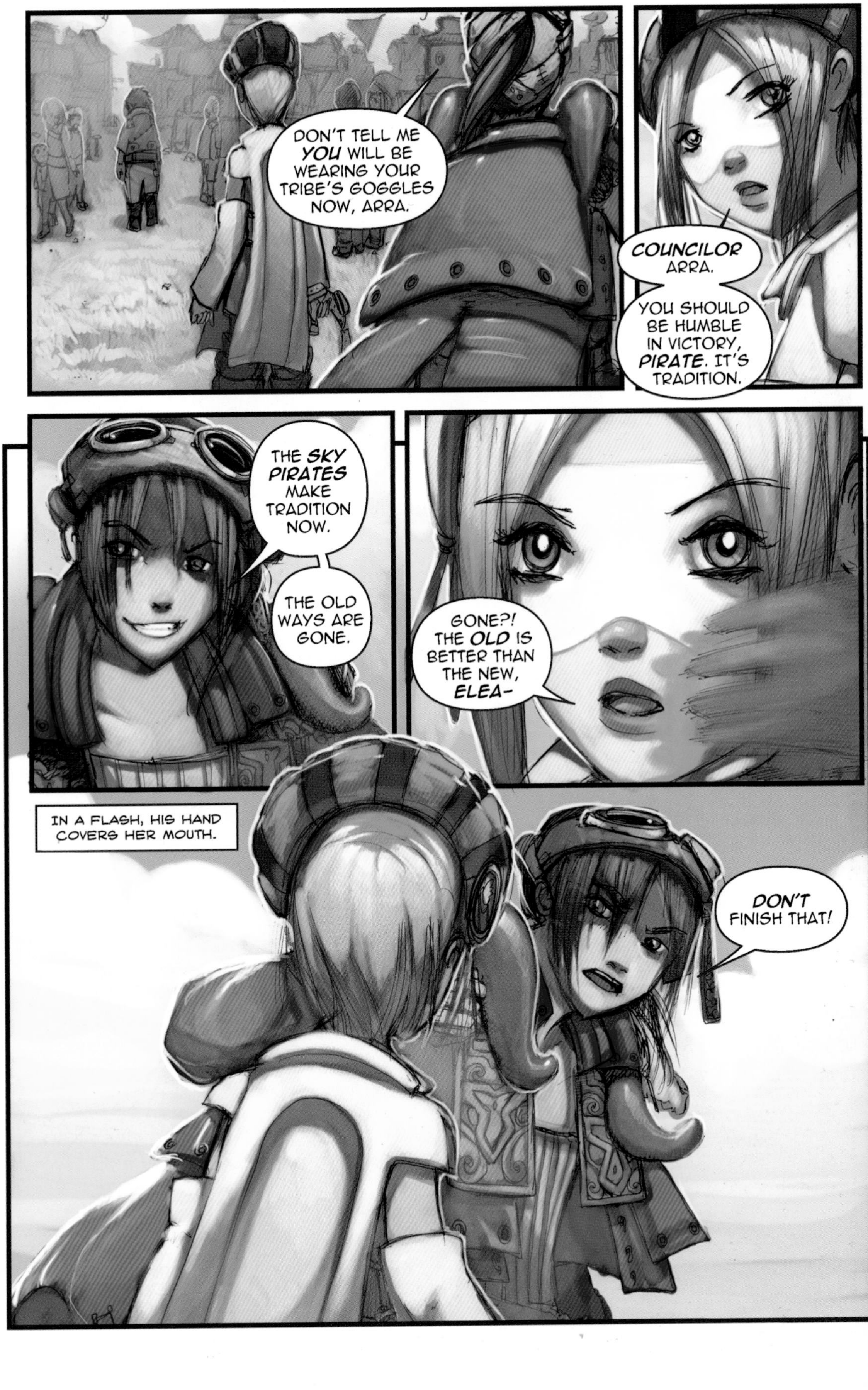
DON'T TELL ME *YOU* WILL BE WEARING YOUR TRIBE'S GOGGLES NOW, ARRA.
COUNCILOR ARRA.
YOU SHOULD BE HUMBLE IN VICTORY, *PIRATE*. IT'S TRADITION.
THE *SKY PIRATES* MAKE TRADITION NOW.
THE OLD WAYS ARE GONE.
GONE?! THE *OLD* IS BETTER THAN THE NEW, *ELEA-*
IN A FLASH, HIS HAND COVERS HER MOUTH.
DON'T FINISH THAT!

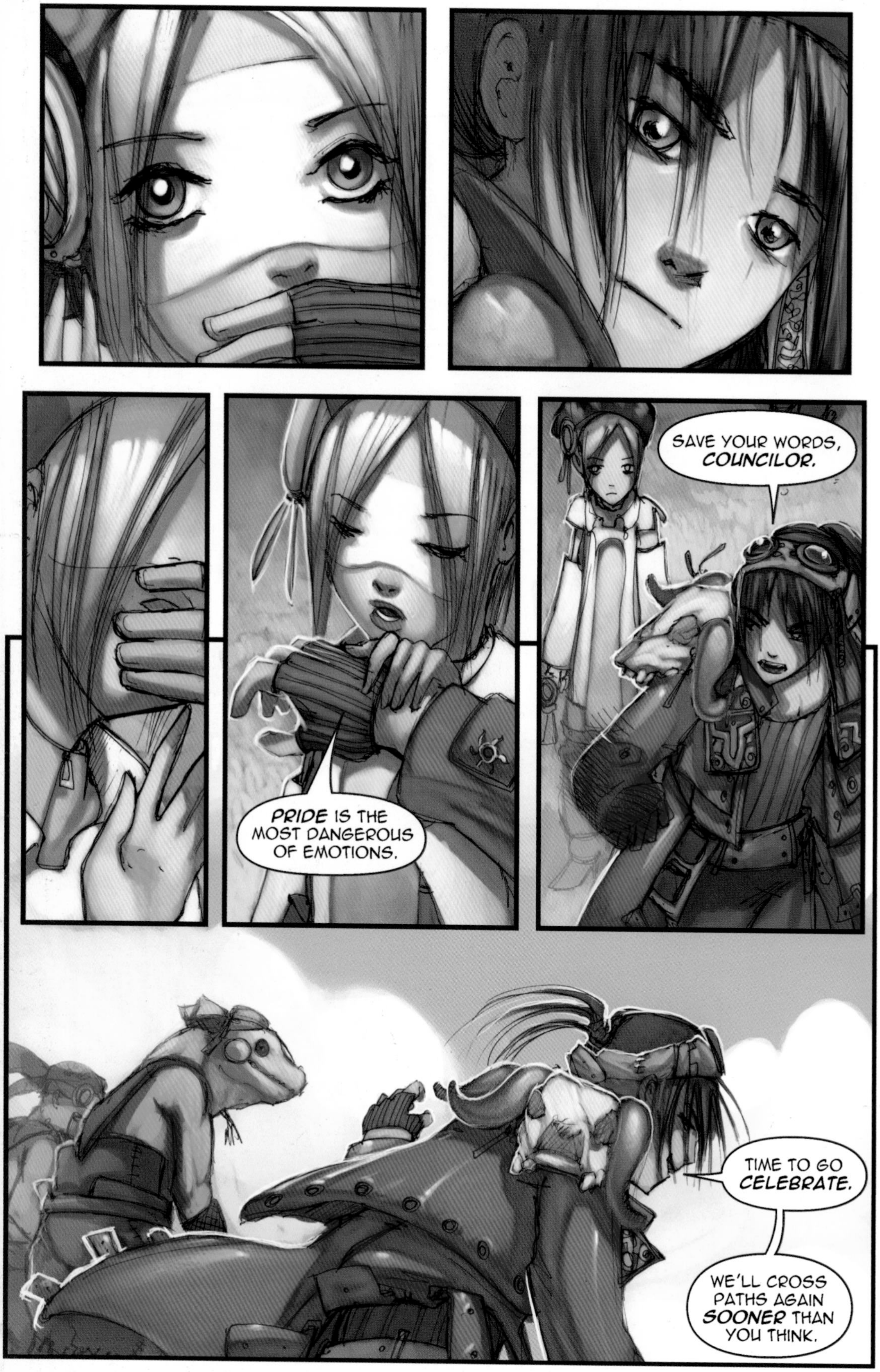
PRIDE IS THE MOST DANGEROUS OF EMOTIONS.
SAVE YOUR WORDS, COUNCILOR.
TIME TO GO CELEBRATE.
WE'LL CROSS PATHS AGAIN SOONER THAN YOU THINK.

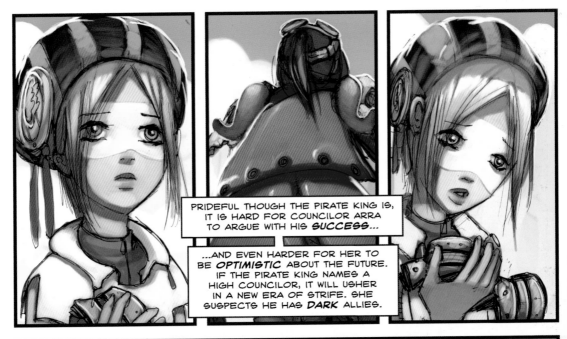

PRIDEFUL THOUGH THE PIRATE KING IS, IT IS HARD FOR COUNCILOR ARRA TO ARGUE WITH HIS *SUCCESS*...

...AND EVEN HARDER FOR HER TO BE *OPTIMISTIC* ABOUT THE FUTURE. IF THE PIRATE KING NAMES A HIGH COUNCILOR, IT WILL USHER IN A NEW ERA OF STRIFE. SHE SUSPECTS HE HAS *DARK* ALLIES.

THAT LEAVES ONE YEAR TO FIND SOMEONE THAT CAN BEAT THE *BEST PILOT* IN NEO TERRA.

AN IMPOSSIBLE *TASK*, IT WOULD SEEM.

BUT THEN, ARRA REMEMBERS SOMETHING... *SOMEONE!*

BUT IS HE TOO YOUNG? TOO *RECKLESS?*

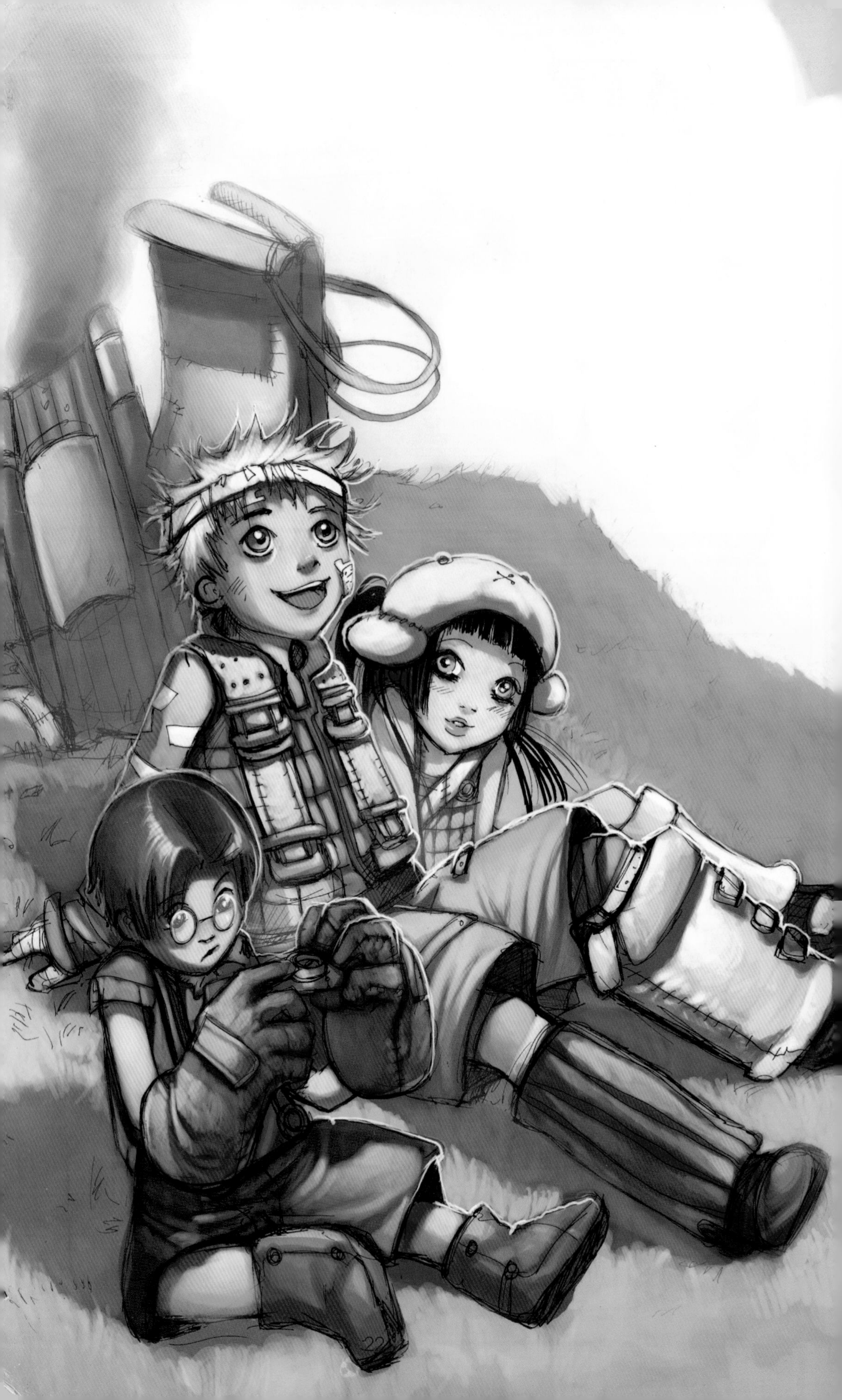

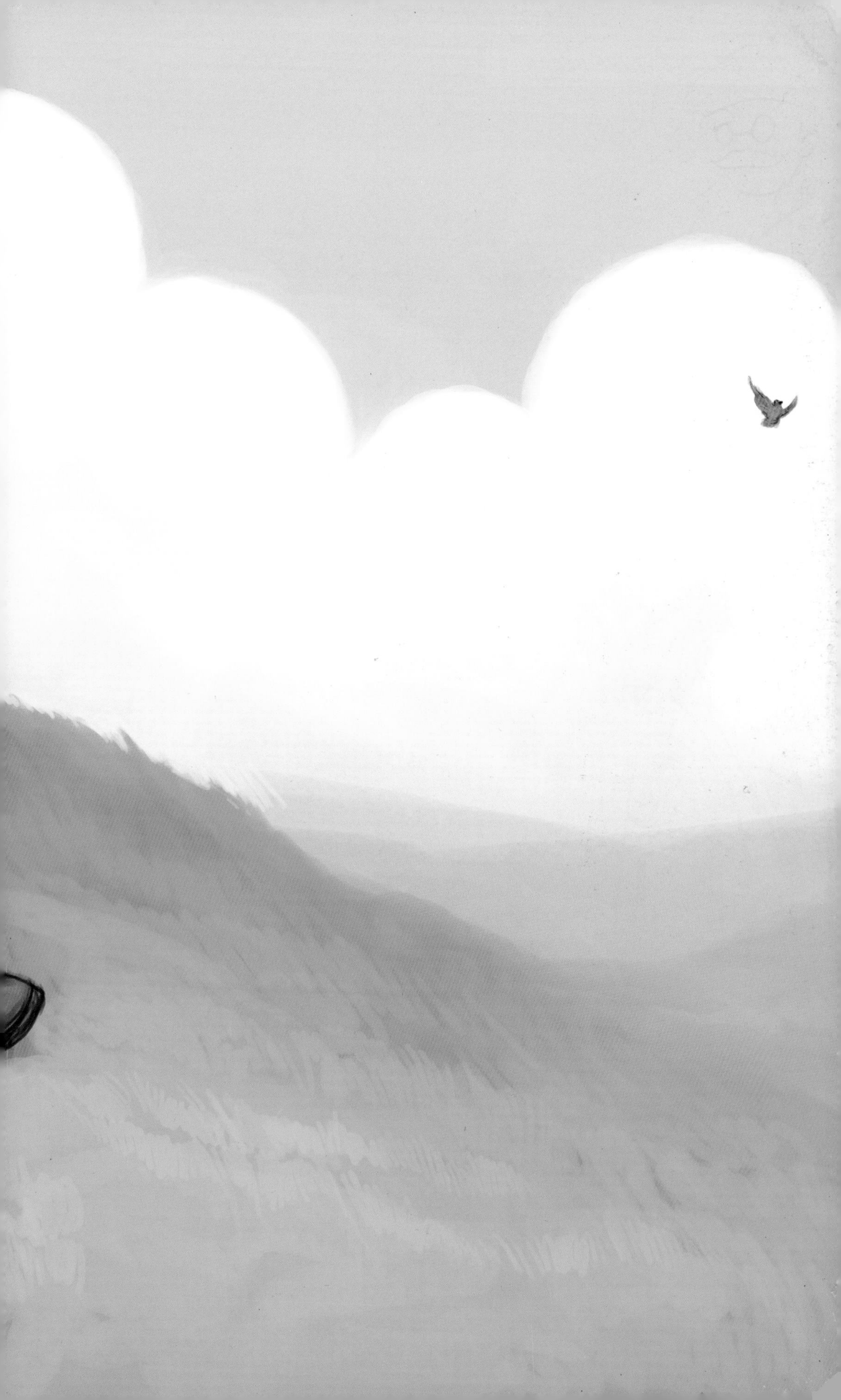

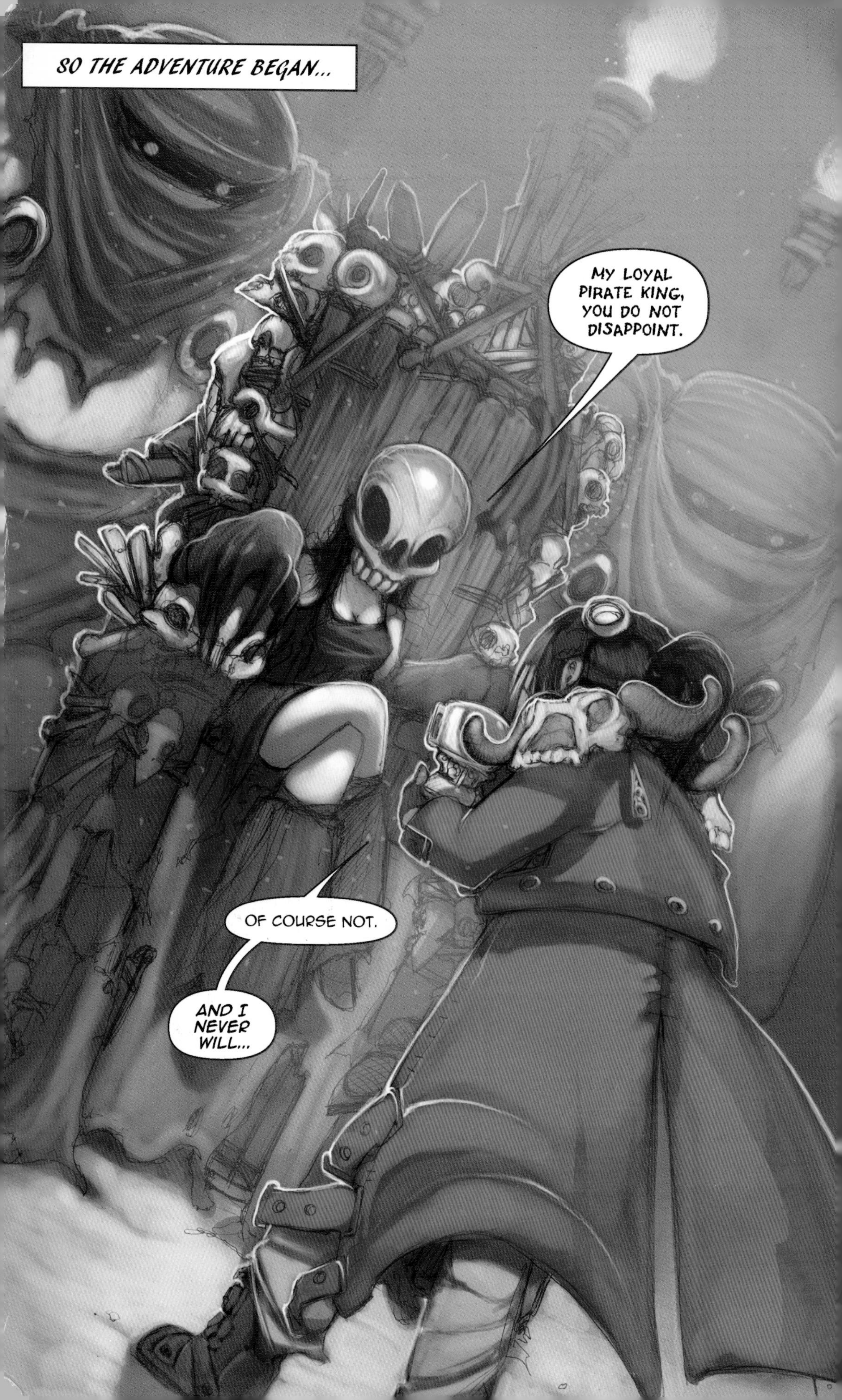
SO THE ADVENTURE BEGAN...
MY LOYAL PIRATE KING, YOU DO NOT DISAPPOINT.
OF COURSE NOT.
AND I NEVER WILL...

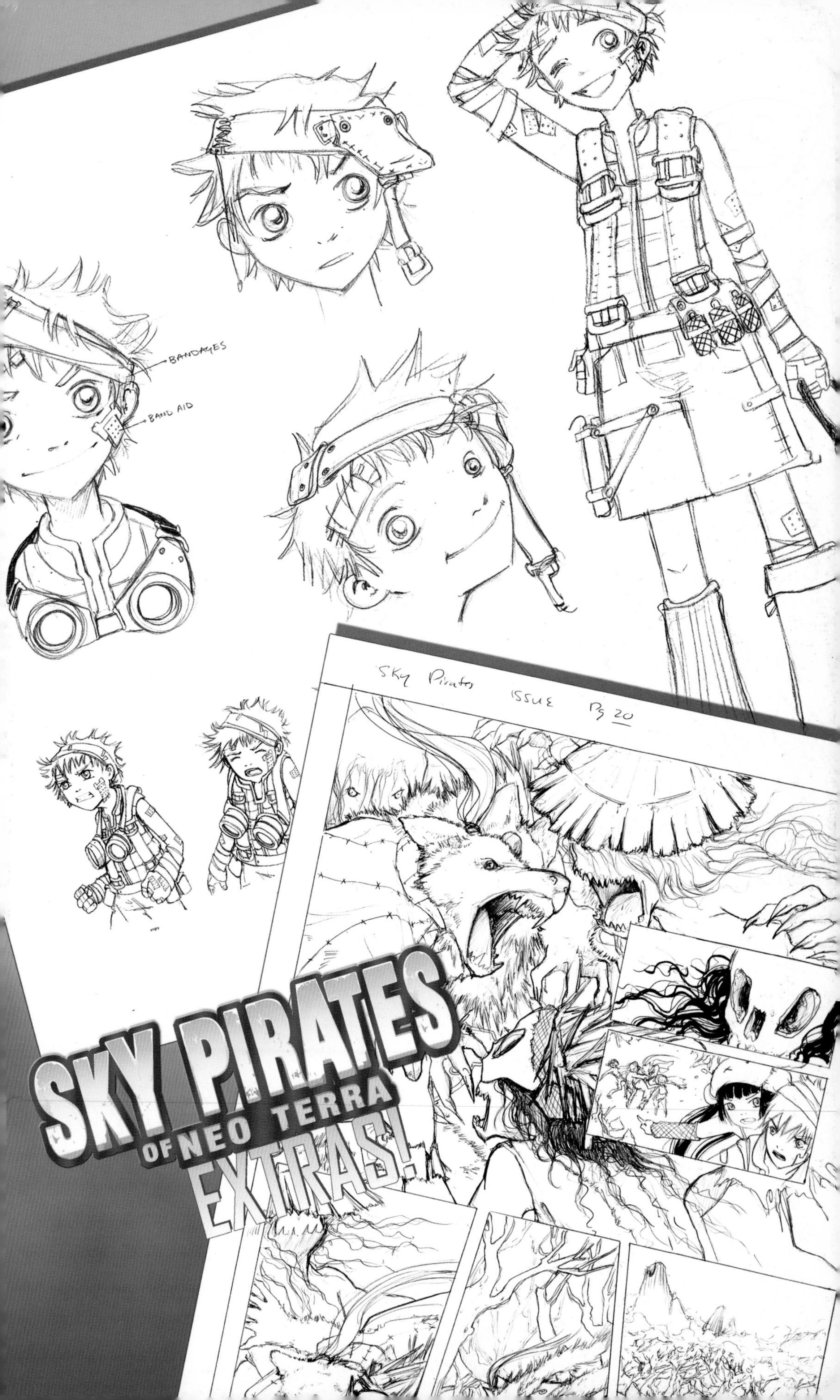
BANDAGES
BAND AID
SKY Pirates ISSUE Pg 20
SKY PIRATES OF NEO TERRA
EXTRAS!

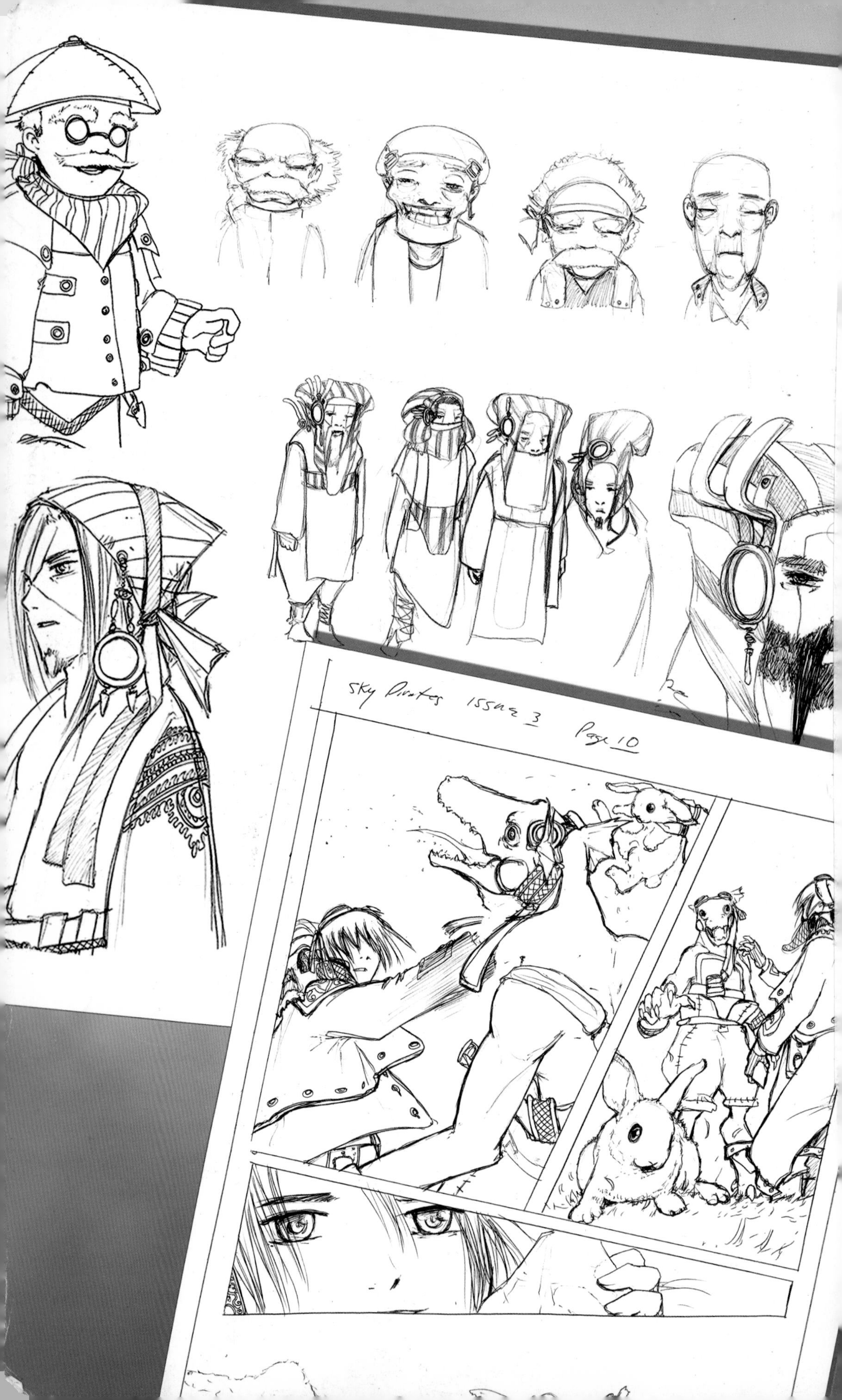
Sky Pirates Issue 3 Page 10

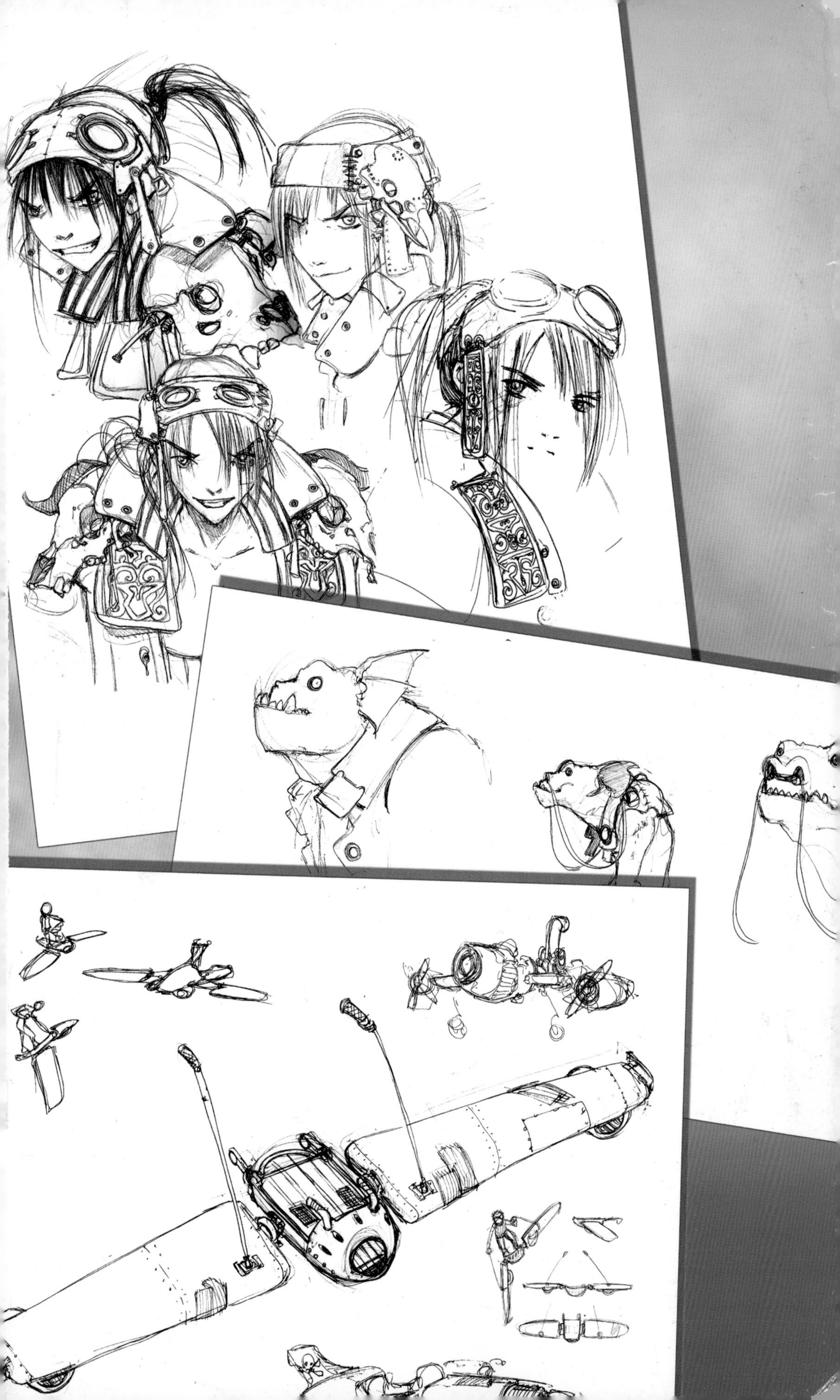

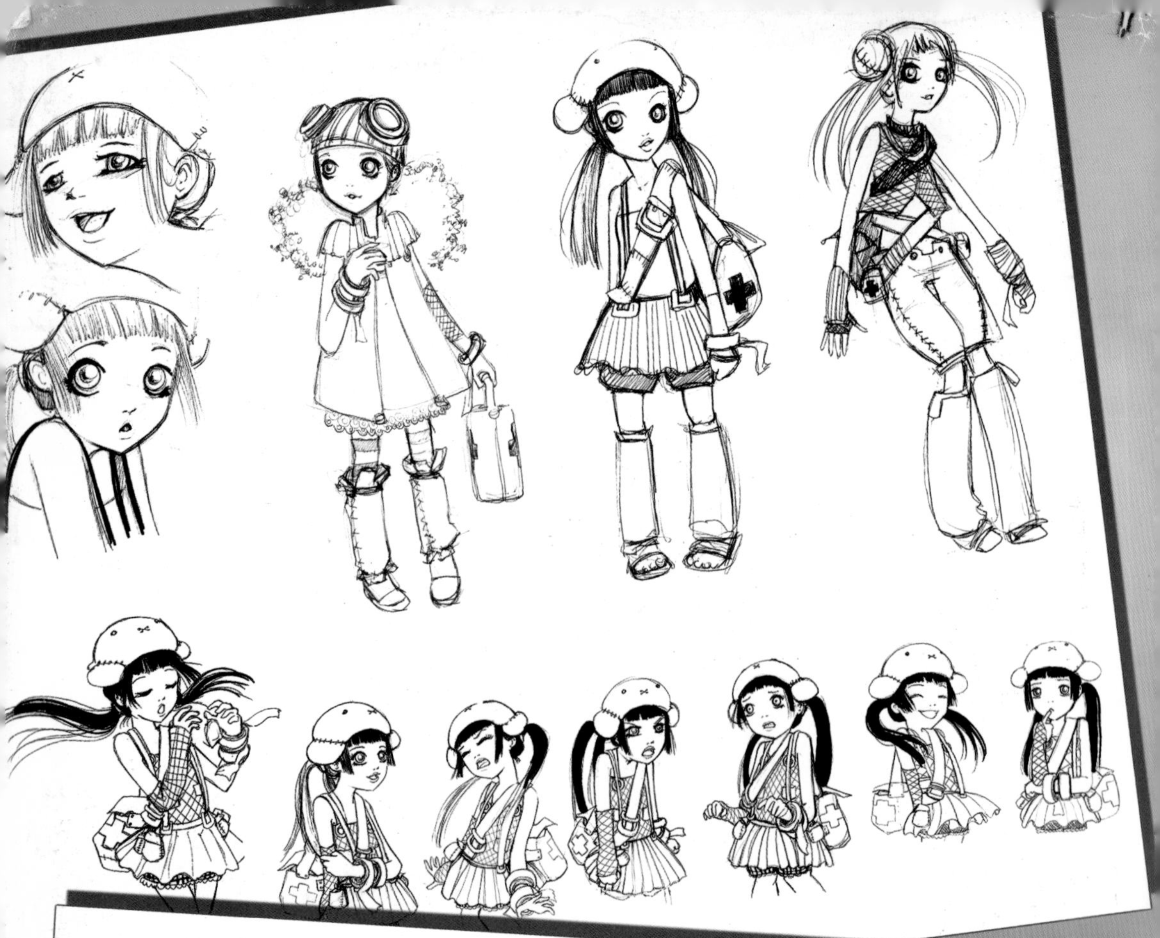

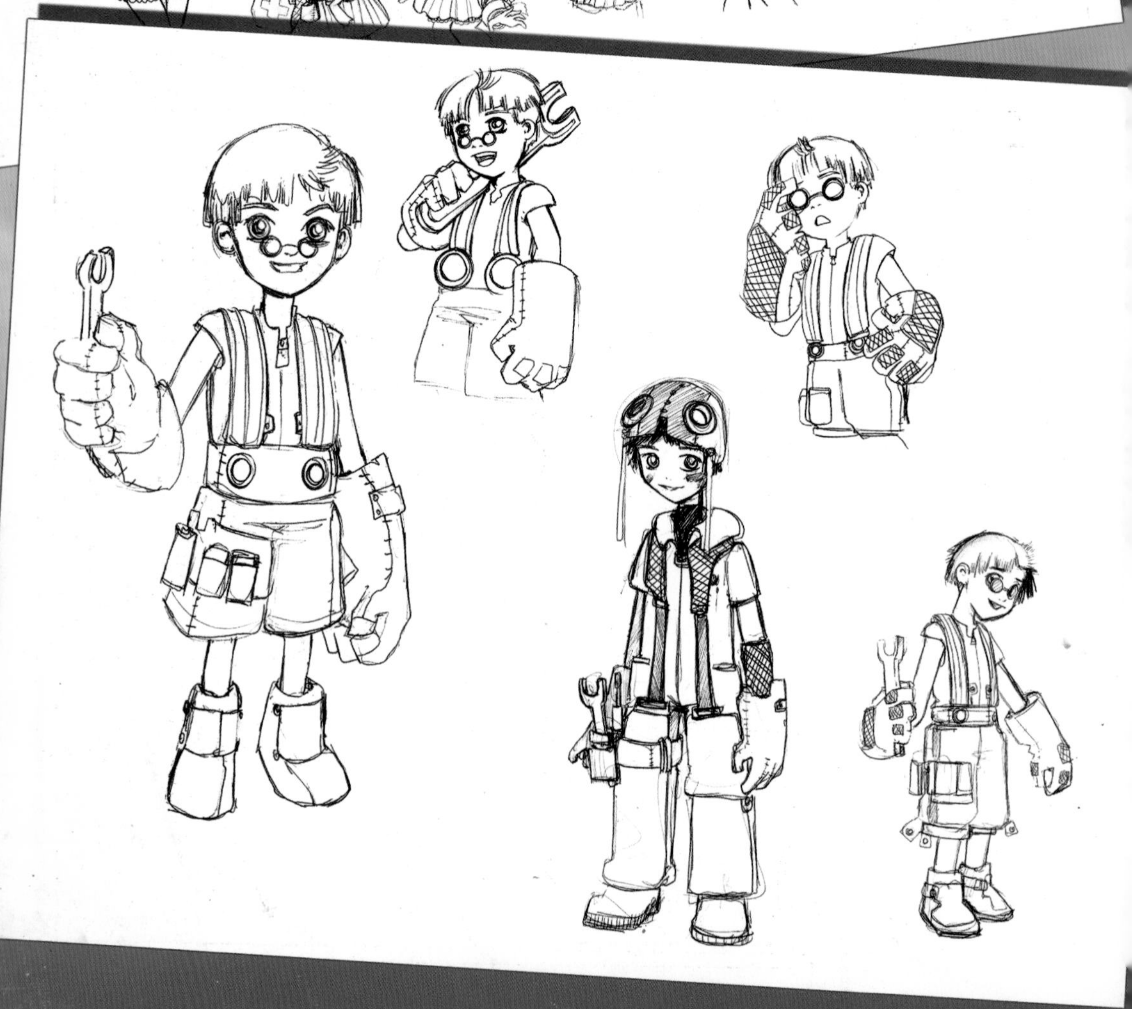

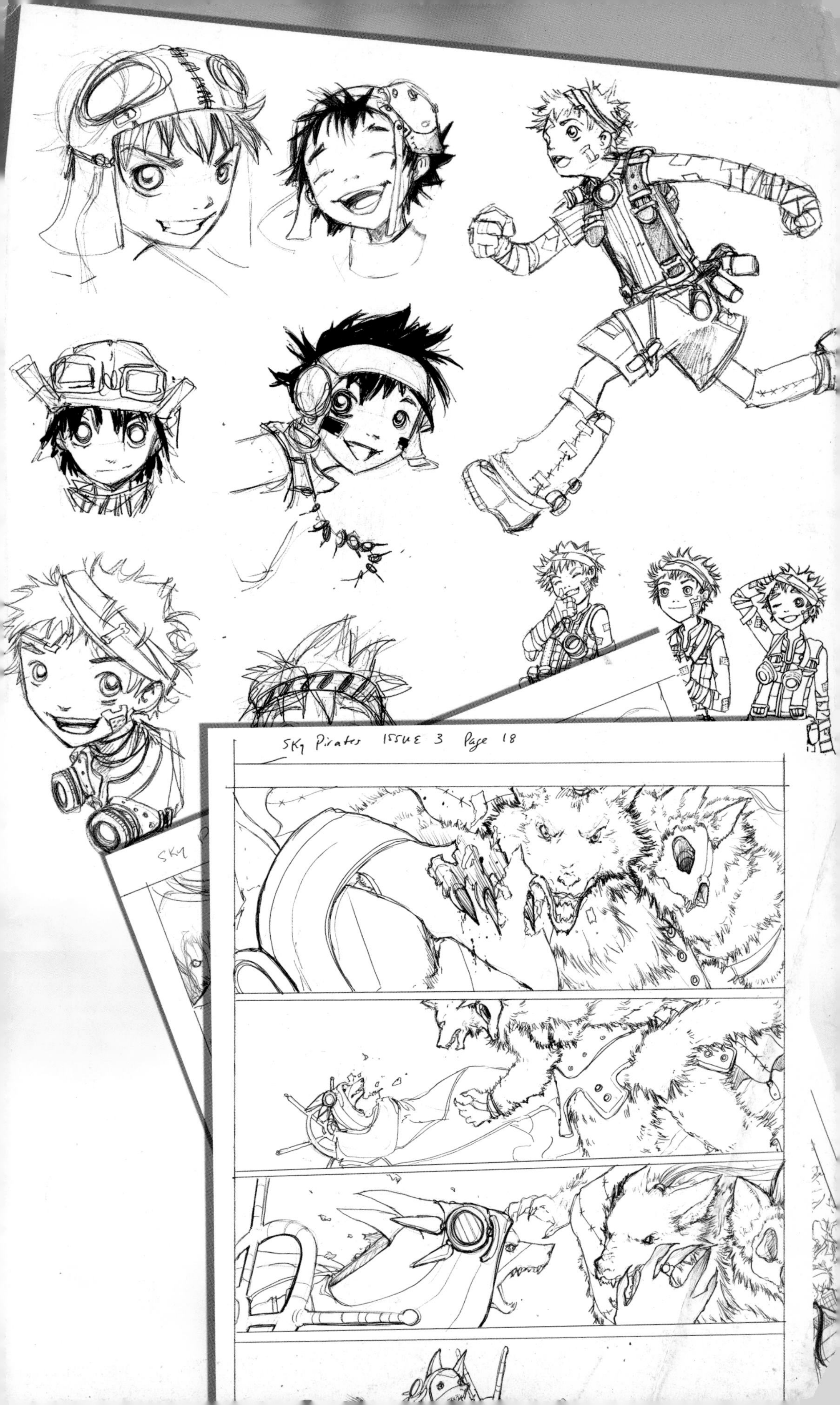

SKy Pirates ISSUE 3 Page 18

TIME FLIES...

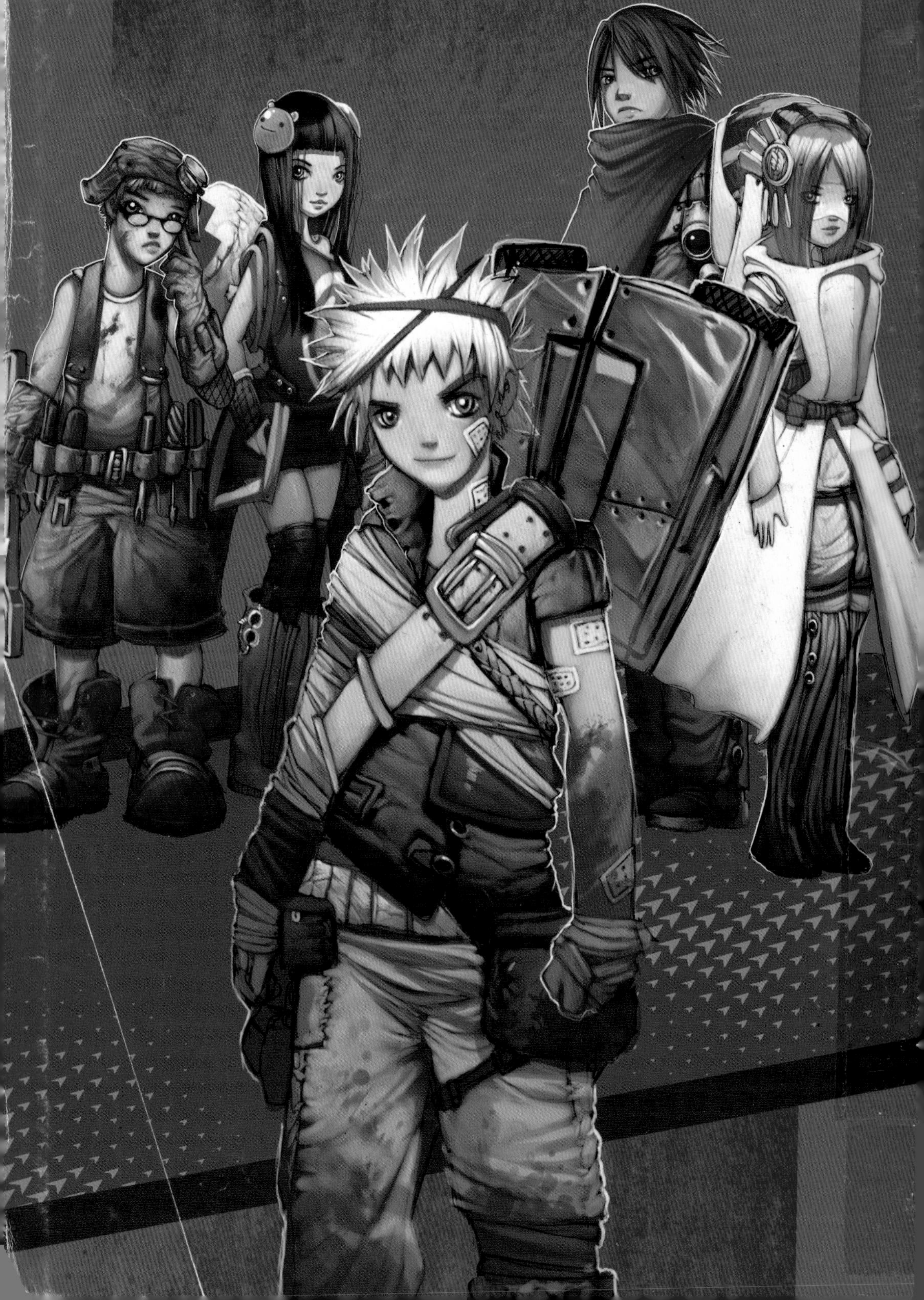